UNFOLDING
OF †HY
LOVE

Unraveling of the Mysteries of the Universe
by Unfolding the Unchanging and Eternal
Love of Its Maker

SAMUEL PAK M.D.

PRESS

UNFOLDING OF THY LOVE
Unraveling of the Mysteries of the Universe by Unfolding the Unchanging and Eternal Love of Its Maker

by SAMUEL PAK M.D.

Printed in the United States of America

ISBN 9781628713732

Unless otherwise indicated, Bible quotations are taken from the New King James Version (NKJV) of the Bible.

The New International Version (NIV) by BibleGateway.com.

www.xulonpress.com

TABLE OF CONTENTS

DEDICATION

M y mom, Ho-Jah Lee, born on November 14th, 1944 and a survivor of the Korean War, was a quiet and unassuming godly woman who loved the Lord with all of her heart and soul, mind and strength, honored her husband, loved her children and her neighbors. Our family moved

from South Korea to the United States in 1985, and she had endured much hardship in this great nation in order to provide for her family and set me in the path of righteousness in Christ. Things were beginning to turn the corner in 2003. I was finishing up my medical internship, and my sister and her hubby were still in their honeymoon bliss with their first baby. My parents were retiring and, it had appeared for the moment, the better days were not far off.

It was then that mom was suddenly diagnosed with a highly aggressive form of brain cancer. Doctors gave her 3 to 6 months to live. Through two major operations, radiation and all the subsequent complications, including that dreadful shingles, she, with dad who never left her side day and night, would try to rally from the brink of death for two long, arduous, but precious years. However, God had a higher plan. She went on to be with the Lord on May 22nd, 2005. It amazes me, and often puts me to shame, whenever I think back to how she had never once complained or despaired through the hour of most severe trials. What a strong and noble lady she was. She would always be praying in her suffering, not only for the healing of her body, but for the true cleansing and the healing of souls of all the people that Christ came to save. Her departure created such a big void in me that I realized, for the first time, what a magnificent human being she was. I didn't really know who she was until she was gone. But she, too, was a human being. I believe the disciples felt the same kind of agonizing emotion, only much stronger and deeper, when Jesus ascended and left them to carry on with His work. It was only then, in His absence and by the power of the Holy Spirit, that the disciples KNEW who Christ really was. You begin to appreciate the full extent of a great love only when that love is taken away; leaving us with that terrible vacuum of pain and longing; pulling us into that love of great divine destiny with the supernatural power and strength we would not have known otherwise. That is the Divine design.

When Jesus turned all that water into wine, out of obedience to his earthly mother Mary, He went as far as to step outside of His God-ordained schedule. The Son, who was the very essence of love, knew how to love and be loved and obey his earthly mom like no man ever could — in the humble spirit of celebration and love that supersedes and surpasses all knowledge and edifies all souls. I wish I had known the Son better so I could have been a better son to my own mom and a better man to the people around me. So, with my feeble hands and a weak mind powered by the Spirit Himself, I muster whatever and all that God has given me, who was entrusted to my mom's care for a time, to write this book in loving memory of her.

UNFOLDING OF YOUR LOVE

The heart is deceitful above all things and beyond cure. Who can **understand** *it? – Jeremiah 17:9*

The unfolding of your words gives light; it gives **understanding** *to the simple. – Psalm 119:130*

My goal is that they may be encouraged in heart and **united in love**, *so that they may have the full riches of* **complete understanding**, *in order that they may know the mystery of God, namely,* **Christ**, *in whom are hidden all the treasures of wisdom and knowledge. – Colossians 2:2-3*

I praise you because I am fearfully and wonderfully made. Your works are wonderful. **I know that full well**. *– Psalm 139:1*

If you would, please read the following with me…slowly.

We are fearfully made because God is holy. We are wonderfully made because God is love. All of His works are wonderful because He is love. Our hearts were forged in the heart of our loving Trinity, because it was originally designed to be nothing less and nothing short of being the glorious holy dwelling place of His perfect love…for God and for one another.

But we have walked so far away from the Maker of our hearts and souls. The heart of humanity has been running away from its Maker ever since the fall of Adam and Eve and became engulfed and shrouded in the mystery of sin and death. Our hearts that were originally designed to be free in the love of our God, who gave us the whole world to rule, became shackled to the sin and evil that continues to rage against God and one another in this fallen world. Our hearts became deceitful above all things and we, ourselves, became deceived by our own hearts. We have walked away from the Garden of Eden, where everything was inherently and instantly understood by the love of its Creator and the Giver of all gifts.

True gifts come from love. And the true love comes from the Giver of all good gifts. And God's love makes us understand the workings of His creation because He designed everything out of His love for us. We are His masterpiece, special possession and the royal priesthood of His coming kingdom. Understanding His love is the key to unraveling the mysteries of the universe, which was built by God of love. The unfolding of our destinies, intertwined and hidden in the heart of Love, reveals the foundation of the universe: Jesus Christ our Lord, who is the author of Love. Jesus Christ is the Gift from God to end all gifts. Christ came to die for ALL. Christ came to save ALL. Christ came to love ALL. His love was beyond anything we have seen or heard, or else we would not have crucified Him. All the treasures of wisdom and knowledge, worth living-fighting-dying for, are hidden in the life, death and the resurrection of Jesus Christ. As kings and queens who belong to the King of love, we will come to understand, with painful regret and unspeakable joy that the King of this universe has designed our hearts to be united in love through Him and Him only. Our God is Holy and His love is self-sacrificial, but our hearts have become prideful and selfish by our fallen nature. God sent His Son to save us all from all of our self-advancing, self-loving, and self-destructive unholiness because our hearts were originally designed to be the indwelling place of His HOLY Spirit and Lord Jesus Christ: the loving, self-sacrificial Lamb and the coming King.

Our divine destinies were forged in the heart of the King of love to be embraced and united only by His Love, and to be His Love...to ALL.

SUPERMAN COMPLEX WITH A RIGHTEOUS TWIST OF THE LORD: LOVE MYSTERIOUS AND TECTONIC.

*What makes a superman a hero is not that he has power but that he has the **wisdom** and **maturity** to use the power wisely. – Christopher Reeves, an American actor*

*When I was a child, I talked like a child, I thought like a child, I reasoned like a child. **When I became a man,** I put the ways of childhood behind me. For now we see only a reflection as in a mirror (a crude metal reflector in the days of the early church); then we shall see face to face. Now I know in part; then I shall know fully, even as I am fully known. And now these three remain: faith, hope and **love**. But the greatest of these is **love**. – Paul, an Apostle of Jesus Christ (1st Corinthians 13)*

High above the atmosphere, the bomb detonates safely thousands of miles above the earth. But Superman doesn't have a moment to waste as he now turns his focus on the San Andreas fault-line in California, where the other missile has just landed and exploded. He descends with all the speed he can summon.

As he watches the earth approaching him at a sickening speed, he can also hear people crying out in terror and shock of the earthquake. He can hear all the people in distress and panic as they are trying desperately, but unable, to find stable grounds. Things are getting worse to impossible rapidly as Superman tries to scan, with his X-ray vision from the bird's eye view, to visually define the tectonic plate that is about to tear away from the continent and violently drag the part of the western California into the ocean. As his mind is racing, his heart is being overloaded with all the sounds of agony and desperate pleas he is hearing. He can hear babies crying and men and women running and shouting. Some were even calling out his name. "Superman, where are you? We need you! Please save us! We are going to die!"

He sees the drifting of the Pacific tectonic plate through his vision, and he is very close to finding the foundation of the plate. But he has to find the critical entry point into the constantly shifting, rocky crevices, which is continuously and violently caving in on themselves. He can blast through them but that will likely worsen the earthquake so he must quickly find a shortcut through the ever crumbling and unwelcoming jagged gaps! He slows down just above the earth, and just enough to make his final adjustments mid-flight before plunging in. When people see Superman coming down, they exclaim with joy, "Superman, you are here to save us! Thank God for you, Super...." And before they can finish thanking Superman for the anticipated rescue, they see Superman disappearing into the ever changing, raging abyss.

People are confused. Some are yelling, "Where are you going, Superman?! We are here! I thought you came here to rescue us!" Some are mumbling, "I don't understand. Why is he flying away from us? We need to be flown out of here and over to a safer ground!" Some people are expressing doubt: "Maybe he is not interested in saving us anymore. Maybe there is someone more important that he needs to save...I guess we are just not that important. We are just going to die with no one to save us." All the while, others are beginning to express anger, frustration, disappointment and maybe even hate. "I knew he was a fraud. He rescued all those people, but I guess it was just for a show...heh? He is like any other fame and power-hungry celebrity. Who needs you, Superman? We don't need you and we never did! I hope you *die* like the rest of us..." But a handful of people are still optimistic with hope in Superman that there is a very good reason for this disappearing act. They are thinking, "The Superman we know wouldn't run away from this kind of situation. He has always stood by our side. He has always helped us in times of crisis. Maybe he is going down there to help us or save us somehow. We don't know exactly how he is going to do it, but we have no choice but to believe in Superman. He is the only one who can save us now." But their words mostly fall on deaf ears that are stricken with terror and turmoil of the *present* situations. And as the time passes, with each and every cry of panic, anger and despair, they themselves begin to doubt if Superman will ever save them. To make the matters worse, some of the people are beginning to shove away and step on each other, as if they can actually find a safer place in this ever-progressing chaos and destructions befalling around them and within their hearts.

Superman doesn't have the power to read minds but he doesn't need to. He can hear all the things that are being said. He can perceive all things that are going on above him. But he is not distracted. He is determined. He does not waste any time. He never wavers from his focus on the foundation of the tectonic plate, which no one sees but only himself. He knows exactly where it is and how to get there and how fast he needs to get there. Nothing can deter him from his objective, which is to save as many people as he can. He knows that he is not only saving them for who they are, but who he hopes they are going to be...

After negotiating and zigzagging through many "violent shortcuts" at a blinding speed, he finally finds the foundation of the tectonic plate...not a moment too soon or too late. He begins to lift the plate on his shoulder. He has to move the plate very slowly, lest his efforts become a trigger point to another earthquake. All this is more than knowledge to Superman. This is wisdom based on...LOVE. What else can this be? Superman doesn't have any other ulterior motive. He is Superman. He can pretty much do anything. He can get everything by himself. He is wise above all men. He doesn't need anything or anyone. He doesn't need to do all this to win the "affections" of the people because he knows that the same "affection" can turn to anger and hate quickly...as it is being evidenced and unraveled above him. He knows exactly what that "affection" or "popularity" means. He knows what exists in the heart of every human being. He *could* be a master politician but he refuses to be one because that does not bring about the permanent, true solution. However impossible it may be, even with his power, he wants to somehow remove the THING that causes all these people to say what they are saying now in fear, doubt and hatred. He does everything out of that which just may change the human heart. And given the choice between the two, Superman always takes the path of the most number of people he can save. Each life is equally sacred to him. It is the path that is the toughest to travel and even tougher to be understood by men. Superman is always about all men at all times. A man is always about himself first and his current situation that he sees and feels.

Superman is just about done easing the tectonic plate back to its original position. The earth and the rocky grounds within the gaping holes quickly stabilize and many of the gaps are filled. Some parts of California are still shifting and shaking, but Superman realizes that he had just saved over 99 percent of the people, who would've been seriously injured or even dead had he not intervened. He comes up out of the ground to the cheers and shouts of all people. He sees people converging on him.

He is covered in ashes and the residuals of some of the molten lava. People's hearts are being moved by the heroic deeds of the Superman. They don't understand exactly what he did, but they know that they have been saved by him. All of them love Superman and many of them cannot even bring themselves to thank him because their hearts are now being pierced with guilt for what they were saying about him earlier. All of them stand in awe of Superman and they want to celebrate their new lease on life with him. It is then that Superman lands on the ground and begins to announce, "People, you need to listen to me. On the way up here, I saw a bunch of families trapped in the houses less than a mile that way and I saw a big sunken hole that a school bus is trapped in just around that corner. I can sense that all these people are OK for now but they need to be rescued, and they need your help as soon as possible. I have to fly over to a town and save the people from an impending flood right now. When my work is all done, I will come back and really celebrate with you all. I believe in you!" And before they can say the words, "You Da man, Superman! Thank you and we love you!", Superman takes off and leaves them in a cloud of dust.

People scramble to help the others out of the houses and the bus. They also look around to see if there are any other people in need of their help and rescue. They are seeing the Superman for who he really is now. Somehow they are beginning to understand that the love of Superman is not like the love they have experienced or known in this fallen, but beautiful, world. They are beginning to understand in their hearts that his love is mysterious beyond their understanding, because it has always been too foundational for their limited minds. The love of Superman was just too much and too strong to be recognized right away. But now, they trust him as to why he had to descend first when they thought they needed him the most. And they trust that the same love that took him down into that raging abyss is the same love that is taking him away up in the sky...

They still cannot make the sense out of the very last thing that Superman said, however. They cannot make the connection between the flood and the earthquake, but trust and hope that he will save as many lives as they have been saved by him. They realized that whatever complex that Superman appeared to have was in their own minds. They have experienced the love of Superman. They are turning away from that complex. They are running away from it in their hearts. Strangely, the peace, joy and hope, which supersede and surpass all of their limited knowledge and understanding of the world and men, begin to wash their hearts and souls. And they are looking forward to the day when Superman will return for the honor and the celebration and the love for all...*for now.*

Why did Adam and Eve fall? Why did they commit the first sin of eating the fruit from the tree of the knowledge of good and evil: the only thing that God withheld from them? They fell because they *doubted* that God really loved them. Their hearts became engulfed in sin and darkness because they didn't believe that God has created all things out of love *for* them. In their minds, God had some kind of ulterior motive or hidden agenda that were not really *for* them. That's how the first sin entered into our world and how *any sin* enters any of our lives, even today. When we doubt the perfect love of our Holy God, we become caged in our own fears, and sin enters into our lives. When we do not believe that God is really *for* us, and that He creates and orchestrates everything out of His love for us, the gate of our hearts opens to all things outside of God. As we continue to run away from God because of our doubt, fear and disbelief, we continue to perpetuate and build upon the garrisons above and around the walls of our hearts, and blind ourselves to the life-saving truth of God's eternal love.

The Superman in the movies is just one of numerous and imperfect projections of our highest ideals and dreams for all humanity. The moral of the storyline is still limited by how far our collective ideals and morals can take us. But as with any superhero story, whether it is Superman or Batman, there is the universal truth of love and sacrifice that we are all undeniably and inevitably drawn into because our hearts were designed by God of such sacrificial love. In fact, the great love of God through Christ is beyond our understanding. This is the main reason why we are truly inspired and moved to tears when we watch certain movies or read certain books but can't explain *exactly* why we should be so moved in our hearts. The foundational love of God is beyond comprehension, but it itself becomes the explanation for everything that our loving God created, including our hearts. No illustration or example, including the most noble and sacrificial acts in this world, is a perfect reflection of the perfect love of God in Christ, but each of them does reflect a part of that glory of love for which all our hearts were originally designed for. We have been made to not only receive such unexplainable and perfect love, but to demonstrate the same love to one another in this fallen world full of hate. And we know in our hearts, at least in part, that this life has no meaning and there is no real hope for the humanity if there was no possibility of such foundational and transformational love. As we grow in the knowledge of the perfect love of our Lord Jesus Christ and His perfect sacrificial love, we will begin to abandon the mentality of the immature-selfish spiritual child, and begin to see and understand all things that are shrouded in the mysterious and surpassing love of Christ...as in the verses from 1 Corinthians 13 at the beginning of this Chapter. It is His **love** that begins to unravel the greatest of mysteries in His universe. Will you let Him show you how...through this book?

You notice in the Superman story that people did not understand why Superman had to descend first. Although some of us may know why Jesus Christ had to descend into the depths of suffering and pain of the Cross at the surface level, none of us understands the full extent of the terrible suffering on the Cross. He had to die that way in order to first expose within our hearts the thing: the sin that wants to destroy one another and even God Himself...if it could. And we, as the humanity, did just that on the Cross. He wanted us to see **what** we are being saved from by being the perfect canvas on which we could pour out all that is within us that we did not want to see. Jesus did NOT come to merely save us from the consequences of our sin — as He could have easily done that without His coming — but came to destroy the very sin by which all of these destructive consequences were brought into the world. It is the kind of supernatural, deep, global and foundational love that even the disciples did not recognize or understand until after His resurrection. The suffering of Jesus Christ is explored from several spiritual and physical perspectives in the **chapter** titled **FINISHED.** In the chapter, you will find many things about the suffering of our Lord Jesus Christ that you have not known, and it is my hope that this story of the Cross will convict our hearts and make us love Him more, and really compel us to move and love all people as He commanded. We will come to know that the Lord's command, "Love God with everything you have and love your neighbor as yourself", is not only the new law replacing the old law of the Bible, but the true desire of every human heart at its inception in God of love. The power of resurrection of Jesus Christ is the proof of His love, that *while* He could have easily and rightfully destroyed all of us for our sins, He *instead* has gone through all that incomprehensible and unbelievable pain and suffering for our utterly undeserving and glorious salvation.

Moreover, the people in the story did not understand at first why the Superman could not stop to celebrate with them after they were saved. But with the newfound knowledge of the incomprehensible and global love of the Superman, they begin to see in themselves the spawning of the new knowledge and wisdom of the true love: that the most powerful and sacrificial love is most difficult to understand and shrouded in mystery when we are always distracted, limited and consumed by our own selfish, temporal needs and desires. **Self-entitlement, or self-love, is the number one roadblock to understanding God's love, especially in America today.** People in the story finally began to understand and believe that whatever Superman does, He does out of his love for all people all the time. Understanding global, foundational and eternal love of God through our Lord Jesus Christ is the key to understanding God's impeccable timing and His divine orchestration of events for all of us. Jesus Christ did NOT come down to save just you and me, He came to save all, AND He will save as many as He can through *us*. We will explore why Jesus had to ascend soon after his resurrection in the **chapter titled Ascension.** If you are a Christ follower, you already believe, just like the people in the story above, that Jesus left us because He knew that leaving us was the best possible action by Him for the best possible outcome for all of us.

In this book, we will be empowered to find many powerful spiritual weapons and arsenals to win all arguments against the forces of evil and bring down spiritual strongholds and bondage in our lives. The Love of God is *the weapon of mass destruction* against all evil. And I pray in Christ to convince you that all of these life-altering/building revelations came to me from the Lord because I am finally coming to an understanding of the love of our Lord Jesus Christ, who designed, and who is orchestrating, all things out of His love for us ALL. (Notice that I didn't say "I understood" but "coming to an understanding"). My friends, I'm a person just like you who have made many mistakes in ignorance and stupidity in my own life. It is my desire and prayer that you do not repeat my mistakes in ignorance and continue on wasting your lives as I have for so many years.

I did not write this book so that we can learn how to win arguments against our unbelieving friends, families or co-workers, and make ourselves look good at their expenses. That will actually contradict the very purpose for which we have engaged in such conversations in the first place as a loving Christian. The purpose for anything we do in life is so that people can see the love of Christ that saves — not destroys or demoralizes — through us. If we cannot speak the truth of God in love, we should not speak at all. There is no truth of God in the absence of love because, "Whoever does not love does not know God because God is love" (1 John 4:8).

The Chapter called **Genesis to Revelation** is not exactly a leisurely reading, but it will be worth your time. *My people perish from a lack of knowledge*, the Lord said (Hosea 4:6). And we are dying spiritually as a nation because we have become intellectually lazy when it comes to God and all things spiritual. Read it as often as you'd like and try to understand everything that the Holy Spirit has written down through me. You will be able to understand everything in the chapter because the same Holy Spirit who lives in me also lives inside of you if you are a Christ follower, and He will help you understand what I wrote down through the word. And if you are an unbeliever, the same Holy Spirit will give you the understanding if you simply ask Him from your heart in sincere desire to know the truth. We will also look into the often misunderstood concept of **predestination** and the idea of **true repentance** by **righteous, tormented souls**.

If the knowledge is power, then the knowledge of our Savior Jesus Christ is the soul-saving power for all eternity. If all else fails in your efforts to communicate your hope in Christ that is so often rejected and ridiculed, you can let the person in question borrow this book or you can buy the book for him. Please, do not so easily give the book away because you will probably need to read the book as often as even I will have to come back to read what I have written down. When the Holy Spirit reveals something eternal to us or through us, we always have to go back to that truth because we, including me, are forgetful by nature (1 Cor. 9:27). We are all humans, after all. **The ultimate reason why I'm writing this book is for us to finally begin to take hold of that Love of Christ for which Jesus Christ took hold of us for all eternity.** We cannot allow ourselves to forget His great love. We have been originally designed not only to be the indwelling place of this love of Christ, but *be the love of Christ* to all people. That is the true meaning of Philippians 3:12. That is our divine purpose and that is the very reason why we have been so fearfully and wonderfully made in the beginning. We will take a journey of redemption of our hearts to finally see that this reality of Christ-likeness, or royal priesthood, is our ultimate divine destiny — of king's true justice and intercessory love of high priests — in Jesus Christ. I chose **Joseph** as my main character of this redemption journey story to demonstrate that our hearts are still in desperate need of redemption by the love of Christ, even though our souls may have been saved by our Lord. There is another character in the story that most of us, including myself, would readily identify with — maybe even more so than with Joseph. I will not tell you who this character is now, but you will find out soon and you will be edified like you wouldn't believe! It is only by the redemption of our hearts daily through the Word AND the outworking of the mutual love of Christ within the lives of the redeemed, the Church, that we can begin to 1) see the real love of Christ 2) share in that same love and 3) save this great nation of ours through His great love. Now, every time I mention a verse in this book, it would be ideal for us to read the entire chapter of that verse in which it was found. I promise you will understand the verse much better that way as the verse is placed in its proper context.

Obviously, the Bible is the primary reference for this book. But I also used Wikipedia in order to ascertain the logistics of the road traveled by Joseph in search of his brothers as a 17-year-old boy. Even though I did not directly quote C.S. Lewis in this book, I cannot help but to incorporate and apply to this book the beautiful and clarifying logic found in his books. I bought 5 of his books over 10 years ago, not including Narnia series that I have also read. I did not turn to his books or any other resources in order to absolutely make sure that I did not steal or plagiarize anyone's original ideas. But my memory is better than some, and I must give this man of God a tremendous credit for giving me the solid foundation founded on the mind of Christ, which was a great help to me, not only in writing this book, but with my Christian walk daily. We all build upon the ideas of our great spiritual forefathers and we all have the same Spirit, the revealer of all mysteries, working in and through all of our minds and hearts.

I cannot teach you or change you. None of us can. I cannot even change myself as my own nature is my witness. We are unchangeable except only through and by God and His supernatural power of love. That, too, is the divine design. Only God can change the essence of our being through the illuminating power of His Holy Spirit, who reveals and searches all mysteries of God and men (1 Cor. 2:10), and through the mind of Jesus Christ that He promised we already have (1 Cor. 2:16), as His blood continuously washes away our sins and cleanses the eyes and ears of our hearts. His love is washing our hearts even now. I want you to know that our Lord is redeeming my own heart through the revelations in this book even as I'm writing them down. So, I can only show you where I'm going and I'm running to our Lord Jesus Christ, the foundation and the King of the universe. So with the **Bible** on the other hand — yes it is required for you to come with me if you are my brothers and sisters in Christ — would you join me as I race to the King of love and our High Priest, our Lord Jesus who holds all mysteries of the universe?

Chapter 1

GENESIS TO REVELATION

A conversation with my atheist friend…

I enter through the door and immediately recognize my roommate sitting at the counter in the kitchen. He is a very smart guy with a PhD in physics. I've been kind of careful with him in terms of sharing my faith because I know he is an atheist and has gotten into several arguments with other Christians before. I've been praying that I would be given the opportunity to share the Gospel with him in a non-confrontational, non-pressured setting. He looks up and says,

What's up, Sam? How are you doing?

Pretty good. Thanks! You?!

Not bad…not bad…hey, you were kind of in a hurry to get out of here yesterday morning.

Yeah, well….I was kind of late to the church…

Oh, so…you go to a church, I didn't know that. How's that working out for you?

Pretty good. Uh…maybe you want to join me sometime?

Nah…I know you are a nice guy Sam, but I don't believe in six-legged flying frogs.

Flying frogs? What do you mean? I don't understand.

The Bible basically is full of fables, myths and legends. Illogical and impossible stories…You believe in the evolution right? The systematic evolution and advancement of species to effect higher function of cognition and faculties by selective environmental pressures, resulting in mutations in our genes for that same ever-escalating, ever-advancing goal. That's the absolute truth! You are in medicine. You should know this stuff better than I do…The idea that all these things just popped up out of thin air is just… ridiculous. Six-legged flying frogs, my friend.

Well…I believe that we all came from God. We didn't just sponta- neously happen. You are a physicist, right? What about the Big bang?

Well, what about it?

Where did the Big Bang come from?

Well…maybe there was a beginning of some kind of black hole that was super hot…The mass that is so dense and energetic that all life came from it when it exploded 13 billion years ago. And the universe has been continuously expanding ever since. By observing the universe around us, we know that things are moving further and further away from us. The ever-advancing science is coming up with all kinds of incredible theories too! It's the result of the scientific observation of the universe my friend… science, not creation. Science, not fiction or religion…you get my drift? Nothing can come from nothing…all right?

Sorry but again, where did all THAT come from before the Big bang? Where did all that dense matter packed with such tremendous energy come from? What was there before that? There had to be something in the beginning all by itself that everything else came from because it's always been there. Like you said, nothing comes from nothing…and yet, here we are.

Sam, the Bible doesn't make any sense at all. The evolution is how life happened. The evidences are overwhelming!

OK…You know those amazing deep sea creatures with florescent eyes and projections…you know, to help them see in that dark abyss to find food and stuff?

That's right. That is the perfect example of the product of evolution over millions and millions of years! I can't believe I'm actually having this conversation with you. You are a scientist, too! You walked right into it, Sam…

Well…just bear with my questions…why would they descend all the way down there in the first place? If they were hiding in the dark for such a long time…did they just wander around in the dark, probing and prodding that vast ocean floor for food while 'hoping' and 'wishing' with all their might that somehow, some of their appendages or even their eyes will begin to grow…before they begin to glow? Did they strain the head muscles really hard for millions of years as they were morphing into higher beings? Wouldn't they have died in matter

20

of days if they couldn't find food? Even if they started out as simple cells in the dark and were able to find food in the dark without the lights — as I'm sure according to the evolution that it would've taken millions of years to develop senses such as lights — how would they even begin to 'think' that they would need the light with all of its bio-chemical reactions/designs, the light that they wouldn't really need by that time? Cell itself is by no means simple and you know it too. The whole theory of evolution sounds like some kind of magic or witchcraft to me...don't you think?

What are you trying to say?

I'm just saying, wouldn't it make more sense if all the creations were designed and programmed by some intelligent, mysterious and infinite God to reflect such intelligent and mysterious designs that we are just beginning to understand? And that you and I are having this conversation about God because God, who is extremely patient, is allowing it? Look, you already know that I'm not perfect; none of us are...only God is. I'm just saying He's been very patient with me, as well as with you.

I want to know God's thoughts — the rest are mere details.– Albert Einstein.

For "who has known the mind of the Lord so as to instruct him?" But we have the mind of Christ. — Isaiah, the prophet, and Paul, the Apostle — 1st Corinthians 2:16

This is what the Lord says, he who made the earth, the Lord who formed it and established it — the Lord is his name: "Call to me and I will answer you and tell you great and unsearchable things you do not know." — Jeremiah 33:2-3

The earth is filled with your love, Lord; teach me your decrees.– Psalm 119:64.

The Unfolding of His Love

B efore there was universe, there was "God's universe". It is the "world" that was there before the creation of this world and will still be there long after this world is gone. It was not the sphere that God existed in, but rather the sphere that existed within God Himself. God created this present universe and set it into motion in the beginning in Himself. This universe is vast. But the size and scope of the universe does not even begin to compare with the magnitude and the infinity of God's being and the universe He operates in. This is not even the case of our universe contained in some kind of "marble" in God's shoebox. That would still be like attempting to somehow project infinite God in our finite frame of mind. There is absolutely no possible way that we, as a finite being, will ever come to understand the infinite God by our own will, power, device or methodology.

However, let's continue on with the "marble in God's shoebox" analogy so that we may possibly, by the grace of God, understand the way through which we can discover and know God. Imagine that this universe is a tiny particle trapped in this marble, and we are human beings who are trapped in that "vast" particle. The scientists tell us that this universe has always been expanding since the "big bang". Perhaps God has placed this marble on a slowly heating pan in His kitchen and the marble is slowing expanding, and along with it, this particle called our universe. In all seriousness, if God was all-powerful and all-knowing, He would be too big to be contained in this universe. This is not a metaphorical statement. That is to say, the totality of His infinite being, His "physicality" alone, cannot be found anywhere in this vast universe because this universe is still extremely finite and tiny compared to God's being. God would be too big to fit himself in "here". God would have to "stand" outside of this universe. All we see is a very small, partial reflection of His being in this universe. Our physical world still may overwhelm our senses to the point of acknowledging that there has to be a being much greater us. However, the fact remains that nothing we observe in this universe will help us truly understand God or prove His existence while we are in this finite universe, because the laws of this finite universe do not apply to the creator God who is infinite. God does not exist in this universe, but the universe exists within God. God is not a part of the universe, but the universe is a small part of the infinite God!

Can you imagine if the totality of God somehow manifested itself to you right at this moment? Even without knowing or acknowledging the attributes of God, such as holiness or righteousness, you would be so overpowered by His presence that you will not live to tell anyone about it.

Even your very soul would be consumed by His presence. We experience a tiny fraction of this type of "death/paralysis" or "consumption of our spirit" when we meet someone we really respect or may even idolize. I recently witnessed a teenage girl on TV who broke down and cried as she was hugging, while trembling, a rock star that she had been idolizing and dreaming about. She had to sit down because she was too weak to remain standing. As I was watching, I was afraid for her that she would faint. Has anyone taught her that's how she should react to such an encounter, or was she moved by her heart and soul to act that way in spite of how ridiculous she would appear? She didn't want to behave that way, but her heart compelled her to react to that situation involuntarily. She could not help herself. But we also remember how God demonstrated just a fraction of his limitless power to Job by giving him the vision of that terrifying and indomitable leviathan. Job, more righteous than any of us, not only repented, but despaired and despised himself in the presence of such power. The response from Job came from that eternal core in all of our hearts, designed by God to correctly recognize and resonate with the presence of the Almighty God that our feeble intellect has rationalized away in His absence. If creations can elicit such powerful and involuntary reaction to the point where we can feel the very life force just ebbing away from our being, what do you think will happen if the Creator of this universe were to appear before you right now right where you are? Do you think we will live after seeing God in His full glory and power? He cannot reveal Himself in totality because His full presence will completely annihilate us. None of the prophets believed that they would live after seeing a mere "representation" of God. And those of us who have stood before the majesty of Grand Canyon, Niagara Falls or other natural wonders of the world remember such overpowering emotions that we have never known we had.

We should be ever so grateful that the ever-patient God will not let that full revelation of Himself to *happen* to us while we are living in these weak bodies. That in and of itself is the reflection of the most enduring, unexplainable, and the most incredible character attribute of God. There is no one more patient and God is the essence of love that begins with patience. But it is in our human nature to take God's love down to our level and reduce them in scope in an attempt to somehow make a sense out of Him in our own unredeemed minds.

When my mom was alive, I barely acknowledged her existence at times. But I'm not the exception in this and you, as the reader of this book, know it in your heart also. I thought I loved her in my childish ways but it is only when she was gone that I realized with much pain and sorrow in my heart how much she really loved me. In fact, this is the story of all of our lives. Her love was finally made real and powerful by the absence of her love that I didn't really appreciate while she was present in this world. So, perhaps the love of God is too great in this great nation of USA because we are living in it? Perhaps the love of God is too near. Maybe that is why we don't feel it at all? The observation of our own human nature bares witness to the fact that it actually is.

What about the science, you say? It's not the science that disproves God's existence, but rather our corrupt human nature that filters out all the sound and logical approach to science. Let's look at a concrete example. There are numerous, near perfectly-preserved ancient fossils trapped in the rock formations that span several layers "representing geological time tables". Supposedly the several layers of the formation translate into several layers of earth and dirt that have accumulated over thousands of years. If that was true, shouldn't we see only the bottom 10 percent or less of the fossil in the first bottom layer, while the rest of the fossil, exposed on the top, either decayed or washed away in the next thousands of years? The preservations of these fossils can only be explained by sudden and massive shifting of earth and quick trapping of these creatures in matter of hours and maybe even seconds, not years, and certainly not thousands of years. Massive flood in global scale would be a good theory indeed. It is more than a theory but the clue for that absolute unchanging truth. The clue is in those rock formations along with many others in the universe. But most of the scientists, even the most brilliant ones, have chosen not to use their scientific approach in the matter of the origin of the universe simply because they have put their faith and trust in the limited universe that must have "happened" without God at the inception of their "scientific" mind somewhere along the way. So, God may choose not to reveal Himself to them unless they repent and see that the existence of God, in which we all exist and have our being, is not only a definite possibility, but inevitability. And as a fellow scientist, we all know that this vast universe, in both at the cosmic and subatomic level, has many elements that continuously defy the traditional and established scientific logic! The very foundation of science is changing as our understanding of the universe changes, but our God is the same yesterday, today and forever. He never changes! He is beyond this *changing* universe.

We cannot be so arrogant to presume that God must somehow be demonstrated in this finite universe. Even if the science eventually reaches its perfection, its power of interpretation is still limited by the observation of our finite box called universe. Again, God in His totality is simply too big, too much for this universe to contain. God does not have to exist in this universe or follow any of its rules to make Him known. Why would He subjugate Himself in that manner? But rather, if there really is God, the universe may exist within God because God allows it and sustains it. He *must* be love. And who is to say that God, who created this universe to obey certain physical laws, will one day decide to create another universe with completely different set of rules? By the way, that day will come. The Book of truth says this world is temporary and passing away. He will bring us the world that is so far above and beyond our expectations and imaginations that no one will be able to describe it while we are in this world. It is the world that no eye has seen, no ear has heard and no mind has conceived.

We can only know and understand God when and if God decides that we can know Him. In other words, God has to reveal Himself to us in order for us to know Him. Again, I say that we can only know and understand God when and if God decides that we can know Him, not the other way around. That is a very simple and yet a powerful piece of logic, is it not? No amount of scientific data or secular philosophy will enable us to grasp the totality of God. At best, they will only help explain His partial, but still magnificent, shadows that He chose to leave behind when He created, and while sustaining, this universe. If you would just take a moment to think about this, then you will begin to understand the nature of God and His great love. Again, if there really was God, the question that we need to be asking is not, "how are we going to find out if He really exists?" or "how can we get to God?", but rather "how is infinite God going to reveal Himself so that finite beings like us can finally understand Him, who is infinite in every way beyond our imagination?" All other religions, scientific methods and philosophies are men's attempts to find the foundational or absolute or eternal truth that built this finite and limited universe. To say that in a different way, all of these are men's efforts to reach God if there really was God. And therein lays a self-contradiction. Men simply do not have the capacity, ability or the will to get to God, who is bigger than anything we can see, touch or understand in this universe. He is beyond this universe! We cannot figure God out, but it is God who creates us and defines who we are.

Christianity is the only logical belief system that says the omnipotent and omniscient God had to reach down and, somehow, make Himself known to finite beings like us, who are too prideful to see that there could be anything beyond this universe. There was no other way for us to know the infinite God but only by His own Revelation to us. That is the foundational truth of Christianity. God had to somehow mysteriously "package" or "fold" His infinite being into a finite flesh, while retaining His full God-self in the way only He knows how, so that we can begin — yes it is only the beginning — to scratch the surface of who He is and begin to understand His great love and mercy. And Christianity is the only universal belief system proclaiming God's ultimate Revelation that has already come in the most intimate, humble and personal way so everyone can know God, from the least to the greatest because He is love first and last. Again, we know God only through God's own Revelation because He alone has the ability to make Himself known to us, AND because He is love. He didn't have to, but He did it all out of His great love for us. And the culmination of the Revelation of God is the love of God revealed in the life, death and the resurrection of Jesus Christ.

The love that was forged in the heart of God was finally revealed in full measure on that terrible Cross 2000 years ago. The power of forgiveness through love was the first and the last thing that we, the unredeemed, desperately needed more than anything in the world. That love could not be found in this world. That is the reason why the Revelation culminated on the Cross. We are all sinners and fell short of that overwhelming glory of God. The infinite God, in a mysterious way that only He is capable of, had to "package" Himself so that we, finite beings, can touch and begin to understand who He is. That is the Revelation of God to us. He would not have made that choice to reveal Himself this way if He was not love. Why the Cross? This unforgettable act of sacrifice was designed to drive home the point into our very souls that this is the most relevant and necessary revelation of who God is and why He made us. In spite of who we are and what we have done, we were originally made to be loved and to love. And He loved so magnificently and sacrificially on the Cross. The love of God, which is and will always be beyond the man's understanding, is the most powerful and relevant truth to human beings and God knew that His love would be the first and the last of all that entails in our eternal journey with Him. It is the kind of unimaginable love for which we are being saved but we ourselves has not yet taken hold of.

With the most frustrating kind of emotions and intellectual struggles in your heart, that you cannot even begin to verbalize or prove, all of us will eventually understand that this love of God is the ultimate reality for our hearts. Every knee shall bow and every tongue shall confess that Jesus Christ truly is the Lord of our hearts. The ultimate reality of love culminating in Jesus Christ is what built this world. And that same reality of love built our hearts and souls.

Colossians 1:15-17 says, *"He, Christ, is the image of the invisible God, the firstborn over all creation. For by him all things were created; things in heaven and on earth, visible and invisible, whether thrones or powers or rulers or authorities; all things were created by him and for him. He is before all things, and in him all things hold together."* And in John 3:16, it says, *"For God so loved the world, He sent His only begotten Son, that whosoever believes in Him should not perish but have everlasting life."*

His entrance into the world was so inconspicuous and humble that only the wisest, noble AND humble men and women on earth were given the wisdom to decipher and recognize it. God resists the proud but gives grace to the humble. The uncontainable Word, Jesus Christ, who was with God and who was God from the beginning, became contained in the flesh. In His everlasting mercy, He bounded and limited Himself so we can finally begin to understand God. He was the light of the world, but this world, distracted and blinded by its love of darkness, did not recognize and understand Him. We were too immersed in the darkness to know that this painfully bright and abrasive revelation was the light that we needed so desperately. We were too busy elevating ourselves at the expense of the souls around us. We despised the One who came to cleanse, reclaim and rebuild our inner beings that were originally designed to build our souls and multiply. He came as a baby in a manger, born of the Virgin Mary. Our physical procreation and multiplication were meant to be the reflection of ever expanding glory of God who is holy and who is Spirit. We indeed have come so far from the Garden of Eden, haven't we?

God began His Revelation to humanity on this planet with patience and humility so that we can come near and see and touch Him. Love is patient. Love does not boast but rejoices in the truth. And Jesus Christ is God's truth and love personified. The record of His teenage years is nearly non-existent. He humbly fulfilled the role as the loving and dutiful son. The Maker and Builder of the universe became a son of a carpenter. One would be right to assume that he was the most loving son any mother had in the history of the world. At that wedding, before His "time" of ministry had come, Jesus had turned water into wine at the request of His earthly mother Mary. Only God can step out of His own schedule and still be on time! In obedience, He has 1) saved the party hosts from certain shame and 2) honored His mom in the presence of others, while 3) giving us the first glimpse of the ultimate revelation in which the wine, representing His blood, replaces the water in the ceremonial jars, representing the works of the law and self-righteousness. In other words, grace, grace and GRACE! Only the Christ can accomplish three in one act! And He said His time had not yet come? He was in the zone when He was not even in the game. How amazing is the grace and the work of God and revelations in Jesus Christ!

In Him, we receive true forgiveness through His amazing grace that is not found in this universe.

God has revealed Himself to us in Jesus Christ through His birth as a humble baby, His untold preparations and the magnificent redemptive work of His ministry. Then of course, there was His suffering, death and resurrection. His unimaginable suffering was caused by our equally unfounded and confounding rejection and hatred — fueled by the sins of our pride — toward that love and truth that we did not recognize, but desperately needed. He was fully man, fully God and the only bridge between men and God, and it will take all eternity to fully meditate on what all that means and all that it entails. He is not from this limited universe. He came as the Lamb of God, the ultimate manifestation of His sacrificial love. Our hearts were made by and for that kind of love and nothing else will satisfy. He is the maker of our hearts. He is love that the world has not seen or heard. He was the Lamb of God who was crushed by His own Father God for our salvation. But our salvation from what? Salvation from...OURSELVES.

He died for us and rose victorious over our sin and death. The resurrection is the proof that our sins, seemingly insurmountable, could not overcome Jesus Christ. But the story does not end there. He will come again to claim His people as the Lion of Judah, the Lamb of wrath and the ultimate Judge and King. He will come, riding on that fearsome white horse with many crowns, which replaces the crown of thorns, with His eyes blazing and the sword of truth coming out of His mouth. He will set all things right and wipe tears from every eyes. We will live in that magnificent city of crystals and precious stones with our new eyes and bodies and hear unspeakable awesome things that St. Paul dared not describe. We will see all things anew through Him who makes all things new, EVEN NOW. He will bring down all that are haughty and deceitful and throw them down into hell, for He will not allow those things to waste and destroy our souls any longer! The justice of God designed out of His love for the protection of our souls is the purpose of hell.

In the end nothing else matters but the love of God. This world and all of its realities, even the undying love of our loved ones and the world itself does not matter without His love, which gives true meaning of love and life to all. This temporary world and everything in it will pass away, but the love of God is forever and His mercy endures forever. All of us will eventually come to understand, with deep yearning and regret in our souls, none of what we deemed true, pure, noble, and worthy of our most enduring pursuits in this world really mattered without the love of Christ, which compelled Him to save even the very people that killed Him! I was one of them! We were all there! Our sins killed him in the most gruesome way imaginable. But He rose victoriously from sin and death and is now sitting at the right hand of the Almighty Father, until Satan is made his footstool! And only in Jesus Christ, we can find ourselves in true love that is eternal, that is beyond ourselves and our universe. This love is the very thing that our eternal hearts, made by the King eternal, yearns for.

The Revelation of God in totality is our Lord Jesus Christ, from Genesis to Revelation and everywhere in between and BEYOND. Now to the One who is sitting at the right hand of God; to the One who is the very foundation and the capstone of this universe; whose conquering love surpasses all knowledge, power and wisdom; we give all the honor, power and glory, forever and ever. Thy kingdom come. THY WILL BE DONE. Amen.

Chapter 2

HIS KINGDOM COME...INTO THE HEART OF AMERICA AND THE WORLD

The psalmist recites: *how can a young man keep his way **pure**? By living according to your **Word**.*—Psalms 119:9

John says: *the Word was with God and the Word was God. And, the **Word** became flesh, Jesus Christ.*—John 1

Jesus said: *blessed is the **pure** of heart for he will "see" God.*—Matthew 5:8

Our great nation has never faced such challenging times. Never before have we seen so many of our young generations "boomerang" back home to their parents after being *equipped* for real life in colleges and universities across America. We are seeing an entire *millennial* generation who are growing up *connected* to the world through the social media with hundreds and thousands of *friends* on cyber domains, but totally disconnected from their own families and the reality of their own spiritual deprivation. We have a whole new *sandwich* generation who are desperately trying to hold the family together by saving and providing for both their children and their aging parents. And while most of the adults are too busy making a living for our families physically and materially, our children are dying spiritually. If their time is not being occupied by godly parents being trained in the word and prayer, it will be occupied by the forces of this world and by the evil one who controls them.

Never before have we seen such chasms between the parents and the children, the rich and the poor, and the Church and the State. Are we witnessing the beginning of the birth pang into a dark new era, where we will see the disintegration of the very foundation of our civilization: our families? Have we walked so far away from our God, the Creator and the Sustainer of the universe, and forgotten how to really create and sustain the true and eternal families and relationships in Him, who is the alpha and omega; the beginning and the end? How do we, as the nation and the Church, begin to take the journey of rebuilding of our hearts and souls and bring our children back from the brink of disaster and total self-annihilations? How do we actually begin to see and understand God, who loves us and desires to bring all of us back into his arms of the true healing and re-creation? How do we help our children to fill their spiritual void, and equip them to fight against the ever mounting spiritual forces and strongholds that continuously infiltrate their minds and drag their hearts away from us, our family and our God?

Young parents in this country have never faced so many challenges and they may not even be aware of the true size of the ice-burg of catastrophe that the Titanic America is directly heading into. We have always felt secure and invincible as a great nation, but those days are going away as we are getting away from God, who desires to make this nation truly indivisible in Him. We have become the nation divided on just about every issue. Hatred crouches at the door of our hearts. The schools and the theaters have become killing grounds. Installing metal detectors as a preventative measure will not eliminate the source of our problems that created the need for them in the first place. We must allow God to deal with *the source* now. We must address the sins of our nation...on our knees before God.

The journey of our hearts back to our Maker begins with two simple steps: Getting on our knees in Prayer and getting our minds into the Bible. The true road to recovery and rebuilding of our nation begins with the Church, the body of believers in Christ, founded upon the unchanging truth of our Lord and Savior Jesus Christ. He is the builder of the universe who came as a son of a carpenter. He is the builder of all foundations, especially our families. He did not merely come to save us from the consequences of our sins, but came to destroy the very thing that is destroying us and our nations: the sins of pride and self-love. If the people can only see the true sacrificial love of Jesus Christ, the Christ who commanded us to love our

31

neighbors as ourselves in Him, then they will know where the true salvation comes from. It comes from our Lord Jesus Christ living through our hearts. The true and eternal solution is only found in the Maker of this Universe and all we have to do is take that first step of drawing closer to our God. We can simply return to our God, and He will return to us (Zechariah 1:3). It is as simple as drawing closer to Him, and He will draw closer to us (James 4:8). And He has already COME near to us in His only begotten Son on the Cross! *"If my people, who are called by my name, will humble themselves and pray and seek my face and turn from their wicked ways, then I will hear from heaven, and I will forgive their sin and will heal their land,"* the Lord declares in 2 Chronicle 7:14!

When we work out our salvation, who is Jesus Christ the holy word in our hearts, with fear and trembling, we will be purified and sanctified by Christ of love. It is only through continuous purification and renewing of our minds, and redemption of our hearts by the Word, Christ, that we will truly "see" God of our salvation. We need to be purified by the word of the Bible daily. My brothers and sisters in Christ, are we reading the Word? Are we at least listening to the Word? The fate of our nation and our children depend on this simple act of eating of the Word daily...in your bedroom or in your car on your commute or anywhere you can find the time. The Bible is the spiritual bread of life for our mind, heart and soul. The devil, working through our flesh, is doing all he can to keep us away from the knowledge of the truth and love in the Bible. Only Christ through the Bible is the bread that can satisfy that eternal hunger pain. We have been starving ourselves too long. Only the hearts that are being purified by Christ in the Word will truly know and understand who God really is. In other words, if our hearts are still being captivated by the lust, greed, hatred, jealousy, idolatry in the world and the religious hypocrisy in attempts to cover them all up, we will never be able to "see" God for who He really is, and we will surely miss his eternal blessing. God will not be the one who will destroy us but we will destroy ourselves! If Christ does not come again as the ultimate King of justice at the appointed time, no one will be left on the planet for Him to judge! God is holy. God is love. Through his loving hand of discipline and protection of our inner-beings, God will finally enable us to see that He is holy. He loves all people and wants to save us from our self-destructive and divisive unholiness. The time has come for America to unite as one people in the unchanging truth and love of Jesus Christ!

I strongly urge you not only to read, but to examine this book carefully through the purifying Word, the Bible, to really "see" God. Blessed is he who is pure of heart; for he will see Me, our Lord said! Our hearts need to be actively purified by the living word daily. How else would you able to "see" that I'm defending the truth of the gospel, the good news in Jesus Christ, which not only saves us from who we are, but transforms us into what we are going to be for all eternity through the power of His blood? I challenge all of you to be diligent in seeking the truth in the Bible, first. If you search the divine wisdom in Christ as for hidden treasures you will find it, the Bible says. That is the promise of our God. If you cannot find the time to read, will you at least find the time to listen to it? God gives us the gift of time so that we can spend our time to get to know God first; the Creator of all things and the Giver of all things.

Our hearts have been forged and created in the heart of the one true King and the High Priest: Lord Jesus Christ. We have been created in His likeness, in His very image the Bible says. He is holy and true, full of perfect love and justice. He came to reclaim our inner beings so that He can demonstrate His everlasting redemptive power through us while we are still in this world. He didn't save us just so that we can go to Heaven after we die. He saved us in Christ, the King and the High priest, in order to demonstrate His power of true justice and intercessory love through us and for us, the kings and priests in His kingdom. And the power of the Holy Spirit, who searches all things and even deep things of God, will allows us to look into the very heart of God and his true and eternal intentions for ALL people. We will see that He does everything out of his love for us. I mean EVERYTHING. Yes, even in making Hell, as you will see later. I believe that the same Holy Spirit will make the message of this book clear to you as to whether the things I write is worthy of contemplation and putting into practice. This journey that we are about to embark is ultimately about finding the true Jesus Christ: the King and the High priest, whose love and justice are the desires of all nations and all people (Haggai 2:7 and Malachi 3:1). We will be built up to His glory! My beloved in Christ, we need to choose this day whom we will serve because the world is watching and waiting for the true redemption by the Redeemer...through us.

Our soul has been fully purchased in Christ. But our hearts are yet to be redeemed to its full measure because we still do not fully understand why the Lord truly is the desire of ALL people. It is only through His love that you can see and understand everything, including God's perfect timing. Until the very end of time, the truth of the Word and the power of His blood will continuously expose, purge, cleanse and heal this heart of ours unto the redeemed hearts that will truly see God, and His people for who we really need to be in Christ. We are made to be loved and to love one another with nothing less than the love of the one true King and the High Priest. When the Lord comes, we will fully know and understand that the love of Christ is the very purpose for which all of us have been created, but we are still very far from taking hold of this true and eternal love of our Lord Jesus Christ — or Christ-likeness— which already has taken hold of us for all eternity (1st Corinthians 13:9-10, Philippians 3:12).

The prophet Joel prophesied that in the last days that God *"will pour out (His) Spirit on ALL people, Your sons and daughters will prophesy, your old men will dream dreams, your young men will see visions."* If I perceive myself worthy of being counted among those to whom the revelations and the visions of God have been poured out, I also know through the Spirit that I have only begun to scratch the surface of the surpassing love of our Lord Jesus Christ and what He has in store for us here and now as well as in heaven. None of the revelation in this book is new. They are simplified and different ways of understanding the eternal and unchanging ways of God that is more powerfully and mysteriously articulated in the Bible: the only perfect Book. By the way, the same Spirit of Revelation who is being poured out on me to write this book, is also being poured out on you if you are in Christ! Please believe in the word of God because His promise does not depend on our emotions or awareness. If He said it in the Word, it happened, it is happening and it will happen. We have to understand, however, that He doesn't want any of us to miss the glorious partaking in it or perish in ignorance because we didn't know what the promises were in the first place.

> *For the word of God is living and active. Sharper than any double-edged sword, it penetrates even to diving soul and spirit, joints and marrow; it judges the thoughts and attitudes of the heart. Nothing in all creation is hidden from God's sight. Everything is uncovered and laid bare before the eyes of Him to whom we must give account." Hebrews 4:12-13*

Let the deconstructing power of the Word of truth, Jesus Christ in our hearts, break down all the barriers of lies within our hearts that we have set up in order to hide all the lust, greed, and the darkness of pride; especially the religious pride. All these things, insidiously or openly, have been systematically defiling our hearts, destroying our families, our friends, our nations and our very souls. In order to be set on the path of redemption and truly find the love of God that saves, we have to first see and understand what we are being saved from and all of its devastating consequences. Let the Word expose the core of our unredeemed hearts for what it really is so that we can give them up to God, who is full of mercy and grace of transforming power, with the Holy Spirit illuminating and guiding our paths through the Word and helping us reclaim our Divine destiny in God's kingdom. That is the journey for all of our hearts while we are in this temporary world. We remain in this world for that exact and glorious purpose.

But where exactly is God's kingdom, we ask? The kingdom of God is where Christ is the King, breaking down all the barriers and destroying all the strongholds that resist the coming of His Kingdom... in our own hearts. The kingdom of God is within you and me, our Lord declares (Luke 17:21)! If we have truly received Christ into our hearts, we will see that this is the eternal reality that our hearts were made for from the very beginning: our heart is the domain for the King Jesus and hence His Kingdom! Christ is waiting for us to hand over the throne of our hearts where we have been sitting on. Let us abdicate ourselves so that we may truly see the glory of the King of love shining through us...for all of us. God did not waste his time when He created you and me in his very image and He wants to reclaim it now with the love of Christ for our own sake.

Our hearts and souls have been made to be magnificent in Christ the King! Our future, our generations, our nation and our very souls may depend on our decision of relinquishing of the self-throne and self-entitlement. That would be the beginning of our journey to become true kings, queens and priests, God's true justice and love, in the eyes of God, and eventually, all people. And as you take this journey, you will begin to truly understand that it was actually our desire to make the Lord the King of our hearts all along. Things of this world will grow dim and unattractive; for the Holy Spirit will illuminate through our hearts to expose all of their deceptions and empty promises. You will discover that there is nothing or no one worthy of your hearts except the Maker of your heart, Jesus Christ. We will be righteously angry at ourselves and ecstatic beyond measure at the same time for all the time that we have needlessly wasted, and all the love that we could've had that is STILL waiting for all of us in the ever patient, longsuffering and loving arms of our Lord Jesus.

Chapter 3

LOVE, JUSTICE, HELL AND THE WRATH OF GOD.

*And I saw the seven angels who stand before God and to them were given seven trumpets. Then another angel, having a golden censer, came and stood at the altar. He was given much incense, that he should offer it with the **prayers of all the saints** upon the golden altar which was before the throne. And the smoke of the incense, with the prayers of the saints, ascended before God from the angel's hand. Then the angel took the censer, filled it with fire from the altar, and threw it to the earth. And there were noises, thunderings, lightnings, and an earthquake. – Revelation 8:2-5.*

And Moses said to the people, "Do not fear; for God has come to test you, and that His fear may be before you, so that you may not sin." – Exodus 20:20.

I'm afraid that the schools will prove the very gates of hell, unless they diligently labor in explaining the Holy Scriptures and engraving them in the heart of the youth. – Martin Luther, a German leader and a true priest.

W ell, this is perfectly a good way to ruin your perfect day...but I'm not apologizing. You know why? Because you will soon rejoice with me in the truth that God creates and designs everything out of his love for us... even Hell. I assure you that you will be edified and be empowered.

You will find yourself in the love of Christ once again. God loves you. He doesn't create anything if it was not meant to build your heart and soul unto eternal redemption and glory in Him. And the truth shall set us free in the Son, even from our fear of Hell.

Hell was created by God to destroy the things that destroy our souls. THAT, too, is love. That is the truth that we have overlooked but the truth that we actually desire. Does that sound strange to you? The above passage from Revelation chapter 8 reveals something about the desires of our hearts for God's righteousness and justice to be revealed. In it, the collective prayer of the saints is the very catalyst for which the justice and the wrath of God will be executed on the earth at the end. Now, we may not verbalize this desire for justice, but we will see this inevitable truth of our hearts in its full destructive power revealed against sins and evil, because our hearts were originally designed to be holy and to be one with the Holy One. Be careful to note that I'm NOT saying we are wishing to exact vengeance on those who have done evil against us. "The vengeance is mine," God says. He is the only one who can bring true justice in His own time. What I'm saying here is that it is our heart's deepest desire for God to bring utter devastation to all things that cause the death of our hearts and souls, and all the pain and suffering that stem from it. In 2 Corinthians 10:3-5, it says, *"for though we live in the world, we do not wage war as the world does. The weapons we fight with are not the weapons of the world (physical weapons against people). On the contrary, they have divine power to demolish strongholds (spiritual weapons against principalities and the forces of evil). We demolish arguments and every pretension that sets itself up against the knowledge of God, and we take captive every thought to make it obedient to Christ."* And we know from the scripture that we are not fighting against the people but the principalities and powers that are continuously raging against God in the spiritual realm to ensnare and destroy all people...even the elect! Because of the power of Hell created by God Almighty, we will finally be validated and vindicated and be raised up in our Lord Jesus Christ. We shall continue to explore.

The word "Hell" is the least favorite vocabulary and the concept of Hell is quite disconcerting and confusing for many Christians out there. Even as I am writing the title for this chapter, I wrote the word Hell after the words, "love" and "justice" in efforts to possibly lessen its negative connotations. But I'm not sure that this arrangement of words actually did the job. I might have even put an unintentional emphasis on the word by this feeble attempt. Is there something about Hell and the wrath of God that our souls may actually identify with but have failed to understand? There is the perennial question, "If God is love, then why would He send anyone to Hell?" He even asked us to love and forgive all, even our enemies and forgive them seven times seventy. Most Christians are seriously perplexed over this issue and cannot reconcile the concept of love with Hell. The idea of Hell or the wrath of God is becoming less and less relevant to our Christian walk and often quickly glazed over or skipped entirely in our conversations. And then there is the issue of "good, non-Christians" out there. Almost all of us have friends, loved ones, and people we greatly admire who have not made the profession of faith to receive Christ into their hearts. What about those "good" people who do not know God or have rejected Christ? What about their fate?

First of all, God says there is no such a thing as good people or a good person. Only God is good because He is the only one who can measure up to His own perfect eternal standards. Our righteousness and everything we uphold as our moral ideals are like filthy rags before the holy God, the Bible says. Our salvation only depends on the acceptance of Christ and His perfect works, never by our own imperfect and shallow/self-righteous works in the eyes of God. But the individual salvation is determined by the state of their hearts and souls and only God knows where they are spiritually. We are not mind readers and cannot presume to ever know the true condition of the hearts of others. So we reserve our judgment as to who truly had the repentant hearts to receive Christ until we see everything clearly in Him, who is the patient love, at the end. But it is absolutely critical for us to understand that God, who is love, also created Hell because it was necessary, not for Him, but for us. Again, hell was designed by God to bring utter and complete destruction to the things that are bent on destroying the things of God; mainly our souls that are being redeemed in Christ. It was built to protect the soul of humanity in many ways, giving it its true validations and vindications. Let's look into it a little further.

What caused Satan to fall? In short, Satan fell because he tried to elevate himself above all creation, including God Himself. It is the sin of pride that caused the fall of humanity and infected our inner beings. It is the pride that is relentless, restless, accusing, seeking and constantly lying in order to subjugate everything under it — not to love, build and restore as with God — but to deceive, abuse and destroy in order to continually feed and reinforce its self-perpetual, self-perceived, self-grandeur. God will not withhold his judgment on such a terrible sin forever. But let's suppose that God, who is abounding in love and mercy, forgave Satan and let him go and along with him, all his dominion and also all those people who have chosen to reject the grace paid for by the blood of Christ. What do you think will happen next? Hold on to that thought.

We have all heard that "nice guys finish last". Have you seen a "nice" person being taken advantaged of or even abused? Of course you have. Why is that person abused time and time again? Why is that person allowing the abuser to continuously assault his heart and soul? What is the answer that we are looking for here? First of all, this nice person is the victim of the fear of man. He is your everyday "yes-man", the crowd pleaser, and he will not let you down but let you walk all over him in the hopes that somehow he will be perceived as someone who really matters in your eyes, and who is worthy of your attention and maybe even your affection. But such validation or affirmation never comes and you know why. Because if you are the abuser who filters everything through human pride, such actions will only fuel your pride that you indeed are smarter and more powerful than the "nice guy", and that will either perpetuate more abuse or at best, pity and mock the fool that doesn't realize the essence of human nature and the ways of the world that you yourself are manipulating to your own advantage — whether knowingly or unknowingly. Both the abuser and the "nice" guy are coming short of the true love and glory of God, in whom we find our true validation, freedom and fulfillment. By the way, if you are one of these "nice" people, in Christ, and being abused physically and/or spiritually, you have the power in Christ to say no and be free. Don't let anyone outside of, or especially in, the church abuse you or take you out of context because you are "nice". God did not create us to be abused in such ways. Do not fall victim to such entrapments.

God is not a "nice" person, nor is he a yes man to petty and shallow requests or desires of our hearts that does nothing but destroy our own lives, nor does He need validations from anyone. And God is not this abuser who would exercise his power to elevate himself at the expense of the souls of the others. God is jealous for His people the Bible says, but we are jealous for our own selfish agendas. He wants us to know that He is God of unimaginable power and domination for the highest and the most glorious purpose for all of us when the time is right. He knows better than anyone that Satan, who has not shown any sign of repentance or remorse since his creation ages ago, will take this "forgiveness" or pardoning of his sins as a license to do and create more evil and bring more destruction. He is the ultimate abuser and the accuser. The "unconditional pardoning" will lift up Satan in his own eyes, justifying and fueling his pride even more! God knows that Satan will up his game in making a mockery of everything that Christ did for us, every single act of suffering that He went through for us, and everything that Christ have done through us by the power of His Holy spirit. All the validations and vindications we will have in Christ will turn into nothing more than garbage and comical tragedies to be laughed at and abused in the eyes of Satan and all those who have bound themselves to him. But he will not stop there. His pride will continue to soar without any real threat of judgment or punishment, and he will eventually try to collect and destroy our souls, and try to get us to destroy one another, and, as if it would be possible, God Himself. In fact, I know that is exactly what will happen if God were to let go of Satan, his dominion and the ungodly. Some of you may have doubts as to how I could have come to this conclusion, but it is not a conclusion. God already saw it through the eyes of John.

At this time, please take a moment to read Revelation 20:1-10.

In the end times, Satan will be bound and thrown into the abyss for 1000 years. You would think that after witnessing the death of God's only Son on the cross, the power of His blood transforming even the hearts of the enemies into His own instruments, and all the redemptive power and the love of God demonstrated through countless saints who died in Christ throughout history, that Satan would finally relent and see the error of his ways and repent like the prodigal son? You must understand that Satan knows the Gospel better than anyone in history. Has he repented yet? As soon as he is set free from that abyss, he will begin to build an army of the world, far greater than any that he had built before and march straight towards the city of God in order to destroy everyone in that city. So, what is the right ending to all of Satan's relentless attack on God's people? The lake of burning sulfur is the right end. This is not some imagined, abstract place of spiritual isolation away from the presence of God. It is a real place that the new, eternal bodies will continuously experience the pain and suffering at the whole new level, and it has to be such a place. Otherwise, the authority and the power of God, along with all of our hopes and dreams in Christ, all of our validation as God's people and vindications for everything that we have gone through because we bare the name of His Son, will turn into nothing more than objects of mockery, abuse and destruction by the forces of evil.

Christ has already suffered all evil, malice, mockery, shame and punishment on the Cross for all humanity. He will not go through all that again and thereby mock Himself and his works on the Cross. He said, IT IS FINISHED. He will not come as the meek Lamb of God but as the Lamb of wrath. He has to come as the conquering King, God of true justice and the ultimate champion of our hearts, in order to exercise his authority and power to bind and destroy all things and beings that are forever bent on destroying our souls. All of our validations, vindications, not to mention the survival of our very souls, depend on Hell created by God. Hell is love for all who are in Christ and utter eternal devastation to all evil.

So, what is the lesson for us, believers, when it comes to understanding real Hell? What does the Bible say about Hell? We should never think so highly of ourselves that we can actually redefine the concept of God's grace and mercy and justice. Trust me; I had been a victim to such mentality for a long time. We are not the one to dispense God's love and mercy on our own terms. God is the perfect judge and we can never be. The word clearly says, without the shedding of blood, there is no remission of sins (Hebrews 9:22). That statement is the reflection of God's grace and justice in Jesus Christ. God's forgiveness of humanity was possible only through the blood of Jesus Christ and nothing else. God's law dictates that our sins have consequences that will *cost* the souls of each other and even God himself, who created our souls to be holy and to be one with Him. Jesus paid that terrible price on the cross by taking on the sins of all humanity of all time onto Himself. Our sins have cost the very life of Jesus, the Son of Man who is fully God. His death was gruesome and monstrous beyond all other murders ever committed. The justice of God had to be judged and executed on the sins that were being poured out on the Son of God on the Cross. We can attempt to imagine the suffering of Christ, but we can never imagine God the Father in His spiritual torment as He was watching Himself killing His only begotten Son for our unworthy, undeserving souls. Therefore, when we say, "How can a loving God send anyone into the lake of fire for all eternity? The real Hell is just a separation from God. That is suffering enough", we are not only far from properly understanding the justice of God that protects and validates our souls in Him, but devaluing that supernatural, sacrificial love of Christ on the Cross. By such manmade notions of grace and love and the rejection of the idea of real Hell, we have unknowingly dishonored the ultimate and precious sacrifice of our Lord on the Cross. It is scary even to think about all this, I know. I myself shudder sometime at the thought of what all of these really mean and have nothing but deep gratitude and reverence for our mighty God of love and salvation. I'm glad that He is God of perfect justice, and He is patient beyond understanding. We are NOT.

Moreover, we simply cannot deny the deterrent power of Hell that keeps us from walking down that path of destruction, the way of our old sinful nature, over and over again. In addition, many people, including myself, have turned to Christ when there was a threat of real hell. We all need grace. We desperately need God's mercy even as Christ followers.

But we overestimate our abilities and think a little too highly of ourselves that the notion of real hell is limited to just a certain immature segment of church populations who have not fully understood the concept of relationship based on "pure grace" as most of us have come to understand. Grace without Hell is not grace at all. Grace cannot exist without Hell. It might as well be a gift from Santa Clause that people may enjoy for a time but soon get bored with and tossed aside while forgetting all about the Santa Clause, the gift giver.

Although most of us including myself love the idea of Santa Clause and what he may represent, (I love Christmas) we know in our hearts that God is much more than Santa Clause and a different kind of Gift Giver. The gift of eternal life demanded the blood of our Lord. The gift was given through the blood of Christ because of our very souls. It was the gift of His own life. And He cannot be forgotten, nor is he going to be abused in anyway by anyone after such unimaginable and impossible sacrifice. He knows our own nature too well, as well as Satan. Moreover, He will not let the blood of all of His children — His saints — who died in His name go to waste or be taken out of context. He is love and He will vindicate all of us in Him but first, he has to be the rightful vindicator, the true King of justice and power, in our own eyes. And we will be lifted up in power in Him! The Lamb in these following passages represents Jesus Christ. These passages from the Revelation are not designed to be terrifying to us, but to be edifying to our souls for all eternity, and now, we understand why. God's judgment and Hell in Christ is the answer to the most fervent prayers of our souls collectively as the Church throughout history. There are other relevant verses, not only from the Book of revelations, but throughout the Bible.

When he opened the fifth seal, I saw under the altar the souls of those who had been slain because of the word of God and the testimony they had maintained. They called out in a loud voice, "How long, Sovereign Lord, holy and true, until you judge the inhabitants of the earth and avenge our blood?" Then each of them was given a white robe, and they were told to wait a little longer, until the full number of their fellow servants, their brothers and sisters, were killed just as they had been.

I watched as he opened the sixth seal. There was a great earthquake. The sun turned black like sackcloth made of goat hair, the whole moon turned blood red, and the stars in the sky fell to earth, as figs drop from a fig tree when shaken by a strong wind. The heavens receded like a scroll being rolled up, and every mountain and island was removed from its place.

*Then the kings of the earth, the princes, the generals, the rich, the mighty, and everyone else, both slave and free, hid in caves and among the rocks of the mountains. They called to the mountains and the rocks, "Fall on us and hide us from the face of him who sits on the throne and from the **wrath of the Lamb**! For the great day of their wrath has come, and who can withstand it?"* Revelation 6:9-17

And the devil, who deceived them, was thrown into the lake of burning sulfur, where the beast and the false prophet had been thrown. They will be tormented day and night for ever and ever. Then I saw a great white throne and him who was seated on it. The earth and the heavens fled from his presence, and there was no place for them. And I saw the dead, great and small, standing before the throne, and books were opened. Another book was opened, which is the book of life. The dead were judged according to what they had done as recorded in the books. The sea gave up the dead that were in it, and death and Hades gave up the dead that were in them, and each person was judged according to what they had done. Then death and Hades were thrown into the lake of fire. The lake of fire is the second death. Anyone whose name was not found written in the book of life was thrown into the lake of fire. Revelation 20:10-15

I assure you that the Apostles and our Lord Jesus himself did not hesitate to expound upon the true nature of Hell and the wrath of God because they all knew that the true knowledge of Hell just maybe the last thing, or the only thing, that will bring to light our true validations as sons and daughters of God, the royal priesthood, and turn us from the ways of sin and the world, that will eventually destroy our very souls. So, please..,do not be afraid. "Do not fear", the great prophet Moses, who was the first priest of the Levitical priesthood, tells us through the scripture! The perfect love of Christ casts out all fear if you are in it. And it is His desire that every single one of us be saved from Hell on earth first: ourselves. We are our worst enemies. I can testify to you that I have been my own worst enemy and so can you. Yes...it's tough to face the truth sometimes. Think about this, "Why would He go through all that HELL on earth and the Cross if our glorious salvation in Him wasn't the very purpose of it?" God truly wants to make you happy through and through. God wants to raise us up with Christ to that glorious heavenly realm where our hearts are no longer subject to sins and pride and all of their consequences, entrapments, pain and suffering. God does not waste His time. There is only one sin that will send you to Hell. Do you know what that is? The Book of the truth says Jesus Christ is the lamb who takes away the sins of the entire world for all history (John 1:29). So the only sin remaining to send anyone to Hell is the rejection of Jesus Christ who took away all of our sins.

He is patient, yes, and painfully so. He is full of love and mercy for all. But He will not be mocked because He does not want us to be mocked in Him. He must be raised to the highest in all of His rightful glory and honor and power for the sake of our own hearts and souls in Him. Why do the principalities and powers of the forces of evil so keen on destroying our souls? They are so keen because we bare His image as His ultimate creation. And they will do anything to make us defile our own hearts. Hell was created by our loving Creator to bring eternal devastation to all evil that is bent on defiling and destroying our souls. Hell is eternal love for all who are in Christ and eternal death and destruction to all evil.

Chapter 4

THE ORIGIN OF OUR INMOST BEING AND ROYAL PRIESTHOOD

I t is estimated that the human body can contain up to 100 trillion cells. That's 100,000,000,000,000 cells. What's even more amazing is that each one of these cells contains about 100 trillion atoms, the scientists estimate. Just like any manmade machines or computers, there are components in the cells that work like machines except it is much more precise and complex than anything we have ever imagined. The DNA, or the program, is usually secured and protected by the protein "housing" complexes when it is dormant. But our body is dynamic and the cells have to continuously replicate and regenerate themselves to replace the old and worn out cells. For a cell to replicate, the DNA itself has to make copies of itself. After this division of cells and the DNA, the DNA again unwinds just a part of itself at the right time to allow that part to be copied into a messenger (mRNA). That mRNA then is decoded or translated, if you will, by bunch of translators (tRNA) to make proteins, the basic building blocks all the components in the cell and therefore our body. I have not even mentioned all the microscopic components that work in concerts in machine like precision to make all of these happen in a matter of micro seconds; also programmed by the DNA. I cannot even begin to explain all the complex functions of the organelles and apparatus in the cells and how they are all different depending on the parts of the body they are found. The DNA is not only the program for the building blocks but for neurotransmitters and hormones, and there are protein and chemical signals being transmitted both within and between cells all the time.

All this is a very crude, simplified model of our body and how it sustains itself. But where did it get that kind of sustaining power? How was the DNA made? And what gave the DNA the "desire" or the "need" to replicate itself continuously in the first place? If the DNA programmed itself to self perpetuate in such precise fashion every single moment year after year, why would it program itself to terminate or "kill" itself after 80 to 120 years after its inception? Doesn't that contradict the very core foundation of theory of evolution? Wouldn't that continuous evolution of DNA have continuously escalated to the point of near immortality after millions and billions of years? And how come the very same DNA with all that "wisdom" of the mother nature failed to bring into our consciousness its own existence until these guys, Watson and Crick, began to finally see that we are more than what we see on the outside...after "billions" of years?

We are more than what we see. We are built that way. Understanding the ways of the DNA and the physical world is just the tip of the enormous ice burg called Divine wisdom of love in our Creator. If it took the genius and relentless-systematic application of logic and science by Watson and Crick to finally understand and establish the model for the DNA — the seemingly limitless program for the physical building blocks of human body — how long do you think it will take science to unravel the mysteries of the invisible realities existing in all of us such as hate, justice, pride, mercy, grace, power, lust and love? These invisible things are the true realities of the universe by which the humanity live and die! Doesn't your heart just identified with the previous statement? Don't you think we will self-destruct long before we can finally get "there" by "science" as we continue to get deluded by the continuous twisting of the truth of God? Such is the destructive power of knowledge without the divine wisdom of love.

Perhaps all of THESE will make sense when we take a look into the Book of Love, the Bible. God indeed originally made the DNA to replicate and perpetuate for a very long time...in the order of 800 to 900 years or so. We all remember Methuselah, who lived to be 969 years according to the Bible, as well as other men of old ancient time at the beginning. So...what made God *reprogram* our DNA to self-terminate after 120 years or less? (The theory of a protective water layer in the atmosphere in the pre-Noah era may very well be true, I believe, but that alone does not explain the dramatic reduction in our life span. I will explain in one of my next books, God willing.) Let's look into Genesis Chapter 6:1-3 and 5.

When human beings began to increase in number on the earth and daughters were born to them, the sons of God saw that the daughters of humans were beautiful, and they married any of them they chose. Then the Lord said, "My Spirit will not contend with humans forever, for they are mortal; their days will be a hundred and twenty years." ...The Lord saw how great the wickedness of the human race had become on the earth, and that every inclination of the thoughts of the human heart was only evil all the time.

This was about the time when the self destructive wickedness of the humanity has reached its pinnacle. The incredibly long life given by God to each individual has given the humanity the time and energy to accumulate the kind of super evil wisdom for each one that is self indulgent and self advancing at the expense of each other and everyone except Noah, who found himself in God. The violence and sexual sins were rampant in those days and everyone was being violated either voluntarily or by force. God could no longer allow Himself to see us continuously violating and destroying each other's bodies and souls. That is why God programmed the DNA to self-terminate after 120 years or less: to protect the humanity from itself as much as He can, while still giving us the chance to find true redemption in God and His Son while we are here. Our God truly is love after all. Knowledge without wisdom is irrelevant. Wisdom without love is deceiving. And love without its Maker in our hearts will destroy us all.

Our body is an amazing specimen indeed. But when God said through King David, "We are fearfully and wonderfully made", He wasn't exactly talking about our bodies...

The best and the most beautiful things cannot be seen or even touched. They must be felt by the heart.–Helen Keller, a deaf-blind visionary

He has made everything beautiful in its time. He has also set eternity in the human heart; yet no one can fathom what God has done from beginning to end.–Ecclesiastes 3:11

God is infinite in every way we imagine. God is not bound by time or space. But let's just suppose for the sake of argument that God somehow operated in time and space. Would He waste His time like we do so often? We find this to be the absolute truth: that it would be against His very nature to waste His time. Everything he plans and creates has a specific Divine purpose. And God certainly did not waste His time when He created you. Let me say again that God did NOT waste His time when He created you and me in His own image. God would not have spent so much of His "time" creating His ultimate prize and masterpiece, men and women in His own likeness, if He knew it was going to be a total waste of His time.

In Genesis Ch. 1:26, God said, *"Let us make mankind in our image, in our likeness, so that they may rule over the fish in the sea and the birds in the sky, over the livestock and all the wild animals, and over all the creatures that move along the ground."* He created you and me so that we can have the authority over all of God's creation. He goes on to command the man and the woman to *"Be fruitful and increase in number; fill the earth and subdue it. Rule..."* So, we can conclude that God's purpose in creating us is for us to rule and subjugate all that God has created because that is who God is, the ultimate supreme ruler. Our very existence itself implies special power and authority that have been vested in us by God Almighty. We were meant to be the kings and queens of our world. We were meant to rule it in the harmony and the love of God.

Again, if God operates in the sphere of time and space, how much time do you think God had spent creating this universe as opposed to creating you and me? God SPOKE this vast universe into existence and everything in it. In Genesis 1:3, God said ""*Let there be light, and there was light.*" He then proceeded to create everything by speaking it into existence...EXCEPT the last creation. And the last creation was humanity.

He did not just speak us into existence. You see, He got down and got his hands dirty. He got personal. He began to mix dust with water to make the clay. He was working on his ultimate creation, his masterpiece! Yes, God took his sweet time and special care to create the first man, Adam. Then He did the most incredible thing. He put His face right over the face of this clay man and breathed into him. Genesis 2:7 it says, *"Then the Lord God formed a man from the dust of the ground and breathed into his nostrils the breath of life, and the man became a living being."* This was more than a personal touch. We see here that God literally breathed a part of Himself into Adam, the first man. It is the picture of the imparting of the Divine, eternal soul into a finite being. What was happening as God breathed into Adam, the first of all human beings? He was doing more than just giving Adam some kind of life force or energy. God was forming Adam's mind, heart and soul, which is the reflection of His own eternal image.

When David, the man after God's own heart said in Psalm 139:14, *"I praise you because I am fearfully and wonderfully made; your works are wonderful, I know that full well"*, was he just talking about his physical body? Our body, first of all, is an amazing specimen. The science continues to reveal the depth and complexity in which our bodies have been formed. But if God took his sweet "time" putting together our physical body, how much "time" do you think he spent designing our heart and soul? David says in the preceding verse, (Psalm 139:13) *"For you created my inmost being; you knit me together in my mother's womb."* These verses are not about physical creation. What David is talking about here is the essence of his being, his heart and soul. That's what he meant by "my inmost being". He is talking about our heart that was initially designed to be the indwelling place of the Spirit, God Himself. Therefore, it had to be fearfully and wonderfully made or God would not reside in it! He simply cannot. We are fearfully made because God is holy. We are wonderfully made because God is love. God's dwelling place is none other than our hearts. We are actually inviting Him to live in and live through our hearts when we first receive Christ into our hearts. You are receiving Him into your heart because it was originally designed by God for Him to dwell in. Even though our body is amazing in its own right, God spent much more of His "time" planning and designing our heart and soul. It is no wonder that God cares much more about the condition of our heart and soul than our physical body!

One of the most powerful and uplifting verses is 1st Peter 2:9, *"But you are a chosen people, a royal priesthood, a holy nation, God's special possession, that you may declare the praises of him who called you out of darkness into his wonderful light."* Once we have been called out of the darkness by the blood of Jesus Christ who cleanses our hearts, we will truly see ourselves as who we are in Christ. Our magnificent and mysterious hearts forged in the mind of the Trinity were buried deep in that dark cess-pool called sin when Adam and Eve fell. The powerful cleansing works of Christ on the Cross removes all of our sins and reveals God's glorious original design; our heart that was made to be the indwelling place of Jesus Christ who is the undisputed King and the high Priest of the universe. He is the King of true justice and High Priest of intercessory love for ALL of us. All we have to do is repent and believe, the Bible says. Then the Christ will come into your heart and begin to cleanse your heart. We still have residuals of "self-love and pride of destruction" covering our hearts. God will remove them but only through the destruction of our flesh, which will continuously feed the residual self if left unchecked. Why are we being allowed to persist in the flesh? We are still here because the redeeming power of His blood is best demonstrated when His blood overcomes our flesh...that's why. He wants us to participate in that death and resurrection power through us while we are here. That gives our lives true meaning that we have all been searching for. Certainly this man who is writing this book is coming to experience the redeeming power of His blood as I struggle with my own flesh! We can never underestimate the power of His blood. It will overcome ALL, including our flesh.

That is the beginning of our heart's redemption journey with Him. And when Christ works through our hearts that is continuously being transformed by Him, we can't help but to demonstrate all the attributes of the King and the high Priest. We have the ultimate authority and power to rule and subjugate all creation in Christ now with love and we will examine the life of Joseph to see what that power looks like or why it should be given to us. So often, whether in our personal lives or throughout history, this authority has been taken out of context and became the subject of misun-derstanding or a vehicle for abuse... both in the Church and the kingdoms/ governments throughout history. We must surrender our notion of power, justice and love to God so that we can receive true love and justice that is found in Christ. And to say that Joseph ascended into the position of unexpected and indescribable power by Divine timing would not do any justice to the process in which his heart was trained and galvanized by the omniscient God, so that he can finally become the person worthy of claiming this ultimate divine authority. God made him worthy, not himself and he was, and had to be, fully aware of that too. But as Joseph began his journey in the pit, we must begin our journey at the cross at Calvary two thousand years ago where Satan was also there. We must SEE WHAT we are being saved from and who is saving us before we can truly be saved and redeemed. Let's look into what may have transpired.

Chapter 5

FINISHED

*Then he showed me **Joshua** the high priest standing before the angel of the Lord, and **Satan** standing at his right side to accuse him…"Listen, High Priest Joshua, you and your associates seated before you, who are men symbolic of things to come: I am going to bring my servant, the Branch." – Zechariah 3:1 and 3:8 (revelation of the Lord to Prophet Zechariah)*

Then the Lord said to Satan, "Have you considered my servant Job, that there is none like him on the earth, a blameless and upright man, one who fears God and shuns evil?" So Satan answered the Lord and said, "Does Job fear God for nothing? Have You not made a hedge around him, around his household, and around all that he has on every side? You have blessed the work of his hands, and his possessions have increased in the land. But now, stretch out Your hand and touch all that he has, and he will surely curse You to Your face!" – Job 1:8-11

*Then I heard a loud voice saying in heaven, "Now salvation, and strength, and the kingdom of our God, and the power of His **Christ** have come, for the **accuser** of our brethren, who accused them before our God day and night, has been cast down." – Revelation 12:10*

It was a glorious day for Satan. Looking at the bloody mess of a body on that cross gave him a certain dark satisfaction. But his day was not over.

Seeing Christ through this kind of long and drawn out agony would just be an icing on the cake compared to what he hoped to witness at the end. There were accusations to be made and the ultimate glory to be claimed, Satan mused. He entered Judas Iscariot the day before and helped him betray Jesus. The Pharisees and the religious leaders, blinded by their own greed and self-righteousness, behaved just as he predicted. Most of the people there, whether by envy or ignorance, went along with their leaders. Even the disciples, now full of doubt, abandoned Him because of fear of men. Many of the women and a few men were distraught and heartbroken, but helpless to do anything about this monstrosity that was being done to their gentle Master and doubted all the things that He said about Himself. What a useless and yet comical, worthless display of God's ultimate failure!

Satan himself had personally orchestrated, with permission from the Lord of course, a series of tragic events as well as that unrelenting and festering sickness for Job in order to test the Lord. Satan killed and took away all that Job held dear in his heart: his entire family! Sparing his wife was a nice touch because, as it turns out, even she would provoke him to curse God and die in his unjustifiable suffering. It wasn't just about testing Job. Job, without question, was the most righteous person who ever lived until Christ. Job was the prime example of the reason why God created man in the first place. And Satan just could not stand it. He could no longer tolerate this man's existence that was the expression of God's abundance, power, wisdom and love. Job's life was a celebration of the glory of the Lord. His life was the perfection of God shining through a being so imperfect and yet so perfectly in tuned with his Creator. It was the kind of beauty that Satan despised. Job was the ultimate example of God's power made perfect in weakness. Satan thought if he could somehow get Job to disown and curse God and sin in his heart against the Lord, it would do more than to justify his own rebellion. It would have been a tremendous victory for Satan and his dominion. It would have been, he bitterly remembered. But he would live to fight another day. He knew he must seek out more opportunities to bring shame and dishonor to God and His people because that was his sole purpose of existence. If he could not ascend above His throne, then he will do everything in his power to bring God down below him.

Satan's mind shifted back to the present. He was amazed at how Christ was still able to hold on. He asked himself, "Why is He still holding on?" All the physical beatings, the lashings, and the long agonizing walk that finally culminated in the crucifixion would've killed any man twice over. On top of this, Jesus was already severely dehydrated from the intense prayer of painful pleading and intercession at the garden the night before.

But Satan understood very well that the physical pain was only a small part of what Christ was suffering here. The unfounded hatred and evil of humanity directed toward the Creator was something that even Satan could not fully comprehend and yet...reveled in. This kind of psychological and spiritual pain could not be expressed in human terms. All he knew was that he enjoyed this moment. This was unquestionably the Jesus' weakest moment in His life and Satan's best, and probably last, chance to expose the Trinity for the incompetent impostor that They really were.

Satan remembered how weak Jesus was at the end of his forty days of fasting. Forty days! People hallucinate and lose their minds after such arduous and agonizing physical deprivation. He thought he could break Jesus but exactly the opposite happened. His flesh was at its weakest point and yet He seemed more powerful than ever! So he went away defeated, looking for a more opportune time to test and tempt Jesus, and the most opportune time has finally arrived and he took it! Just as Satan entered into Judas Iscariot, he had sifted Peter as wheat, and saw him to deny Jesus 3 times. He whipped up a spiritual frenzy, if you will, in the minds of all who were there before the Cross, especially the priests and the teachers — the supposed men of God — to deny, defame and defile Christ with their words of depravity, jealousy, blasphemy and violence. What they didn't know was that they were condemning and defiling themselves.

He began to muse in his mind — part accusatory and part mocking — knowing that God can also perceive his thoughts, "Do you see what's happening here, Son of Man? Look at all these men and women that You and Your Father have created...in Your image. Their hearts are raging against you. They look at you as if you are no better than their worst criminals. They are destroying you from inside out, killing you. Do you call these your ultimate creation? Will you be glorified through THIS? Do you see how they have nothing for you but hatred, jealousy, and at best, apathy for you? Even the ones that professed their love for you have either deserted you or helpless to do anything about what's happening to you. What a pathetic and comical display of the ultimate divine mistake. Just yesterday, you were in that garden all by yourself, praying earnestly to your Father, 'please remove this cup from me!' You knew exactly what you were getting into and you did have a real choice to either accept or deny. No one knows the depth of your suffering but I do. Now, come into your glory Son of Man! Denounce them. Deny them. You should not have created them in the first place. Wipe them out and come into your glory now, which is rightfully yours! Did you know that your great love and mercy has created this perfect canvas on which they can pour out all of their malice, jealousy and greed without fearing any consequences? This Cross is of your own making and nothing more...So let the righteous judgment of the Father come. The Father is leaving you but He will be here the instant you call upon Him. This is the burden that you needlessly volunteered for. You know you don't have to do this. Purify and purge this place of this filth and make this place holy again! You can start all over. Just watch what has unfolded before your very eyes."

Then, Jesus began to move his lips, as if to say something. Satan became very nervous because he knew what Jesus was about to say just may alter not only the destiny of the mankind, but his own as well.

Jesus began to mouth the words with what little strength left in Him but He pronounced each word carefully and slowly so that everyone near him, including Satan, can hear:

"Father, please forgive them...For they do not know what they do."

Satan could not believe what he was hearing. Then, a deathly silence ensued...

With all the commotions around him, Satan could hear nothing. This kind of response was not what he was used to. He has had thousands of years of practice. Every man has a breaking point. And Jesus is now all alone, even without the Father. He knew that Jesus was God but also fully man. Jesus was bearing this burden that was totally nonsensical and unnecessary for God to bear. Justice of God had to come now. It just had to...for the destruction of His ultimate creations, these so-called fearfully and wonderfully made beings...

But in this most critical moment in history when the fate of humanity hung in the balance, Jesus stood his ground when He had absolutely nothing else to stand on but His love for us alone. He was truly alone, deserted, dejected and utterly rejected by all. For what? For whom? Even the Father is abandoning Christ. Satan never believed such demonstration of power was possible and yet here he was, witnessing something that is just... humanly impossible? Satan could barely utter, "What kind of power is this? What kind of...LOVE is this? This power...this unimaginable power to CONTROL unleashing of His own rightful justice that's been held back since the beginning of time? To what end?!"

In fact, Satan could barely think. Then, a gradual and despairing understanding began to dawn in his dark soul. He began to understand why Jesus was still holding on up to this point. From his perspective, a part of the reason why Christ went through all that unbelievable suffering — hell on earth — for such a long time was to clearly bring out every argument and pretension, all that are being on display before them at this very moment, including all that is within and of Satan that has set itself up against Christ and His children; that Satan would be absolutely convinced, beyond the shadow of any doubt, that all of his "creative" attempts to bring dishonor to the name of God by the way of His ultimate creation and His people would utterly fail and turn into nothing worthy of attention. NOTHING but lies full of garbage. And Satan could NOT stand this.

The full extent of the suffering on the cross by Christ was the beginning of the absolute and complete defeat by Satan because the love of Jesus Christ for His people was just too much, just too...STRONG. It was simply beyond comprehension. It was the ultimate LOVE that was too deep and mysterious to be recognized by His own creation and even Satan himself. Had the creation known the love of Christ, they would not have crucified him. Had Satan known what kind of supernatural effect that the Cross would have on God's people now and forever, he would never have helped Judas to betray Jesus in the first place...or would he do it again if he could? He will not be given that chance.

Then Satan witnessed the instant salvation of one of the two thieves on the cross. He probably failed to see this coming and therefore, likely failed to grasp here the full impact of this particular salvation story that will be told over and over again until the end of time; instant salvation of the truly repentant heart that Christ himself will enter to make it holy and worthy of eternal paradise. Satan was getting kicked in the teeth now.

Satan slowly turned in order to take his final flight away from Jesus. The pride in him began to surge again like never before. He will NEVER admit defeat. He was about to go out like a roaring lion ready to devour anybody in his path...even God's elect. Then Satan heard these last words by Christ:

"It is finished."

Three days before the Resurrection and the Revelation of God's ultimate victory over sin and death, Satan knew that he, too, was pretty much...finished.

By the way...the same righteous and complete judgment on us that Satan so craved (all because we bare God's image) has instead come down upon all sin, death and evil when Christ rose victoriously from the dead. You see, even with all of his super evil wisdom, Satan could not have foreseen *how* our God was going to deal with the impossible problems of sin and evil in us until he witnessed the working power of death and resurrection of our

Jesus in its full glory. Had he known that Jesus would go to *that* extreme loving measure — all the way to the end of His own life at the hands of his own children — in order to bring us back to Him, Satan would have never helped to incite God's people to kill Him on the Cross. Again, God's plan of love for His people could not be understood or anticipated by anyone because it was just too deep, too strong and too foundational...even for Satan. Therefore, Satan helped orchestrate the crucifixion of Christ *because* he did not understand the magnitude of the universe altering love of God through His Son on the Cross.

Now, we know with absolute certainty that Jesus Christ has won the victory on our behalf and is now sitting at the right hand of God until our enemy, Satan our constant accuser, will be made His footstool! None of us deserve this kind love AND that's exactly why this love by Christ is the only thing that can transform us unto His glory for all eternity. Nothing else will! The indescribable and uncontainable power and strength of His LOVE ALONE made our salvation possible. His love is beyond this universe. And that same love of Christ desires to work among and through us for ALL of us. Now to the only Victor and our Savior Jesus Christ, we give all the honor, power, praise and glory!

Amen.

Chapter 6

ASCENSION OF CHRIST. INDWELLING OF THE SPIRIT

He could not believe this was happening. It seemed like only yesterday that he had denied Him 3 times. He was trying to wipe away the fountain of love and sadness streaming down his face but to no avail. "You really are leaving us," he may have thought. "You are really leaving me. Only when I thought I was given a chance to redeem myself for what I have done, You are leaving me... Lord please, you don't have to leave us...You are the only One worthy and true. I, your first chosen disciple, betrayed and disowned you and let you die...yet You came back for me. You are the only One that matters in this wretched and fallen world! Please, don't leave me..."

His memory would have taken him back to the very first time they met. He had never seen so many fish caught in one net divided into two boats, and the boats were sinking before his very eyes! The overwhelming, supernatural and undeserving love compelled him to say to Jesus, "Go away from me, Lord; I'm a sinful man!" He may have also remembered that fateful night when he had supernaturally walked on that deep and dark water toward the Master.

All the things that the Master and they did together, all the lives He touched, all the sickness He rebuked and healed, and all that the Master went through for them; including all the events leading up to the horrifying death on the Cross; continuously rushed back to catch up with the flow, which he could not stop. Did Peter think, "Lord, how can I redeem myself in You if You are not here?"

Then he might have remembered the Master telling him 3 times in the most loving way only He knew how, "If you love Me Peter, then feed my lambs…"

Please realize that as the people wept during their farewell to Paul on his last journey to Jerusalem, I'm confident that Peter cried when our Lord left him and the world. In fact, I believe he wept…even afterwards and frequently for a very long time. If we know Peter to be the man of unsurpassed passion and conviction, then we are right. Weeping is one of the ultimate signs of love. You will see in the story of Joseph that he wept with sadness and joy multiple times as he was in the process of reuniting with his brothers. We don't usually see us or other people weeping for and over the souls of the people too often nowadays, do we? There is no mention of Jesus laughing or smiling in the Bible, but we know He wept over Jerusalem and the family of Lazarus, his dear friend. Do you think Jesus often wept in secret as well? In the last days, the love of many will grow cold the Bible says… Are we becoming a part of that stone-cold tragedy? Are we weeping for our children who are becoming so lost in this world? Do we even know that we are losing them? When Jesus said "feed my lambs," who do we think he was referring to? Just the adult flocks? And what does "feeding" mean? Physical feeding or Spiritual? Or maybe…Both? The book of Acts is full of stories of the early church doing both in the power of the Holy Spirit.

But very truly I tell you, it is for your good that I am going away. Unless I go away, the Advocate will not come to you; but if I go, I will send him to you.–John 16:7

But the Advocate, the Holy Spirit, whom the Father will send in my name, will teach you all things and will remind you of everything I have said to you.–John 14:26

When the Advocate comes, whom I will send to you from the Father –the Spirit of truth who goes out from the Father–He will testify about me.–John 15:26

...The Spirit searches all things, even the deep things of God. For who knows a person's thoughts except their own spirit within them? In the same way no one knows the thoughts of God except the Spirit of God. – 1st Corinthians 2:10-11

Ascension of Jesus Christ was necessary to create the supernatural longing and desire in us for the concrete presence and the knowledge of the love of Jesus Christ in this passing and temporary world; in order to be powered by the Holy Spirit to do the same kind of loving, redemptive, saving work of Jesus Christ... for all.

The power of the Holy Spirit, our Advocate, is maximized in the knowledge of Jesus Christ in His physical absence. Our Lord Jesus Christ has finished his work on earth as the Son of Man, resurrected and ascended to claim His authority over heaven and earth. We take over where He left off and begin our journey with the power of the Holy Spirit. It is not only the journey of our heart and soul. It is the journey into the heart of our God and the ultimate Divine Revelation, Jesus Christ. We must understand that if Christ had remained after His work was finished on the Cross, His physical presence would have prevented our spiritual journey with Him in the Spirit because we would constantly seek to be with, to be seen with, and to be seen by him physically without ever truly knowing Him spiritually.

He is more than his flesh that He has overcome. He is God and the Spirit. His physical presence would have again produced, through our flesh and pride, our unhealthy physical dependence on Christ. Our hearts, which are eagerly awaiting full redemption in Christ at the end, are still lazy, selfish and deceitful. Yes, even as we are being saved! As long as we have this flesh, this would be the inevitable truth. We would even begin to depend on Him for the things that we ourselves can easily accomplish! Such is the nature of our ever digressing nature of our hearts unchecked by the foreknowledge and the preemptive wisdom of our Lord. Our souls have been saved when we received Christ into our hearts for all eternity. But our hearts are still in desperate need of redemption by the King until His coming. Christ knew His physical presence will actually interfere with that redemption journey of our hearts by the Holy Spirit. Again, our souls are saved but our hearts require the journey of redemption every day of our lives through the work of Christ by the power of the Spirit. So, **the first reason** that the Lord ascended soon after the resurrection was to actually prevent us from physically depending on Him for all of our physical and temporary needs. He is concerned about the eternal condition of our souls in the Holy Spirit, first. Without the salvation of our souls and the redemption of our hearts in Christ, all of our physical blessing in this temporary life becomes meaningless and will actually turn on us to destroy us and our loved ones. Many of you know this to be true. Certainly, I'm kicking myself for wasting so much time up to this point on the temporary things of the world!

As we begin to know more and more about our Lord, we will begin to miss him. Even though you have never met Him in His physical form, you will miss His presence in your life when you know more and more about His love. Your heart, as it is being cleansed and redeemed, will say, "I want to be with Jesus now because the real concrete presence of His love is what I need right now in this world of deceptions, empty promises, ulterior motives/agendas — religious or otherwise — hate and self love." Psalms 14:2 -3 says, *"The Lord looks down from heaven on all mankind to see if there are any who understand, any who seek God. All have turned away, all have become corrupt; there is no one who does good, not even one."* Paul uses the same verse in the book of Romans chapter 3 to drive home the point that in the world, with no one knowing what is good or how to do good in the eyes of God, the world itself will prove to be worthless to us as well, because we will never love one another with the same genuine and eternal love that can only come from the goodness and love of the Lord. The power of longing for the true love in Christ compelled St. Paul to confess, *"For I am hard-pressed between the two, having a desire to depart and be with Christ, which is far better. Nevertheless to remain in the flesh is more needful for you" (Philippians 1:23-24).* Paul, seeing through eyes of the true love and the righteousness of Christ, saw all of the empty promises and counterfeit affections of the world. He was missing the concrete presence and knowledge of the Christ badly in his heart while he was in this shifty and temporary world. The only reason why he would want to stay was because he wanted to help the people understand and experience the same eternal love of Christ that he himself is coming to understand. In fact, this is the confession of all the Lord's disciples. You can turn to the very end of the Bible to witness John say to our Lord, "Even so. Come, Lord Jesus."

Have we ever failed to deliver our most genuine affection and help promised to the others because of our own shortcomings, doubts, fear or just plain selfishness? I certainly have failed to do so many times as I look back. But when Christ comes into our lives with the power of the Spirit working through Him in our hearts, we are the ones breaking that vicious cycle of chain called fake love and shallow affections. This is Paul's version of fulfilling "feed my sheep" command by the Lord. Paul is feeding the love of Christ to the people in the church, then and now...in His physical absence as we become hungry and hungrier for His true love in this world full of deceptions and counterfeits.

Therefore, **the second reason** for His ascension has two parts. Part number one is that Jesus left us to create that powerful supernatural longing in our hearts for His constant, deep and supernatural love while we are in this world full of betrayals, disappointments and destructions of our souls; mutual and self inflicted. This supernatural longing based on the knowledge of the love of Christ is designed to change and move our hearts. Our hearts were not designed to be *changed or moved* by anything else except by the love of their Creator. What helps us see or understand His true love standing in stark contrast to the dark reality of the world is the revealing power of the Advocate or the Holy Spirit (1st Cor. 2:10; John 14:26). Here comes part number two. What enables us, who are weak in our bodies — through the power of prayer to do the work of Christ in the necessary absence of His body — is the empowering power of the Holy Spirit. (Romans 8:26; John 15:26). And only through prayer and reading of the Word on a regular basis can we be filled with the Holy Spirit to do the work of Christ (Acts 4:31). If we are saved, we have the Holy Spirit in us. But only when we are FILLED with the Holy Spirit, can we be like Christ to speak and demonstrate His love to others (John 15:26). This, again, is a part of our purpose in life as the ones being redeemed, to learn, cultivate and advance the love of Christ for the souls of other people. That is the work of the Christ or the fulfilling of the command "feed my sheep/lambs", by the Lord.

But what is **the third reason**?

Another reason why Jesus had to leave us soon after the resurrection was because we, as the humanity, would have suffered his righteous and true justice in its full and devastating power if He didn't. He could no longer be perceived as the meek Lamb of God after the resurrection and let the unredeemed mock his work on the cross, accuse him of being insane and eventually crucify Him all over again. Our collective human nature dictates that THIS is true and inevitable. He left so that His incomparable love on the Cross and victory would do its patient and supernatural work through us without His physical and immediate, and now the most frighteningly powerful, presence. We can ask ourselves, how would we have reacted if the people dismissed us as being insane and delusional, following some guy who claimed that he came back from the dead as the Savior of the world? Would we have asked Jesus to show his true power of resurrection by *"putting in some Divine fear in them to convince them...a little? You know... to give them a little nudge of supernatural encouragement?"* Well, that's not redemption, my friends. That's exactly the opposite of what Jesus did and thwarts the very purpose of His loving sacrifice. We don't know who will receive Christ and who will not at any given time. God's love works in mysterious ways all the time. We also remember that every one of us was like one of these unsaved people needing the love and the grace of God before we received Christ into our hearts. We are made to express His glory in the true freedom of His love, not to be cowards and be paralyzed like robots or zombies under the control and spell of fear. If the Son frees us, we are free indeed because He is the true love we have not found in this world. And His perfect love casts out our fear of men. Therefore, He ascended so that His love can now be understood in proper context according to God's patient timetable without His imminent and rightful justice.

And you are going to love **the fourth reason** for His ascension! It is very simple. He went up there to prepare a place for us. Yes, the Heaven! But you say "Wait a minute, didn't He already have all that planned out even from the beginning?" You know...God and His predestination and stuff." Yes...that is true in a way...But there is every indication in the Bible that he was going back there to actually "prepare" the place for us. That's why He used the word "prepare". Even now, there are things happening in the spiritual realm that we cannot even begin to imagine. Daniel, the man highly esteemed in the eyes of God, waited earnestly for the answer to his prayer but did not receive the answer for 3 weeks. (Daniel 10) He didn't know at the time of the prayer that there was a great spiritual battle in the angelic realm between the principalities that kept the *Man of white linen and lightening* (looking suspicious like our Lord in the book of Revelation) from coming his way sooner. (The answer to his prayer was divinely delayed if you will...and by the way, the answer to his prayer was not something he expected...such vision of power and magnitude! Check it out in Daniel Chapter 10. Moreover, what is the ultimate answer to all of our prayers? The ultimate answer to all of our prayers is none other than Jesus Christ Himself. This is why, though I do not know with 100 percent certainty, I believe that this man of white linen and lightening is the Angel of the Lord who came as the answer to Daniel's prayer. Of course, you may disagree with me on the identity of this unnamed man and that's OK!). But we trust that our Lord, with the ultimate and indomitable power of His resurrection, is setting things right and putting things in order in the spiritual realm. Perhaps the Lord will give me an opportunity to share with you in the knowledge and revelations of Heaven in the future.

It is hard for us to understand all of this because we are temporal and God is not. We always return to focus on the physical time and space, God does not. He love is eternal and constant. The time does not exist for God and yet He wrote the Bible in human terms so we can understand it. He was crucified for us. Even as the Son of God, He fasted 40 days in preparation for His ministry. He did many things as examples for us to follow...but 40 days of fasting? Come on! We cannot follow THAT without losing our mind...or dying! That is simply love incomprehensible! We trust that the love that "made" him who He was is the same love that He is operating in right now in both spiritual and physical realms. Just like the Superman story that was given at the beginning, we look forward to celebrating Him and His love in and among us even more at the end...not just for a time but for all eternity! And all these, call for our wisdom and patience in our great God who is working things out...behind our backs! People may talk behind our backs. God always works His labor of love behind our backs. And it is the desire of the Lord that we learn to do just that. We will learn to labor with Him in love behind people's backs if we are followers of Christ. Isn't that one of the strongest and the most glorious things you have ever heard? Nobody really knew why Jesus came until He left! And He is getting our heavenly mansions ready for us for all eternity with Him while we may be complaining about our very short and temporary trials and situations in this life. Again, His love is too strong and too much. It is too foundational and too beyond for us, and that's precisely why it can change our hearts while nothing else can. But as we are filled with the Holy Spirit, we will *begin* to understand his incomprehensible love.

In conclusion, He left so that the Helper can help us understand more clearly who Jesus is in His absence and help us do the work that Christ would do if He was here physically. Only in His physical absence, with the power of the Holy Spirit that searches all things and even the deep things of God, can our soul take on this journey and truly come to know Christ and what He will accomplish through us in this temporary world. That's why we are not immediately taken up to be with Him when we are saved. We have been set aside to do the work of Christ and be like Christ and demonstrate the power of His eternal redemption in the process. The fate of all the souls we hold dear and true to our hearts, especially our future generations, depend on how well we travel this road with Christ. Let's travel this road on our knees in prayer and the Word! Our work in Christ proves to the world, and to our own hearts, that we have Christ living in us and our hearts are truly being renewed and transformed. Our works from the flesh actually hinders our salvation because our self-righteousness founded on jealousy and pride, that would have accused Christ of being a blasphemer and pretend, is like filthy rags before God. But our salvation through Christ guarantees the working of Christ through our hearts because He will not be idle in our hearts if we truly believe in Him. Why would He be? Our hearts were created for this very purpose. We are designed to do the mighty redemptive work of Christ by the power of the Holy Spirit. Didn't Jesus say, "It is finished?" Didn't Jesus say we will do greater works than these because He is going to the Father (John 14:12)? He said this not because we will be endowed with some new supernatural power greater than that of Christ when we are saved, but because He foresaw Himself working through us to accomplish the redemption of souls, which would only be possible after His own death and resurrection.

Have you ever asked yourself, "Can a man's heart really change?" The greatest miracle is the transformation and redemption of the human hearts. Only through the death and resurrection power of Jesus Christ working through us can it be accomplished. That's what Christ meant by "the greater works." That's why He left us with the gift of the Holy Spirit. He still is the One working through us to do those "greater works" through the power of the Spirit! We will partake in His authority over sin and death powering through us, as we see our lives being transformed to overcome and rise above this world and ourselves. In that, we ourselves redeem our own hearts in Christ with the power of the Holy Spirit. And there is no other truth or feeling like it. There is no other healing or restoration like it. There is no other redemption like it! No matter who we are or what we have done, you can make the choice to claim this path unto a glorious redemptive destiny of total spiritual healing and empowerment unto eternity in His love. Peter experienced it after he denied Christ 3 times and so can we.

In the next chapter, we will carefully look into redemption journey of Joseph and his brothers. Joseph truly became a king in the eyes of God in every sense of the word. It is important to note that while you will have hard time identifying with all the element of his journey, it is absolutely imperative that you try to understand *all of it* because Joseph was pushed to his limit for the sake of our hearts and souls. He went on that arduous and impossible journey into the hearts and minds of all men and the world so that we do NOT have to…if we truly learn from it. But like I said, most of you will identify better with the journey of another character in the story. Either way, you will be blessed as I have. Many of us will identify with both characters I believe. I will not mention the name of the other character but the identity of the person will become crystal clear to you toward the end of the book.

The physical work of Jesus Christ on earth is finished. Now, it is our turn to be the kings, queens and priests by the power of His Spirit with Christ Himself working through our hearts. And all His works, constantly *changing* and perfecting our hearts in love and truth of the Word, is the work of the one true King and the High Priest by the power of our Advocate. We have been placed in the end times for such glorious purpose of global redemption in Jesus Christ.

Chapter 7

SEPARATION FROM ALL THINGS SELF

**The Beginning Of Our Redemption Journey
Of Hearts Through Joseph (Genesis 37)**

This all transpired when I was in the second grade.

We were at this art festival out of town where I was one of the "artists". But I couldn't draw anything or enjoy the festivities. I was writhing in pain on the grass. My right lower abdomen was killing me and I could not help myself but to coil into a ball. My schoolteacher wanted me to try some soup. I had not eaten lunch, and it was getting closer to dinnertime. I swallowed some but it all came right back out. My teacher said, "What's wrong Sam?" But I couldn't tell her what was wrong with me. I just knew that my tummy hurt and I felt terrible. I was getting feverish. It felt like I was slowly drifting into a nightmare. My teacher and some of my friends were initially skeptical at first and said, "Sam, are you faking it?" I told her and everyone, no, this really hurts! I was getting angry at them for not believing me. But as the pain got worse, I couldn't even have the energy to fight them or try to explain. It was only when I was nearly COMATOSE that they finally believed me and knew something was seriously wrong. But they still didn't know exactly why I was in such pain and neither did I...

When I came out of the anesthesia-induced coma, I was feeling groggy, but much better. My senses were alive again and I came back from the dead! They told me that I slept really well and the surgery was a success. My Dad told me that all of our friends and family were praying over me through the whole process. He also told me about my inflamed, ruptured appendix that he saw in the hands of the surgeon. He saved it for him! I wanted to see it but Dad told me that the surgeon just threw it away after he saw it. "Bummer," I said, "It would've been so cool." But the surgeon later came into my room and described the "thing" to me. A very wise-looking old man, that physician was. He said I was very lucky because my appendix was bigger than any of the other appendices that he had taken out (including those of the adults) and it had ruptured, but folded back on itself so that the infection and the inflammation of the tissues around the appendix was minimal. He said it was almost a miracle that I didn't come in with a full-blown peritonitis: serious and potentially life threatening infection of the entire belly. (Of course, I didn't know what all these meant at the time but I remember most of the words he said).

I finally understood what was causing me so much pain at that art festival. It was this "monster" growing inside me. When the good physician took it out for all the people to see, they also knew for sure that I wasn't faking it. The evidence was irrefutable. My pain had the real physical cause. And I know now as an adult that they also believed in the possibility that it can happen to any of them, because we are all made the same way somehow, regardless of whether we believe in God or not. And should something like that happened to them or any of their relatives, they would know what to do...or would they have learned their lesson? It could potentially be a life-saving memory for someone out there, I'm pretty sure. Turns out, I did not have to worry too much about the lessons of pain in this life because they are everywhere and in all types. So, what is the monster that continues to cause and compound this mysterious pain in all of our hearts? And what if someone were to bring all the monsters out of us for the whole world to see...

Love makes life-saving memories endure.

The Love that took all of our monsters on that Cross makes the life-saving memory endure forever because that kind of love is gloriously and indomitably FEARSOME.

*Blows and wounds scrub away evil, and beatings purge the **inmost being**.—Proverbs 20:30*

The fear of the Lord is the beginning of knowledge, *but fools despise wisdom and instruction.–Proverbs 1:7*

*Through **love** and faithfulness sin is atoned for; through **the fear of the Lord** evil is avoided.–Proverbs 16:6*

*But the eyes of the Lord are on those who **fear** him, on those whose hope is in his unfailing **love**–Psalms 33:18*

At the beginning of our journey with God

Have you ever wondered why a loving God would allow pain to exist in the world? Certainly there have been extensive discussion about the topic and it will continue on until we come into the new world with Christ where there will be without pain and suffering. The Bible says there will be no more tears in the new world to come and Christ himself will wipe away our tears. Few of the notable figures may have addressed the issues of the problems of pain. In fact, the phrase "the problem of pain" is the title of the book written by C.S. Lewis, one of the greatest Christian philosophers of our time. His book is brilliant and very deep on the subject of pain but I would like to approach the pain from slightly different angles and use examples in laymen's terms from the Bible as much as I can. Many of you may have come across that book and even read it but probably came away with unsatisfactory understanding of why God allows pain to exist. Certainly, some of us understand to some degree the necessity of pain and suffering on the road to redemption in this fallen world corrupted by sin. Simply put, without pain none of us would know, and thereby even think or want to veer away from, the very thing that causes pain. And that thing is our fallen nature or, in short, sin. In the beginning, there was no pain in the world but only love. But when Adam and Even fell in the Garden of Eden, sin was introduced into the world. And the sin brought forth pain for all humanity.

God sent His Son to save us from sins. But we know, just from our own life experiences, He did not save us from the present and future pain, which are the consequences of all of our past and present sins. He didn't save us from pain because without them, we will never know or address what caused the pain in the first place. God wanted us to SEE what we needed to be saved from by the consequences of it. It is only when we come to the Lord with the repentant heart, seeing and understanding that our sin is finally what causes us to fall, fail and not only receive, but impose pain on one another, He can truly forgive us and save us from sins and thereby the consequences of our sins.

Out of all different types of pain in the world, the pain of separation ranks number one. When the person you love dies and leaves you, there is no other pain like it. That pain is compounded when that person is taken away from you by force or, even worse yet, that person you loved was the very person that caused the separation of pain. When the Son of God was separated from God the Father, it was the most painful moment in all of history and it was clearly demonstrated on the Cross for that very purpose. There is no pain like the pain of physical and psychological beatings and death caused by the people you love and you came to save. Christ went through that for us. But the ultimate pain that Christ experienced was when God the Father turned his back on the Son and the Son was separated from His Father. This was separation by utter Divine rejection because of our sin. They have never been apart for all eternity until that moment. The pain of Jesus Christ has many faces and many dimensions because Christ bore all the filth and the malice of our sin and God had to separate Himself from His Son. We often think, "How can a loving God allow such pain in that godly man or woman's lives, in that family? Or how can God allow such evil to endure?" When you are experiencing the pain, all logic and reason may escape your mind. Even the nice argument for the existence of pain that I have summarize above will not matter to you that much. But even in those trying times of pain and suffering, we have to remember first that Jesus Christ and God the Father, both of them, became separated and went through the ultimate pain of separation in order to save us. He doesn't want to save you from that pain at first. What He really wants to save you from is that thing, that sin nature that caused all those pain in the first place. And it is the pain itself that makes you to see the thing — the sin causes all of our pains — which we need to be saved from.

Therefore, our God the Father and the Son, who was more than willing to go through such unimaginable pain of separation on our behalf, will not be so petty and shortsighted as to allow such pain and suffering in our lives for no other purpose than for the glorious, the most magnificent redemption of our hearts and of this whole world and to save as many of our souls as possible from ourselves. We will not become the kings and queens that God envisioned without the pain and suffering. Joseph was allowed to experience unbelievable pain of separation from his family by his own family like our Lord on the Cross. Our pain and suffering has great purpose! So, do not be afraid! And God is alpha and omega. He is the same yesterday, today and forever. As he had allowed pain of separation to shape and orchestrate the path of Divine destiny for Joseph, He may do so in our lives as well. And remember that our suffering in this temporary world is just a speck in God's eternal spectrum of time and space. If you run the good race in the Lord, you will trade all of these suffering for even a greater resurrection and the crown of life. We will examine how the suffering and pain are integrated into our destiny in more detail in the chapter titled "**predestination vs. persecution**". But how do we begin to know Him enough to trust Him in the first place? Enter the "fear of God", the beginning of all knowledge (Proverbs 1:7).

Nothing can separate us from the love of God, not even ourselves! Our eternal destiny is secure in Christ. Again, this pain that we experience is temporary. It is only a speck in the spectrum of eternal life that we have in Christ. And it is the very short-lived pain of our short lives in this world that makes our eternal life that much more full of significance, meaning, fulfillment, joy, peace, happiness and love. But the inception of this trust in God must be caused by the fear of the Lord. We should not be so concerned about the fear of men or the world that will eventually and inevitably destroy our souls. The fear of God is the beginning of true divine knowledge. The fear of God causes us to steer away from the things that we are drifting into either by choice or by ignorance. The fear of God ultimately leads us to the knowledge of God's love, which gives us protection from all forces of evil; both within and without. At the very basic level, we can imagine the fear of God as a loving and imminent rod of correction for His ignorant flocks, ignorant of the dangers out there, who are constantly trying to stray from the protection of His love. You can respectfully disagree with someone but you can't do that with God because God is always concerned about the matters of our eternal hearts and souls while we are not. God needs you to revere and fear Him and no less…for our own protection from all of our evil and its consequences to our own souls.

Family Divided. Nation Divided.

He was his father's favorite child as the story goes. What is not stated explicitly at the beginning of the story is that Joseph was also the firstborn of his late wife Rebecca, who was Jacob's first love. Rebecca died of the hard labor during the birth of Joseph's younger brother, Benjamin. The death of Rebecca must have been devastating for Jacob. So, in his old age, Jacob poured out his love for Joseph, which became the cause for great envy by his half brothers. The brothers were jealous of Joseph even before Joseph told them about the dreams. We find Joseph in times of a very interesting and turbulent family dynamics.

Joseph had two dreams in succession. They were the same dream in two forms. There was no question about the meaning of the dreams. His half brothers as well as his father Jacob, by gleaning from their reactions to the dreams, knew what the dreams implied. But none of them, not even Jacob, understood what will have to transpire in order for God to make this dream a reality. The dream was ultimately about the redemption of the brothers through Joseph's destiny. None of them knew exactly how the dream will become a reality, let alone why it has to come about through Joseph. All that the brothers could see and feel was that the dream is some kind of aggrandizement that Joseph did not deserve as one of the youngest sons. Whether the dream truly was the Divine revelation or Joseph's own personal concoction was not relevant to the brothers. They were so blinded by jealousy and greed that even if the dreams were truly from God, they were going to kill him anyway. Pride and jealousy not only blinds our souls and dulls our senses from all Divine revelations, but all of their consequences to our souls. The "dream telling" only fueled the hatred and envy of the brothers toward Joseph.

Jacob reacted to the dream a little differently. After rebuking Joseph for telling such an outlandish dream for the second time, the Bible says Jacob kept the matter in mind. Jacob understood that the dreams described by Joseph simply could not be made up in the mind of a 17-year-old. Also, Jacob likely recalled the promise that was made by God before the death of his wife Rachel that kings will come from his own body (Gen 35:11). He may have even thought that Joseph would be the first in the line of many kings to come from his body.

In the preceding Chapters, Jacob had wrestled with God while he was on his way back to his homeland (Gen 32). Jacob was wrestling with God in human form, the Man, because he was determined to get his blessings from Him. It is interesting that God asked Jacob what his name was. Didn't God already know that Jacob's name was Jacob? The question was not for the benefit of God's knowledge base, that's clear. The question was raised by God so that Jacob would realize he will no longer be defined by who he himself thought he was. By this simple question, God is trying to reveal Jacob's new identity in God, which will supersede his earthly identity. For God said, "Your name shall no longer be called Jacob, but Israel, for you have struggled with God and with men, and have prevailed." When we wrestle with God — by that I mean really clutch onto Him like glue and not let him go no matter what — because He is the true source of all of our blessings, He reveals our new identity in Him. Some of us have heard through many sermons that we are not what the world says we are, but who God says we are. That is a true statement and has been a great source of encouragement for countless Christians. However, unless you are in intimate relationship with the Almighty, even to the point of wrestling with Him, your new identity will not be confirmed in you and you will always doubt the validity of the concept "We are who God defines us to be."

God does not force or strong hand any of us to come to Him. He is a longsuffering and loving God, patiently waiting for us to engage Him because He has already given more than what we can possibly ask of Him. He gave up His only Son for us. God cannot do anything more than what He has already done in His Son! Remember, Jacob initiated the wrestling, not God. But God ran into Jacob because He was already there. James 4:8, the apostle James says, *"Draw near to God and He will draw near to you."* Unless you turn from your worldly ways and draw near to Him first, He will not draw near to you. He can't. He has already come so far, covered such a great distance of chasm between God and men, in the form of a humble man to reach out to us in His Son Jesus Christ. If He were to draw any closer, then He will become nothing more than a Santa Claus or a genie in the bottle in our eyes and every single one of us would take His love out of context. He is already HERE. God has already drawn near. Unless you draw near to Him, you will not SEE that He is drawing near to you. Zechariah 1:3, God says to the rebellious Israelites during the time of the Babylonian exile, *"Return to Me and I will return to you."* God wants us to draw near to Him so that we can clearly see who He is. And when we see God for who He truly is, we will see ourselves in Him: our new and true identity that God had been predestined in Christ; the royal priesthood. Just as much as God predicted that the kings will come from Jacob's body, the Church is the new line of royal priesthood of the new Israel and symbolic/ spiritual descendants of Jacob.

This little side story of background on Jacob here gives us a glimpse as to what kind of man Jacob was. He was a man of God who taught his sons, including Joseph, God of righteousness. I believe Jacob raised Joseph well in the Lord. But even Jacob was not prepared to train Joseph for the divine destiny that God had in mind for Joseph, as we will see in this story. God is gracious and loving to bless us with the gifts of our children, but our children do not belong to us. They are not ours to control. Ultimately, only God can control them and thank God for that. Even the most obedient of children in the Lord can become less than who they are meant to be if our instructions turn into life and death truth for their future. We as adults need to raise them to the best of our abilities in the Lord with the divine wisdom from the Bible and on our knees in prayer. And as parents, our job is simply to share in the life-building love of the Lord in our children the only way that we can as parents. Spending quality time with your children doesn't always translate to imposing of rules and regulations to keep them away from the things that will make them less successful in the eyes of the world. If we want them to really succeed as sons and daughter of the one true King, our Lord Jesus, we need to show and demonstrate the love of Jesus Christ to them and to the world while they are watching us. Again, this can only be accomplished as we come to the Word in prayer.

Jacob was a godly man. But he had a certain weakness as a parent like all of us do. You know what that was? He had a favorite child to spoil. When Joseph was gone later in the story, He held fast to Benjamin, the youngest, with all his soul. He spoiled him...perhaps even more so than Joseph. It is tragic to find out later that the tribe of Benjamin, his descendants, was virtually wiped out by the other Israelites in the Lord because of the wickedness and sexual depravity among the Benjamites that had escalated out of control (Judges 20). It is true that excessive control will stifle the souls of children and their destinies. But obsessive and misguided love by spoiling our children and caving into their childish desires will naturally build their sense of self-entitlement and self-advancement: the very seed of sin and evil in America today. Self-entitlement thrives in the fear of men because in the world without God's control, you will have to get everything you want however and anyway you can NOW in fear that the other person, smarter and more powerful, can always take that away from you. That kind of world exists in the minds of every person who are not actively being redeemed by the Lord. If you fear the Lord and shun evil, there is no place for such fear in your life. Your life is in the hands of the loving Father, who is in control of the universe and all the affairs of men. It is hard for us to speculate but perhaps the Joseph's descendants may have suffered a similar fate as that of Benjamin's had God not intervened here to pry him away from Jacob to instill divine fear of God in Joseph. Our children are the privileges and the responsibilities that the Lord had blessed us with and allowed us to enjoy for a time. We can instruct them in the ways of the Lord and enjoy seeing them grow in the Lord while we are being faithful stewards. However, we do not need that impossible expectation and pressure of *making* them who they need to be in the Lord. No one can *make* them who they are. Only God can make them who they are, and that's the reason why we as adults and parents have the responsibility to lead them to Christ. God gave them to us for that very reason. Let us lead by our examples first, by following Christ ourselves.

Many of us have made speculations about the character of Joseph in the beginning of the story. He may have been a little show off, a little too smart for his own good at times. However, he was only 17 years old, already operating in wisdom beyond his years. Of course, he had his own struggles as a human being, but it would be more accurate to say that Joseph was a better son than all his brothers combined. Joseph brought bad reports about his brothers to his father because it was likely that his brothers would always get themselves into trouble by their disobedience and they have their history to prove it. Joseph, on the other hand, was an obedient son who was willing to cover a great distance in order to find his brothers at the request of his father. It is well known that, by being obedient to his father, Joseph traveled over some 65 miles in order to find his brothers, going from his home in Hebron, to Shechem to finally Dothin. Certainly, Joseph could've refused and Jacob, I suspect, would have consented his son to remain by his side. That is a very plausible scenario given that Jacob would never let Benjamin leave his sight after Joseph was taken from him. It is interesting, however, that Jacob sent his son on this mini journey at this time and Joseph obeyed wholeheartedly.

I believed Joseph obeyed his father for two reasons. He loved his father and delighted in obeying him. That is also understandable. But he also cared about his brothers. I'd say that being a 17-year-old, he is showing the kind of maturity and dedication to help and build his family like no other 17 year old, or 37-year-old for that matter, that we know in this day and age. He could've stopped at Shechem (about 50 miles from home in Hebron) and turned back to go back to his father, but he persisted in finding out whereabouts of his brothers...to make sure they are OK. We don't know how many miles that he had wondered while he was in Shechem. And there is every indication that he was searching for his brothers all by himself. What a pursuit!

It is important to note that near the city of Shechem was where one of his sisters Dinah was raped years ago. Upon this news of the rape, two of the brothers, Simeon and Levi, had devised a scheme and killed all the males in the city and carried off all their females and children along with all their possessions. To say that there was a tension between the city of Shechem and the house of Jacob would be a severe understatement. Jacob would have been especially concerned for the welfare of his sons when they were near Shechem where the relatives of the people who were killed still lived. And Joseph, likely knowing all of this, was still more than willing to do this important errand for Jacob. We cannot say he was willing to do all this just to make sure he can bring a "bad report" about his brother to his father. That does not make sense at all.

Sure, there is some indication of freedom and power that he had taken for granted as a favored 17-year-old son of the patriarch. He had freely shared that incredible dream in the open, without reservation or restraint, and got an earful from his father Jacob. And he would always be wearing his colored robe as if to show it off. A discerning soul would have shown a little restraint in such display of affection and influence...but again, we are talking about a 17-year-old. If Joseph was a conniving character as some have portrayed, he would've faked the trip or he wouldn't have even gone on this trip in the first place. It is not at all clear to us why Jacob would send his young favorite son, all by himself with his bright, ornamented robe, to find his brothers in these potentially dangerous lands. Perhaps Joseph was well known by all the people of the land because of his father Jacob, and he would always be distinguished by the robe that he wears? Did Jacob think Joseph was invincible and had the absolute protection of the Almighty? Was this just an ongoing effort on the part of Jacob to continue to train Joseph in the ways of the world and men? Remember these were the ancient days in which boys were not spared of the harsh reality of the true human nature and the world, and thereby became men sooner. Whatever the reasons maybe, Jacob would have never thought in million years that the unthinkable harm would come to his precious Joseph by his own brothers, his own flesh and blood. In short, he failed to protect him...not by intention but his inability to recognize what rages in every human hearts. But let's be kind to Jacob. Who would've recognized this evil that raged in the hearts of all the brothers? Certainly I wouldn't have if I was in Jacob's shoes. Only God knew and God knows.

Ten brothers, driven by envy, conspired to kill Joseph. Their collective murderous intent produced an unthinkable action that was not justifiable in any circumstances or any culture: fratricide. We remember the story of Cain and Abel, Adam and Eve's first two sons. Cain killed his only brother Abel, the world's first murderous act. God blessed Abel more than Cain and Cain became very jealous. Cain's jealousy was aroused ultimately because he thought he had better sense of fairness than God. But God weighs the hearts. He is not swayed by the outward appearances. He is the author of justice and weighs all of our hearts' intent even before any of the actions is produced by them. And one man's blessing may be another man's burden and God's dispensation of blessing and justice is always done out of His love for our souls. Nevertheless, this first murder was not only an act of hatred and jealousy but an ultimate act of defiance toward God. In Cain's mind, God violated His own justice. When God came to Cain after the murder, Cain said to God in not so respectful tone, "Am I my brother's keeper?" That was the statement completely devoid of responsibility or remorse for his actions.

With the type of jealousy not so different than what Cain had for Abel, the brothers meant to kill Joseph. Now let's not cast our judgment on the brothers just yet. This is more than the story of human condition in certain situations. It is about the human nature that exists in all of us that is just biding its time for the right situation to explode onto! That phrase by God, "sins crouching at the door" is the true observation of the human heart at any given point in time by none other than God Himself. Yes...the sin crouches at the door of all of our hearts. But what about God's promise? Didn't God promise Abraham as well as Jacob that many nations will come out of them? How can God allow brothers even to meditate on fratricide? How would the brothers rightfully claim God's promises of their future nations through their lines if they had such auspicious beginnings? However, the question that we really need to be asking is not, "How can God allow such evil?", but "What lurks in the heart of every men (and women) and why do we try so hard to hide it from God as if we actually can?" Jeremiah 17:9 says, *"The heart is deceitful above all things and beyond cure. Who can understand it?"*

How many times have we tried to hide the fact that we hated our own brothers and sisters, both biological and spiritual for no reason except in jealousy! How many times have we said to God in our mind, "Am I my brother's (or sister's) keeper?" and "I'm not your keeper, and therefore you and I have nothing to do with each other. In fact, you are less than who I am; therefore, I don't want to have anything to do with you. I'm not going to stand here while you make yourself appear to be better than me before God and men. And I don't really care about your intentions. Even if you love me, I don't need that kind of love. I will do fine by myself. In fact, I will hate you." That kind of dark spiritual state harkens all the way back to the beginning of time; the time of Cain and Abel. In the name of Jesus Christ, I pray that we be free of such devastating jealousy and hatred. That kind of mentality does not become us, who are sons and daughters of God groomed to be kings and queens in the spiritual realms. When we walk away from our Lord, our mind becomes so desensitized to the point where do not see or feel that we had this kind of dark mentality to begin with. Christ took all that sin of hatred and got nailed on the cross. We are not so different from the Joseph's brothers at times in heart are we? God sometimes allows us into certain situations in order to bring out the hate and jealousy in us so that we can truly see how monstrous we can be in retrospect. We are all sinners. Every single one of us has fall short of the glory of God the Bible says.

But here is the beauty of God making all things new. We will see that this dramatic, life altering tragedy caused by their own hands will haunt the brothers for many years to come, especially Judah. The guilt of selling their brother Joseph into slavery, the fate worse than death itself, will slowly but surely come to weigh down on their souls. It will beat them down into spiritual submission unto God's will and we will look into this, as well later in the book. Judah would become the righteous tormented soul of the repented heart. You see, the acts of trying to kill Joseph or selling him into slavery didn't make these brothers evil. The actions were mere symptoms of the sick hearts. It is their hearts mired in sin that produced evil actions. The brothers, obviously, needed Divine redemption of their hearts but God also knew that certain amount time and season of trials and tribulations, appointed and orchestrated by God, must transpire before the brothers can actually see the NEED for their redemption. If you do not feel the need to be redeemed or forgiven, God cannot redeem you or forgive you. The worst thing God can do is to give the grace of forgiveness and redemption to the prideful heart who does not want it. Didn't Jesus say, "Do not give what is holy to dogs nor cast your pearls before swine, lest they trample under their feet and turn and tear you to pieces?" But the Son of man has revealed Himself to us in all manners of love and wisdom...and got crucified for it! Now, God has to wait until we see the need for His resurrection and salvation because he has already provided the true picture of our sins on that Cross. And in the story, God will wait patiently and let His divine interventions do their work.

God, in His wisdom, knew that this particular tragic event had to happen at this particular time AND the great famine about 20 years later, with everything that would happen in between, in order to make the redemption of all of their hearts possible and acceptable in His sight. This is the mystery of God's timing at work. For God's redemption is true redemption, happening precisely at the right time and making all of our hearts brand new over and over again.

It is the job of the older brothers to protect the younger. But we find the brothers wanting to kill their young brother and the word "protection" was not even in their radar. Everything about the brothers screams out the need for the redemption of their hearts and souls and Joseph cannot be groomed to be a future ruler of Egypt in this kind of hostile and dangerous environment.

The brothers will have to be set on their own path of redemption instigated by their own evil actions. The brothers and Joseph can no longer be together at this time. Joseph's time for departure had come in God's perfect timing. Before we proceed further, however, we need to recognize as the Church, especially here in America, that the visions and dreams of true heaven in Christ will initially set ourselves against all things in the world and separate us from our unbelieving friends and family members. We don't want to... and yet, we are already being separated in the minds and hearts of our families and friends as in the case of Joseph. All of you have experienced this social and spiritual separation with your families and friends to some degree already. This divine separation is necessary so that they can begin the redemption journey of their own hearts toward Christ through repentance as well as the journey of our own hearts in Christ.

Separating from SELF...unto the fear of God.

Now, we can return to the central character of the story, Joseph, and really focus on him. He was 17 years old, full of vigor and having the time of his life. But he could not have foreseen the freight train coming around the corner. Up until now, his life was like that of his dreams that God gave him. To his mind, he may have mistaken those dreams for a reflection of his current life or the life that was to happen very soon. Didn't he say to Pharaoh later that the dreams came in two forms because God was going to make it happen very soon? We will explore in depth this paradoxical interpretation of his dreams later.

His father, who is the patriarch of the whole family, adored and worshipped him. His brothers begrudgingly yielded to their little brother who is always stealing the affection of their father. The brothers, to their outrage, probably thought that Joseph will inherit most of Jacob's possessions. And...they could not do anything about it. They dare not, lest they will experience the fury of Jacob on account of his favorite son! He really owned his little world. The joy of ownership and the budding of self-entitlement were coming to an end, however. His own brothers grabbed him and threw him down into the pit. And as he lay there, he may have overheard the dreadful conversation between any brothers or families in history. In that pit, his dreams ended and the nightmare began. In that pit, he began to experience the kind of fear that he had never known before. The dreams no longer mattered. Terrible and unimaginable things were happening to Joseph and the fear of death gripped him. Very few of us can imagine the magnitude of the horror of listening in on our own family members planning our own death but Joseph was living that nightmare. It was the time to either survive or die for Joseph. Everything he knew to be true and real has been turned upside down. He could not think about anything else except his life and God. There's no doubt that he prayed while he was in that pit. He probably prayed like he never prayed before. As he was being drawn out of that pit, he probably saw his stone faced brothers and knew they would not listen to any of his pleading. He did it anyway. He pleaded with all his might. Can you hear him today? His pleading resonates with the blood cry of Abel. It resonates with all the helpless victims who have been the victims of unjustifiable abuse and death. I can almost hear him say, "Please my brothers, don't kill me! Don't sell me. Please!!! I'm your own brother, your flesh and blood…"

He may have pleaded with God in his mind probably even more so; for it is a natural human reaction when we are totally helpless and on the verge of death or demise. But there is no mention of any of Joseph's pleading in this first chapter of his story. We know now that Joseph pleaded with the brothers for his own life when the brothers recount the event before Joseph later in the story. Perhaps the detail of pleading is irrelevant here in God's mind. No amount of pleading or bargaining will change God's mind when God has already determine that you will be His mighty instrument for your own divine destiny in Him. And He knows that you will not be truly happy until you eventually find yourself in your true divine destiny in Him!

This tragic turn of events was the necessary beginning for the path that was designed not only for Joseph, but for all the people in this story as well as all of us reading the story, and God was not going to deter from it. As for Joseph, he literally descended from the throne of self-entitlement and ownership to the pit of fear and despair. That was a long and hard fall. The situation was out of his control. For the first time in his life, he did not own or dictate the situation. Whatever security or love he thought he had in his own brothers has been revealed as counterfeits and lies. It was a sudden and painful realization that his brothers had absolutely nothing for him but hatred. There was nothing he could do to get out of this nightmare. He was the favored son of the patriarch. Now, he would be a lowly slave; a vessel to be used and abused. He was dead to his brothers by choice and dead to his father by force. He was dead to his old way of life and everything he knew to be his. He was essentially a dead man. Long, painful and sad goodbye was coming but he was still clinging to a tiny sliver of hope in his heart that somehow the dream that God gave him will still be fulfilled somehow. There was only one person who can protect him in Egypt. GOD. There was only one thing left for him to do if he was to live again in this new, dark, cold and foreign world. SURRENDER. He surrendered to God. In order for Joseph to trust God with all of his heart for his unimaginably glorious destiny to be revealed later, the beginning of the journey had to be equally unimaginably painful to order to instill such immovable trust in God and God alone. He had no choice.

There is only one thing you can do when you find yourself in the pit of fear and despair and it does not matter how you got there or how long you've been in there. You still have a choice. You can surrender your life to God, your Maker. This doesn't mean that you should just drop everything and let the chips fall where they may. This is not about abandonment, but exactly the opposite. When we totally surrender to God, our lives are truly brought under God's control. We must realize that He is in control of everything and everyone. We are actually embracing and welcoming into our hearts God's kingdom and His control over our lives. He already controls everything else. Why not our hearts? And as we begin to walk in Him, people will begin to see the beginning of God operating in you. They will see God through you.

There is always my will and God's will. My will is an attempt to bring God's timing, and even God given relationships and God's provisions and His gifts of talents under my control. Everything we have originated from God. It is God's will for you to work hard, with all your energy and creativity, in the job that He has given you. But He is asking you to leave that sphere of destructive influence that wages war against your soul. Whether it is in the marketplace or on the home front, He maybe asking you to leave the sphere of gossip, laziness, false witnessing as well as any activity that encourages infidelity, sexual immorality, jealousy and greed...all to our self-destruction. We need to use all of our knowledge and creativity that God has given us, even to the point of being shrewd like snakes, the Bible says, to separate ourselves from that destructive and wasteful social sphere without being antisocial. God has called us into peace but not at the expense of purity in Christ. Otherwise, people cannot see Christ in us. We must understand that in the minds of our unbelieving friends and families, we are already being sent on spiritual exile. Yes, that's right...Like the divine dream that caused the separation of Joseph from his brothers, our divine destiny in Christ will cause the separation between us and the world. We are in the world but not of the world. Our hesitation or unwillingness to separate from the world will not only cost us the redemptive and glorious work of divine destiny in Christ, but our own hearts and souls — as they will be ensnared, abused and destroyed by the deceptive powers and empty promises of this world.

You may still say that this kind of painful separation may not have been necessary for Joseph and it just seemed a little too much. Surely, God could've separated Joseph from the family without such pain and suffering. But, you see, with one single swoop, God was able to separate Joseph not only from the dysfunctional and counterproductive relationships within his family, not only from false sense of security in anything of the world — including his own family — but also separate him from his own possible delusion of control or maybe even self grandeur. I'm not saying that Joseph was actually self-delusional. I'm saying that if there was any hint of self-entitlement and ownership budding in Joseph, this experience literally crushed all that out of him. And on top of that, this tragic event provided an effective canvass on which the brothers could see the true condition of their own monstrous hearts and souls being poured out on Joseph.

The brothers needed this horrifying event to happen by them to see themselves for who they really were in retrospect in order to know that they needed to be saved and redeemed by God. Joseph certainly is the main character of the story, but the souls of the brothers are the very reasons why this "evil" had to happen by the brothers themselves…for their future selves and their redemption. Certainly God knew that Joseph could properly handle the situation by giving up his control of the uncontrollable situation in the most dramatic and painful way imaginable. God never tests us beyond which we can bear. And God does not tempt us, but it is the desire of our own unredeemed hearts that beckons temptation. And we have the Holy Spirit helping us and guiding us. Most of us have it so much easier than Joseph so we need to meditate on the grace that He is pouring out on us in these last days. There are those who are made to suffer more than the rest for His glory. I will not say anymore than that, but nevertheless, God is orchestrating everything here for the true redemption of everyone in this story even, and especially, here. If Joseph's heart was in need of redemption for his divine destiny through this journey, then how much more in need were the hearts of the brothers! This tragic event was necessary for redemption of all people involved. God is in control from start to finish.

Our control is an illusion produced by our flesh that craves it. Only God is in control. And if God was not in control, this world would have self destructed long ago. For Joseph specifically, God launched him into this journey with this unexpected and unimaginable fear and pain of separation so that he will begin to surrender his life and begin to abdicate himself from the throne of self entitlement and self security, and embrace God's control. It is the fear of God through this event that overpowered and crushed all things out of Joseph that could be desired and worshipped by the world. This was the beginning of the end of fear of men for Joseph and the beginning of the fear of God and all manners of knowledge and wisdom. It is the fear of God that steered him back to the one true God, who alone can truly love the way we need to be loved. This event had to be so fiercely atrocious for Joseph in order for him to see clearly what may exist in every human heart, and for Joseph to totally to depend on God alone in the hope that only He can save him. This event of separation needed to be so devastating and horrifying for Joseph in order for God to build the immovable foundation of his magnificent divine destiny that cannot be overcome by anything or anyone in the world. The beginning of the knowledge that God is the only One, who can save Joseph from humanity, including himself, begins here in the pit of despair called the knowledge of all things that instills the fear of God.

The journey of knowledge of God and men is about to begin for Joseph and all of us...but it will not begin unless we are on our knees in the fear of our mighty God. Again, *the fear of God is the beginning of all true knowledge...including, and especially, the knowledge of love for all.*

Chapter 8

DIVINE WISDOM TO OVERCOME ALL THINGS HUMAN
(GENESIS 39)

Jesus said: "Ask and it will be given to you; seek and you will find; knock and the door will be opened to you. For everyone who asks receives; the one who seeks finds; and to the one who knocks, the door will be opened. Which of you, if your son asks for bread, will give him a stone? Or if he asks for a fish, will give him a snake? If you, then, though you are evil, know how to give good gifts to your children, how much more will your Father in heaven give good gifts to those who ask him! So in everything, do to others what you would have them do to you, for these sums up the Law and the Prophets." – Matthew 7:7-12

If any of you lacks wisdom, you should ask God, who gives generously to all without finding fault, and it will be given to you. – James 1:5

My son, if you accept my words and store up my commands within you, turning your ear to wisdom and applying your heart to understanding – indeed, if you call out for insight and cry aloud for understanding, and if you look for it as for silver and search for it as for hidden treasure, then you will understand the fear of the Lord and find the knowledge of God. For the Lord gives wisdom; from his mouth come knowledge and understanding. – Proverbs 2:1-6

Ask, seek and knock for divine wisdom above all else

There are many larger than life questions posed by both believers and unbelievers. If our desire is to truly know God and the mystery of His love, we cannot just ask these questions and walk away, not really wanting to hear the answers. If we are simply asking questions without really desiring to find out the answers, God will not give us the answers. Now let's examine the above 3 passages that give us further insights regarding the answers that our hearts really desire.

So often, we project the physical on the spiritual. When we do that, our understanding of the scriptures becomes dull. God is spirit. He cares more about the condition of our souls than anything else. Our flesh, and all of its desires, and all of these 'misperceived physical blessings' that we thought resulted from it, interferes with our perception of God, who desires to first impart true spiritual blessings. He knows better than anyone that the true blessing comes from having the right spirit and the right mind that is constantly being renewed by His Spirit as we offer our bodies as living sacrifice (Romans 12:1-2). God designed us to be happy in our spirits first. God himself is the Creator of all things and designed our hearts to enjoy them in peace. The peace of God will not be found in your heart if you are outside of His will, and you will not be able to enjoy your wealth, fame and prosperity because they are also under God's control. We really shouldn't be surprised that this is so obviously true. God is the creator of all things, talents AND desires of our hearts because HE had wired them that way at the beginning. Everything has been created by God including wealth, sex and power. But we cannot really enjoy any of the blessings in this life if we are not faithful to the Designer. Happiness is found in the heart of its Designer. Once we enter into His domain of wisdom and love, we will be able to truly enjoy all the things that God created within His intended Divine context. When we try to obtain God's blessings outside of His divine context, the very same blessing will turn into a curse, as evidenced in the lives of so many celebrities and the wealthy. That, too, is the divine design.

As we have already seen, the journey of Joseph began in the fear of the Lord. And we know that the fear of the Lord is the beginning of all knowledge. When we begin our journey with the fear of the Lord away from the fear of men — that God and God alone is in full and ultimate control of our lives — then we will begin to understand the wisdom of all things God and men. But in this world, we will experience and encounter so many questionable and perplexing things and elements that we will be constantly asking God for wisdom. Asking God is actually a good thing!

That's exactly why God instilled the fear of God in us so that we will continuously go to Him and ask Him for all answers as opposed to running to the world and seeking to find answers that it doesn't have. It is only when we stop asking God that we could easily fall prey to the intellectual laziness about all things spiritual that saves. And again, the Lord said that we will perish because of our lack of knowledge.

Ask, seek and knock, Jesus said. He is not telling us to persist in asking for physical blessings like so many of us have assumed. He was actually talking about the Divine wisdom that we will be given clearly and generously when we persist in asking. The passage cannot be understood in any other context in light of the other passages that were given above. This verse is specifically tailored for our spiritual needs above the physical needs. And this wasn't his recommendation. He is COMMANDING us to ask, seek and knock in order that we will find the Divine wisdom to decipher the mysteries of God: that He does EVERYTHING out of His love for us, His people. He wants us to know that we are being protected and loved by the Almighty. If we do not continually ask, seek and knock, if we do not call out, cry aloud and look as for hidden treasure, we will not understand the fear of the Lord that is the beginning of all knowledge (Proverbs 1:7). Certainly Joseph understood the fear of the Lord that led to the beginning of the true Divine knowledge as it is evident in all his life. As He continually set himself apart in fear of the Lord, refusing to compromise his faith, he was continuously being purified by the stories of God and the precepts that God has given to Abraham, Isaac and Jacob to walk with the Lord and seek His righteousness. It is the divine cycle of pursuit that begins with the desire to seek divine wisdom that fuels the need to understand and seek more divine wisdom. Once you get into the cycle, you can never have enough. And the continuous byproduct of this ever-escalating divine cycle of wisdom is the golden rule. You might be saying right now, "That doesn't make sense." Let me show you below in the section, "**Fear of God leading to the knowledge of...love?**", why the golden rule is not only the mandate but the inevitability of this divine cycle of fear leading to love leading to fear continually leading to the love of Christ for all people.

Purity by living according to the Word

The wife of the captain of the guard may have been very beautiful. I believe that many of the scholars came to this conclusion because of the pervasive, openly sensual culture of that time in Egypt. People with power, like Potipher, probably had the power to choose his wife among many potential candidates. Another angle of speculation that may reinforce this fact is the way Potipher reacts to the lie that his wife tells after Joseph refused her. "He burns with anger," it says. There is no trial, no inquisition and no time to waste. Joseph was immediately put into prison. You should raise your eyebrows at this point and ask to yourself, "Is this not the same Potipher, the captain of the guard who was observant and wise enough to correctly identify the workings of the divine leadership and blessings in Joseph?" You can see in the text that Potipher saw (understood) that the Lord was with Joseph and the Lord gave him success in everything he did. Potipher, with his great power, had the wisdom of discernment and delegation. This kind of wisdom is not always found in people with such power, so it speaks volume about the Potipher's character as well. He entrusted everything in his household to Joseph that everybody, including all the Egyptians, would have to answer to Joseph. This sort of power transfer is unthinkable for a Hebrew slave because Hebrews were an abomination to the Egyptians. He had the wisdom to overcome the cultural and ethnic prejudice, which were nearly impossible to overcome in those times. Potipher not only trusted Joseph's ability and talent but also his character. If Potipher had any inclination that Joseph will somehow steal from his wealth, he would've never put Joseph in charge. We can reason, then, that Potipher lost his perfectly good sense of judgment and put Joseph in prison because his wife was really beautiful, and that the possibility of this unholy union was somehow real despite Joseph's impeccable character. Potipher lost his mind over a woman...like many of the men before and after him. He was actually expressing his jealousy and anger that overpowered his reason. Also, the battle to fight the temptation in young Joseph's mind, and the power of God to overcome such temptation, becomes more worthy of contemplation and inspiration if we assume that she was an undeniable, beautiful temptress.

Furthermore, If Potipher's wife was not beautiful, she likely would not have behaved in such ways and there would be no lie for Potipher to lose his sense over. In Proverbs 2, 5, 6 and 7, you can see the pattern of these beautiful women who are always seeking to ensnare men, even the wise and strong, as their trophy cases. Both the weak and the mighty throughout history for all kingdoms and empires have lost their souls over women like these. They are relentless in their pursuit like the wife of Potipher, who was relentless in pursuing Joseph. In Proverbs Chapter 7: 26 it says "many are the victims she has brought down; her slain are a mighty throng." And the entire chapter 5 of Proverbs speaks about the deceitfulness of the wayward women and the devastating consequences of infidelity and impurity. Men, we just need to flee all situations or medium that will cause us to be ensnared. Do not give your mind a chance to rationalize or, more accurately, lose itself. Flee.

Flee from such temptation and run into your divine destiny. The place of sexual sins outside of holy matrimony is the furthest point from the place of your God ordained destiny in God's eternal spectrum. The wisdom for all us men is that we should be wise to steer clear of all situations or mediums with potential for any sexual sins to enter our lives. Some of you men are saying right now, "But our jobs *kind of* require that we need to frequent such places." Then ask yourselves, who gave your job in the first place? And do we think we can make the job more secure or less by catering to the fear of men, who are always bent on making a joke out of our God and His people, which are us? Separating yourselves from such "opportunities" may earn the ridicule and social isolation for a short time, but God who sees all things done in secret will rewards you in ways that you can never imagine...like Joseph. And we will see some of the very men that made a mockery out of you become pierced in their own hearts later for doing so...unto their own redemption in Christ! Imagine that. Few of us may or will have stories like that, I can sense, even as I'm writing. We have to find ourselves strong in the love of God and trust Him for His protection when He says the sexual sins are the most destructive sins of all (1 Corinthians 6:18-20). Let us be men of Christ. Men, we can do this but we have to unite as the men of Christ. Let's not willingly destroy the temple of our God, which is our body. And this is the only way to turn the hearts of the wayward women as well in the end. We are not doing this for just ourselves but for our wives and especially our children. Men, are we leaders? Are we men?

Joseph lived in the era of story telling and traditions. His Father Jacob instructed him regarding the stories of their ancestors and the Divine precepts. Remember that it was Moses, generations later, who received the 10 commandments from the Lord. The written instructions did not come until the time of Moses. Unlike the rest of us, Joseph did not have the luxury of reading the Bible when he wanted to. In comparison to the richness of the knowledge of God that is readily available at our disposal today, Joseph had to hold on to the words of these stories with everything in him and practiced it daily. He kept them deep in his heart. And as he recited the lessons of his ancestors in his mind over and over and trying to put the precepts into practice everyday, he was being purified and set apart.

"How can a young man keep his way pure? By living according to your word" (Psalm 119: 9). Joseph was living according to the truth of God that had been tested and lived out by Abraham, Isaac, and Jacob. It was not the

amount of book knowledge of God that mattered. He was LIVING out the precepts, which is meager in volume compared to all that has been made available to us in these last days. The lives of the forefathers were set apart by God, who is, first and foremost, holy. They walked with God in spirit. The very word holiness means to separate and be set apart from all things human. In this foreign land where there was no one to depend on or trust, Joseph put his trust in the Lord who is the deliverer and provider in all situations and separated himself from all things ungodly. Just like Abraham was called out of the land full of idols, Joseph kept himself pure from all idols in the land of Egypt. He knew that Holy God desires holiness and purity in His people, and Joseph understood this better than anyone.

As He dedicated himself to be purified by the words of God through his ancestors, he began to really understand and know God for who he really is. It was only through LIVING in and living out the precepts and the principles of his fathers on a daily basis that Joseph came to understand who God really was. He was *seeing* God. Jesus said, "Blessed is the man who is pure of heart for they will see God." When our Lord said *see God*, that true *visualization of God* is not just limited to a select individual(s) who has actually seen God in person physically and just barely survived. It means that we will truly see or understand God for who He really is and what He will accomplish through us, if we are willing to be purified and set apart by His precepts: the word. Again, I ask you, how can a young man keep His way pure? If your life is being purified by the word of God, then you will truly see who God is and what He has in store for us. Men, let's purify ourselves by getting into the word every day. Let's not try to deceive our Lord by doing a quick cursory glance at the word for 5 minutes or less a day. We all know that the word will never be internalized that way. If reading cannot get you in that meditative mode, then there is Bible on CD or MPD available for you. Let the word of God find you wherever you may be. We will not be able to overcome the forces of evil or temptations any other way. Men, our families and friends are counting on us even though they may tell you they do not. Trust me when I say that God made their hearts the same way that He made ours.

The text says Potipher's wife tested and tempted Joseph day after day. It is amazing how Joseph was able to stand his ground on the truth of God's righteousness in the face of this constant attack on his spirit through his own flesh. Joseph was able to resist the temptation day after day because he understood that he was under God's tremendous grace and that same God was, and is, holy and love. He persisted in His holiness and His love. In order for us to properly pay attention to God who is holy requires the understanding that He is love. And in order to fully understand God's love, which is vastly different than the love in the world, we must first come to fear the Lord, who is holy. The fear of God requires the knowledge that God is both holy and love.

Joseph was in awe of holy God who snatched him from the jaws of death and placed him in the most unlikely position of power, an abominable Hebrew slave who became the functional master of the house of Potipher because God gave him success in everything he did. He understood that God's love was demonstrated in supernatural way through his life because he was actively putting God first in everything. He knew that everything physical and spiritual, including the souls of everyone and himself, belong to holy God. Joseph could not have come to know and understand such magnificent love of God without the fearsome working of the Lord who put him in severe trial and tribulation for a time in order to separate Joseph unto Himself and to bring out the love and protection of God in proper situation as to make it certain that all these miraculous blessings had to come from God and not of Joseph's own making or from the world. Joseph feared the Lord above everything because of His awesome, daily provisions flowing out of His love that is undeniably obvious, even to the pagan master Potipher.

Fear of God leading to the knowledge of...love?

And in His fear of the Lord, Joseph came into the knowledge of God that eventually culminated in true love. You may ask, do you mean to tell me that the fear of the Lord that resulted in the knowledge of God, who is holy, eventually led to the understanding of God's love? Look at the end of the passage out of the book of Matthew 7:7-12. After commanding us to ask, seek and knock continuously for Divine wisdom that all of us seriously lack, Jesus says, "So do to others, what you would have them do to you, for this sums up all the Law and the Prophets." This is the golden rule that suspiciously sounds like the other great command that the Lord gave us, and that is, "Love your neighbor as yourself." What Jesus is saying is, when you come into the true wisdom of God by the fear of the Lord (because you asked, sought, and knocked for it) you will not only be inspired but to be equipped to love your neighbor by the true love of God because God is always about ALL people all the time. **The fear of God always leads to the knowledge of the golden rule because all true knowledge and wisdom of God is summed up in the golden rule as Jesus said.** We must remember that any divine knowledge begins with the fear of the Lord and the knowledge of love is no exception. You will see that pretty much all the events in the Joseph's life has been designed by God to always instill the fear of the Lord first in order to eventually love all people.

Only the fear of God will steer you away from sins and evil — the seed of all destruction — and puts us in the proper training mode to be equipped in His love to impart the same love that truly builds all things eternal in everyone. In the end, the true litmus test of our "living according to his word" is demonstrated by the love of Christ, being lived out and worked out through us by fear and trembling. Christ is our salvation. Holy God who sacrificed His only Son for us desires to unite us in love by removing that sin, or that self-advancing unholiness, which is divisive and destructive by nature. And the power to resist the temptation day after day came from Joseph's putting these principles of God into practice. Joseph understood that the laws and the precepts of Holy God are designed out of love to protect everyone from all potential consequences of such sins. **Therefore, while the fear of God initially steers us away from ever alluring sins of the world in our own hearts, the beginning of the knowledge of God's love begins to shine on all things to reveal the true faces of those same ensnaring sins: deceptions and destructions for our hearts and our families. The fear of the Lord drives us away from all sins and into the true love of happiness for our souls that is only found in the unchanging and eternal love of Christ. The fear of God initiates the divine escalating spiral of fear of God to love of God to higher fear of God to ever surpassing, all conquering love of our Lord Jesus Christ for all people, including you and me!**

Joseph is like that young man in Psalm 119:9, who keeps himself pure by getting into the word of God consistently. The heart that is being actively purified by the word of the Lord will "see", or understand God, who is holy and love for **all people**. When a young man understands that Holy God is orchestrating everything in and around you out of His love for him, he will be compelled by the same love to flee from unholiness…because he can also see that this unholiness, covered with fleeting pleasures of the flesh, is deceptive and destructive for all, including himself. That's the beginning of the golden rule of love manifesting in our fear of God.

But he refused. "With me in charge," he told her, "my master does not concern himself with anything in the house; everything he owns he has entrusted to my care. No one is greater in this house than I am. My master has withheld nothing from me except you, because you are his wife. How then could I do such a wicked thing and sin against God?"

Here in this passage, we understand exactly where Joseph stands. If we were to rephrase the passage, it would read something like, "God has shown me His great love by causing your husband to give me — an abominable Hebrew slave — this unprecedented and undeserving position of power, honor and responsibility to become the master of this house in his absence. If I were to sleep with you, it would be a great sin and insult to Holy God who loves me and sustains ALL including your husband, you and all of us."

Great battle for our children

Now, if somehow in your mind that all of these things that I have described in this chapter in bits and pieces, or as a whole, are not something new, then let's really try to apply the principles of the lessons in this chapter by projecting all of these truths to our own children in this nation who are in the midst of great battle when it comes to sexuality and the values of purity. As their guardians and parents, we cannot just give them lectures for 10 minutes about how they are to continuously flee from the temptations and leave them unattended. Many of us do not feel like we are qualified to instruct our kids in the arena of sexual purity before or outside of marriage. I exhort all of us that nobody, I mean nobody, is perfect in the eyes of God when it comes to sexual purity. Some of us may even have been virgins before we got married but the true purity is established by nothing short of continuous redemption by the Word itself, our Lord Jesus Christ...as in the verse, "How can a young person stay on the path of purity? By *living* according to your Word." We need to radically change our strategy on how we are going to combat these overwhelming and insurmountable problems. We start by getting on the frontline...together. Yes parents and all the adult crusaders, Let us fight alongside with them. Take the first step by reading the WORD...TOGETHER.

For those of you who has less than perfect background and past in this arena of sexual purity, you can actually use your experience as the examples for your children. I'm not saying that we should all share our experiences openly with our kids. That's not wisdom and it will actually work against us. We must face the realities of our own past and understand the devastating consequences that are already taking place and ruining the lives of our friends and loved ones. Just look at all the broken families and relationships around us. I'm just saying we need to be motivated by *that* clear understanding when we approach our kids in love and truth. If we repent before the Lord, the Lord has already taken away all of our sins by the way of His Cross. We can be their parents with all divine authority but let His love do its patient work as you intentionally, lovingly and persistently approach your children in this area. His blood has already cleansed all of our sexual sins in body, mind and spirit. And He will show you and give you the wisdom to combat and bring down the strongholds when it comes to sex in your teens. We must start early and call upon the aid of our local churches where many of the parenting programs are available. But we must also remember that the foundation of the Church is the family. The *program* must start in our homes. We do not have to resign to the fact that the problem has already gotten out of control. That only reflects our lack of faith in God. In God, nothing is out of control EVER. And perhaps we have been born into this dark era precisely because of our divine destiny to overcome such grievous evil in Jesus Christ.

While we begin to instill the eternal values of the truth and love of Christ on our knees, we can also provide them with practical boundaries and protection where they are not constantly subject to opportunities to be exposed to such temptations or experimentations. We can begin by limiting the number of hours spent on TV and internet. There may be homework that will require the use of the internet, but we can program our children's computers to block any unsavory websites. We must get involved in our children's future by putting a tight leash on the gateways such as TV and the internet, for all of these alluring and destructive influences in their lives. This also means that we, as parents, must set the examples for them first. However, setting up filtering programs are not a permanent solution, but a temporary one. We must first *change* the way they view us: the adults and parents. We change their perspective when it comes of sex, power or money by redeeming our own perspective in the truth and love of Jesus Christ. He is the only one who can change you, and thereby, change them. Have a family Bible study at least once a week, not to expound on some theology or doctrine (we can't do it even if we are pastors), but to recite a chapter or two from the Bible (I recommend to start with the book of John and the book of psalms at the same time), and pray to God, who gives us generously all manners of divine wisdom, to give you the understanding through your *lives*. Then, you can discuss whatever may have happened that week or day as you are filled with the Spirit. And pray with them. Pray for them, for their schools and their friends...with them. There are many good Christian children resources out there so...why not go over the book before they do? Yes, if we are their parents, it is our God-given responsibilities as well as the blessings to do so.

Instead of getting kids out of the house, we can invite their friends into our own house. Simple gesture such as a soda or a snack would do wonders for these kids. And as we, adults, continue to grow in the knowledge of love and truth of Jesus Christ, they will grow in their interaction with their friends and the world in the knowledge and the truth of Jesus Christ. Children still imitate their parents...even though a lot of you don't believe that. It is true. Are we going to continuously give into the ever unreasonable and outrageous demands of our children and their peer pressure? We are not their friends. We are their parents! We do not have to give into the fear of men and the world that say, "The kids will hate you and you will lose them if you do not allow them to follow the ways of the ever advancing 'cool' world that they seem to understand better than you, causing them to be outcasts." We have bought into such lies for so long and that's why we are in this mess in the first place. But it's never too late for us in God's book. We can rise again as their guardians in our Lord Jesus! Don't look at other parents or don't get discouraged by what's happening out there. We can overcome all things through Him who strengthens us by the journey of our hearts that begins with the word and prayers on our knees...our spiritual knees.

As for Joseph, however, this great stand of faith in God throws him back into the heart of darkness. Why, we may ask? We should never stop asking such questions. We have to ask hard and ask diligently and ask relentlessly until we find the answer! God promised that if we ask, seek and knock, and search as for a hidden treasure, then the divine wisdom to truly save and build all things, including our families, will be given to us! Joseph was faithful in all things small as he was put in charge over the house of Potipher. Now, he will suddenly be welcomed into that training ground called king's prison teeming with major league conspirators and *unlucky* master politicians. The time has now come for Joseph to really learn about the hearts of all men AND the heart of God! Joseph will really learn to trust God and God alone with all of his heart until that trust in Him will became a part of his spiritual instinct.

Chapter 9

DESCENT INTO THE HEART OF HUMANITY... UNTO DIVINE DESTINY.
(GENESIS 39 AND 40)

Yea, though I walk through the valley of the shadow of death, I will fear no evil; For you are with me; Your rod and your staff, they comfort me.—Psalm 23:4

Because the Lord disciplines those he loves, as a father the son he delights in.—Proverbs 3:12

Were you a slave when you were called? Don't let it trouble you — although if you can gain your freedom, do so. For the one who was a slave when called to faith in the Lord is the Lord's freed person; similarly, the one who was free when called is Christ's slave. You were bought at a price; do not become slaves of human beings. Brothers and sisters, each person, as responsible to God, should remain in the situation they were in when God called them.— 1 Corinthians 7:21-24

But He said to me, "My grace is sufficient for you, for my power is made perfect in weakness." Therefore I will boast all the more gladly about my weaknesses, so that Christ's power may rest on me.—2 Corinthians 12:9

Divine introspection by spiritual isolation from all things familiar... again

It is hard for us to understand why God would allow Joseph to be thrown into prison when he did everything right. He had been a faithful and wise servant to the captain of the guard. He upheld the principles of his forefathers, honoring God in all he did, even to the point of resisting that powerful, relentless, repeated temptations by Potipher's wife. He was a man of character and integrity, full of wisdom and the Spirit of God. He truly was the best of us. At this point, he was more Christ-like than pretty much all of us who profess to know and follow Christ. Do we really know Christ with all the knowledge that we have on Christ as much as Joseph who knew God the Father? If the answer is no, then we really need to know Christ of true love as much as Joseph knew his God of love. I know personally that I need to know Christ now more than ever.

Again, why was he sent to prison for something he didn't do at this particular time? Could he have not gone through this ordeal and still be on the path unto greatness? Could God, who can move heaven and earth, have somehow orchestrated all the elements and people around him as to spare him such unjust suffering? We often hear stories of how bad things happen to good people. Most of us have lost loved ones or friends who were the "best" of us. What about all these children who have been born into the environment of neglect and abuse? "Honest" people often get fired or demoted, and let's not forget, "nice" guys finish last. And you begin to ask yourself, where is God in all this? Where was God when Joseph, a "righteous" man, was sent to prison? It's perfectly OK to ask such questions. It is only natural that our hearts, designed by God of justice, should seek "justice" in everything we see and do. God certainly welcomes all who are skeptical and contrite. He will not shun or despise us from doing so. He will let us get close and touch Him and allow us to feel the evidence of His eternal, unchanging love and be convinced of His truth and not doubt. Jesus said, do not doubt but put your hands and minds where there is evidence of my Love! And the doubting Thomas believed. Let's be like Thomas. Let's be convinced of His love! Let's persist in asking and not give up. Let's look into some of the answers by the grace of God as the Spirit, who searches the very heart of God, illuminates the truth in all things. He wants us to ask, seek and knock continuously...for God to open the doors of His kingdom and wisdom. He will reveal Himself in His time when we earnestly seek His face. He's never early or never late but always on time. Didn't He say He makes all things beautiful in His time?

When God closes one door and opens the next, He wants to make sure that we KNOW it was from God. When Joseph was thrown into prison, I believe that God had given Joseph the insights that the event was orchestrated in the foreknowledge of God as he was meditating on the event. Jesus said in the beatitudes in Matthews 5:11-12: *"Blessed are you when people insult you, persecute you and falsely say all kinds of evil against you because of me. Rejoice and be glad, because great is your reward in heaven for in the same way they persecuted the prophets who were before you."* This was the persecution that Joseph had to endure in order to be reminded of the nature of men in the absence of God in their lives. In the eyes of God, he was being counted as one of the prophets that Jesus mentioned in the passage. And Joseph knew that this turn of tragic events that resulted from following God in obedience wholeheartedly MUST have come from God for a greater and more magnificent purpose yet to be realized. If the persecution comes because we bare the name of God and Jesus Christ, we know it was from God for our eternal and glorious destiny in Him and for all people. We will talk more about the idea of persecution later.

Moreover, we have to remember that Joseph is only around 20 years or so at this time. Even our Lord Jesus did not begin his ministry until he was 30 years old. I'm positive beyond any shadow of doubt that Jesus was more than ready to reveal himself when he was a child. Remember that Jesus as a child had engaged in deep theological discussions with the teachers of the laws in the temple for days while his parents desperately searched for him. You see, the world was not ready for Jesus. The world would never be truly ready for Christ but God had waited the best possible moment in the life of Christ as well as the history of the entire world for Christ to reveal Himself in ways that the world needed to see Him. His revelation still doesn't mean the world was ready to receive Christ but the timing of the revelation of Christ coincided with the necessity of the revelation of His incomparable and amazing grace, first. The sad reality of the human race is that the world as a whole will never be ready to receive Christ as who He really is in His totality. That's why Christ revealed His love first. His perfect and righteous judgment will not be revealed until the very end. Joseph, however, is not ready for the empire and the empire is not ready for some 20-year-old Hebrew boy to take the throne of Egypt. He would have been despised in the eyes of the rich and powerful as so many of the young people are...then and now. And he would've wasted so much of his God-given talents, wisdom and energy on politics instead of managing God blessed wealth and providing for the people.

The world has been rewiring itself in such a way to recognize, and usually reward, our efforts to preserve our pride that exists in every one of us. This is why we have to be very careful when we are being kind or nice to other people in order to win their favor. The devil, the prince of the world, prowls about like a lion and it seeks to devour all, even the elect, the Bible says. Actions leading to the approval by the world — and subsequent *happiness* thereof — ultimately come from our desires to preserve and perpetuate what exist in the core of every heart; the pride that does not see or need the presence of God. But when that very pride of life, along with the lust of the eyes and the flesh, is directly challenged by righteous deeds of a righteous soul following after God, that pride of life will hate the person who made them look and feel inferior although that air of superiority was never the intention of the righteous person. And it is the same pride that looks upon the other hearts filled with the same kind of pride and says, "If I cannot make myself look, sound and feel better than the other person, then ultimately, the other person with the same kind of pride will have to either go or be destroyed." So the cycle of self-destruction ensues. It is only the mysterious working of the grace and love of God — yes, it is working not only in the Church but even in the world of unbelievers through all history including now — that has prevented us from annihilating one another. But in the end, the pride doesn't care because the pride itself is the number one cause for spiritual blindness to realize how prideful we are. And Joseph is getting to know about this nature of pride and sin in every man very well in this prison full of people who are very well versed in the ways of the world.

Joseph knew, beyond any doubt, that this turn of events was from God. It had to be. We can see that Joseph was quietly and diligently obedient to God in this new world of darkness that God himself had pushed him into. He was not being obedient to the authority per se, but to the ultimate Authority of God who put the warden over him. He was doing everything as unto the Lord as long as it didn't compromise his faith in God. He was humble before God who was in control of the present and the future. Joseph excelled in everything he did under the prison warden. But while he was walking in obedience, he also had time to ponder about the very cause of every evil and horrible thing that happens in this world: The pride of human hearts.

Potipher and his wife: the nature of false security fueled by pride in the world

When her desires were not fulfilled on her own terms, Potipher's wife did not think twice about accusing Joseph falsely, in the hopes of bringing devastation to a life that has barely begun in this new land. Her pride, the only thing mattered to her, was damaged. What about Potipher himself? Here was the man who was the captain of the guard, a wise master with insights to see the Spirit of God working in Joseph. Potipher himself put Joseph in charge over everything in his house because he knew that Joseph's vision and character was extremely profitable to him. But in a fit of rage and jealousy, putting his wife's lies above his good judgment, he threw him down into the king's prison, where the only way out would be death or the king's pardon. Joseph was once again reminded of the evil that resides in the heart of every man. Do you think Joseph's mind was brought back to the day when he was thrown into the pit by his brothers? That's a rhetorical question. Just as he was thrown into the prison for being the excellent steward and a trustworthy noble servant, he had been thrown into that pit by his brothers for being obedient to his father in making sure of his brother's safety, the very same brothers that wanted to kill him! Joseph was coming into the knowledge of human nature that Christ already knew; mainly that terrible human pride. God's grace and wisdom flies in the face of our human pride that is hidden so well in our hearts. God's amazing grace through Christ implies our imperfections and shortcomings. Our flesh in its core does not like to be second to anything, including God. Our pride, working through our flesh, constantly wages war against the Spirit. It is our pride that brings confusion and destruction to our lives when the truth of God is clear and redemptive. And our pride wants to kill anything that will make it number two, including God himself.

Our pride blinds us from the truth that we are prideful. The power of the Word divides the joints and the marrows of our inner being and exposes what we try so hard to hide: The human pride. The Word, Jesus Christ, sets the sword of the truth against the thing that destroys our soul: the human pride. The Word pierces our very souls because the Word saves our souls from this pride that resides in the core of every single one of us. In order for us to be fully redeemed in Christ, our pride will have to be systematically and repeatedly...crucified. Our Lord Jesus Christ said, "Deny yourself, take up your cross daily and follow me." Only in that weakened state of *self without pride* that the overcoming power of Jesus Christ is perfected.

Divine Instinct of the King's love formed and driven through God's hammer

Joseph witnessed this human pride in full display when his own brothers tried to kill him out of envy and was once again reminded of the same pride working through Potipher. He was not even given a moment to defend himself before he was thrown into the dungeon. Human pride working through jealousy is the most destructive force known and yet too often ignored because we are so easily ensnared by it. When God repeats something in these stories and throughout the Bible, he is trying to teach us something critical that is very hard for us to learn, accept or understand. God has to repeat the same lesson over and over again. Joseph, even with all of his wisdom, had to be reminded of the human pride working through all human hearts over and over again...in his own life and now in all people confined to this prison.

We tend to dismiss all of our spiritual forefathers as the people of strong faith without much knowledge since we are living in this advanced modern age with all these accumulated "knowledge and wisdom" about the Bible or anything in life perhaps. Once again, our pride working through our hearts blinds us from the truth that our forefathers were much more knowledgeable and wise in the ways of God and the world than we ever thought possible. What we study in theory, they knew by experience as they were walking with the Lord. What little truths we choose to have the Holy Spirit illuminate and reveal to us in the Bible at our leisure, the very same truths multiplied and magnified in overwhelming and often excruciatingly painful ways were "forced upon" them by His Divine timing...all for the benefits of their future spiritual generations, God's people, which is us and ALL people who will stumble upon the truth of God. Joseph was being ushered into the major league of all training, not only for his divine destiny, but for our own divine destiny in God. For such a great future leader, God had in mind to purify and refine him as by fire from a boiling cauldron. God was going to turn him into a king above all political machines and powers that this world has ever seen.

If I may be allowed to use my medical background as an analogy, I would say that the *university of life* with Potipher was over for Joseph. He has finally graduated from the university of life into the spiritual equivalent of medical school, and the grueling 100 hour + a week boot camp training called the residency. A good physician is not made in the classroom. He is made by the knowledge of the healing arts and science of medicine to be confirmed and reconfirmed in countless patients at nauseam so as to make being a good doctor not only a calling but a second nature. Joseph had to be trained in all manners of men and exposed to the darkest corners of their hearts in one of the most hostile places on the planet for what may have seemed like an eternity because he needed to learn how to deal with people of all types in the truth and love of God, and especially the politicians that he will be rubbing shoulders with. Such grueling training of heart and soul was necessary for Joseph because his divine destiny — to become the ruler of this great empire and the redeemer of his own brothers through the Lord — needed to be more than God's calling but a divine instinct...for ALL people! All the knowledge and wisdom gained through the training will be used by Joseph to administer true justice and demonstrate mercy and love in all divine wisdom after God catapults him to the position of power. The severity of the training is proportional to the force of the spiritual hammer that drives such knowledge and wisdom into one's heart until it is firmly and eternally anchored in the love of Christ. And the love of God for all people necessitates such hammer of pain and suffering into being God's chosen instruments. The unmatched pain, suffering and persecution of divine hammer in the life of Paul produced half the New Testament, including the love Chapter, 1st Corinthians Chapter 13. Amen.

We truly live in the age of grace and unprecedented Divine knowledge that we have yet to fully embrace. Our spiritual ancestors, even accounting for all of their sins and the lack of revelations from God, were far more advanced morally and spiritually than how we have come to know them or who we are. Many of them were more Christ-like than any of us even though Christ had not come until thousands of years later. Knowing the mechanism of salvation does not save us, but believing that *God is the only One who can save us* will. Joseph understood this well. How do I know that? To the righteous tormented soul, the peace of God and the revelation of salvation is given. Our salvation is not earned. That is the fundamental truth of salvation in Christ in all of history. There was another individual whose righteous soul was tormented by an unimaginable suffering and pain like Christ before Christ came to earth. To that individual, God has given him the assurance of eternal salvation and his resurrection with the new body. Who is that person? It was Job, who made this proclamation of revelation in Job 19:25-26,"*I know that my Redeemer lives, and in the end He will stand on the earth. And after my skin has been destroyed, yet in my flesh I will see God. I myself will see Him with my own eyes — I, and not another. How my heart yearns within me.*" Now, we must ask, "How on earth did Job know about Jesus Christ and our resurrection in Him at the end with our new bodies?" To a righteous tormented soul, who understands in his heart that God is the only one worthy of our trust and hope, the revelation of eternal salvation is given by our God. It is GIVEN. This topic will be discussed in a little more detail in the chapter, **Tormented Righteous Soul.**

Joseph's own brother's abandoned him. His "new family" and friends in Egypt betrayed him. Through all these tragic turn of events, however, God always stood by his side and provided a constant sphere of safety around him by working through the hearts of those whom God had put in charge directly above Joseph. He has experienced God's protection, saving his life from his own families and friends. Joseph can clearly see that God did not fail him but the very people he was counting on did. He was perceiving through his mind, full of Divine wisdom, that all of our dreams, vision, hopes, desires, pursuits, gains and anything we perceive to be good, true, noble, and beautiful are constantly being filtered through that veil covering over our hearts, and that veil was our sin nature — mainly that destructive thing called pride that we ALL partake in. And given the right situations, that pride will inevitably manifest itself in the form of jealousy that kills. So the predominant question in Joseph's mind was not, "Is there really a God" or "Is God really for me?", but rather, "Why are we this way? why are we so bent on bringing down or destroying each other and, if we could, even God Himself? And why does God, who has protected me from all the evils of humanity, allow such humanity, including myself, to live on and have our beings?" In this sobering reflection on humanity and his own introspection, this man of visions and dreams came to know, perhaps better than anyone in history, that our inner being, which was designed and sustained by and for God himself, has traveled so far from the Garden of Eden — that place of perfect life and eternal harmonious relationships — to the place of mutual and perpetual spiritual death. God, again in his infinite wisdom and protection, has taken Joseph on this Divine journey into the heart of every man to reveal — without being defiled, consumed or destroyed too much by — what was in every man, including Joseph himself. This was the Divine working of God's will and grace being applied to this season of Joseph's journey in life for what he is predestined to become in God's time, not for who is or what he wants to be in his time. God saves us not because of who we were or what we have done but who we are going to be in and through Him.

102

Loneliness, rejection and restlessness of a soul... unto true REST in God.

It is no coincidence that the path of Joseph's trials and tribulations was carved out by the very people, his own families, who were supposed to protect him from such injustice. Here, Joseph becomes the foreshadowing of Christ. Christ had to suffer at the hands of the very people, God's people of Abraham, Isaac and Jacob — mainly the Israelites, in order to reveal definitively what was in the heart of every man. It is strangely and tragically fitting that the religious leaders, or the "men of God" during the time of Jesus, were first in line to destroy our Savior on the Cross. Pharisees, Sadducees and the teachers of the law, men who were supposed to recognize the Messiah before anyone else, men who were the self-proclaimed experts of the scripture, men who were the "first recipients" of God's blessings and revelations, were the same people that took the Son of man, God personified, and crucified him. Why? Because Christ so clearly revealed the true condition of their inner beings, full of death, deceit and decay, that they were trying so hard to cover up and compensate for by imposing extensive and complicated rules and regulations that they themselves could not keep. And their jealousy, rooted in pride, could not tolerate the superior and powerful truth and love of Jesus Christ shining before their followers, building them up to life eternal, while their monstrous destructive hypocrisy was constantly being exposed by the same truth. In their unredeemed hearts, full of pride and devoid of humility, Jesus simply had to die and go away.

Joseph walked with the Lord, demonstrating God's superior wisdom to bring prosperity, both physical and spiritual, to everything he touched. But the people around him, with their inner beings perceiving through the veil of pride and jealousy, did not feel grateful or humbled before God of Joseph. In their minds, Joseph had to die. Proverbs 27:4 says, *"Anger is cruel and fury overwhelming, but who can stand before jealousy?"* Jesus said, *"Foxes have dens and birds have nests, but the Son of Man has no place to lay his head"* (Matthew 8). Also remember that Jesus entrusted Himself to no one because He knew what was in every man (John 2:23-25). Our hearts were designed to be the indwelling place of the Almighty. Our hearts were originally created to be the resting place for our Lord Jesus. But while Jesus was on the earth, he could not find one true resting place in anyone. That's the tragic but true state of the human heart that Jesus was referring to by all these verses and these verses were lived out by Joseph, too. Joseph, like our Lord Jesus Christ, experienced true loneliness of his soul that a very few of us has and will ever experience.

As far as Joseph is concerned, no one could be trusted, not even one. No one has and will ever be proven worthy of his heart. No one was worthy enough to trust or lean on except...God! The heart is always searching for that place of true rest. Our hearts were made to be the resting place of God where He is worshipped. Our hearts were also made to be resting place for each other! But Jesus could not find any soul that he could lean on or rest in because He knew that this resting place, our hearts, has been infected and altered by the lust of the flesh, lust of the eyes and the pride of life all for the cause of *self*. We must labor in Christ to crucify our self-will before we can truly enter His rest, which represents the true Sabbath rest of our souls in Him (Hebrews 4:9-11). Our hearts have been drowning in sin and became unworthy and untrustworthy. Jesus knew that the man's heart and soul, which He had designed to be His dwelling place, became the very thing that defiles the man (Mark 7:15). And this nature of the man that Christ knew so well was becoming more and more obvious and predictable to Joseph as well.

We can assume that Joseph was imprisoned for 10 years or so. 10 plus years in the heart of darkness! This assumption on timetable is based on the fact that Joseph had served in the Potipher's household for less than 3 years and that's not a conservative estimation. Potipher's wife could not have sustained such monumental efforts to pursue Joseph for what she would know to be a seasonal pleasure.

It is likely that Joseph believed he would be released soon somehow as he was thrown into the prison. He could still remember his dreams like it was yesterday. Now he knew that his life back home was not the fulfillment of the dream. He may have believed that God will make his dream a reality this time and soon. I know this to be true because when he is finally brought to Pharaoh out of prison, he tells him that God gave the Pharaoh the dream in two forms because He will bring it to pass very soon. Joseph, too, had one dream in two forms and he knew that somehow God will make that dream a reality for Joseph soon! But how soon? Well...soon, but not very soon like Joseph probably thought because there were many lessons to be learned in the King's prison. Joseph was being groomed to be the future ruler of Egypt and this prison was the perfect school for him, prepared by God himself. And only God knew the exact amount of time and the training it would take for Joseph to be ready for His Divine redemptive destiny as He was simultaneously preparing the world for his triumphal reentry.

Making of the king among the king's prisoners

As the name itself would imply, the king's prison likely had been an imposing and dreadful place. It was designed to house and torture the offenders of the king Pharaoh and the officers and put them to work as the texts suggest. In this place, Joseph was to be trained in all manners of being the most effective and benevolent politician and administrator. Benevolent politician, you say? Anything is possible with God and it will take no less than the act of God to make such a man. But such men, including Joseph, have already come and gone, made and glorified through suffering for the sake of the people they love, even including all of us. And all their suffering and glory culminated within Jesus Christ.

The warden is the law of the prison. And as the right hand man of the warden, Joseph probably knew the story of every man in that prison. He is more than the accountant and the messenger of the warden. He is seen as the extension of the power that the warden has, and the prisoners had better behaved before this favored one of the warden or they will suffer the consequences. It is logical to assume all of these to be true given the intelligence and the knowledge of Joseph in just about everything. And it is also consistent with the character of Joseph that he never abused such favoritism by the warden. And the warden trusted Joseph with all of his responsibilities because he was successful in everything he did. He was successful because he was diligent. He was diligent because he never lost hope in God. With God protecting him, the prisoners, whether innocent or guilty, were able to observe that there was something about Joseph that they didn't know; something otherworldly and beyond this universe. They could sense it but could not exactly place it in their minds. They may have also wondered why a person like Joseph is in there with the rest of them. He truly was the divine oxymoron on which people marveled and wondered. God was with him, protecting him in all he did because he did everything in the Lord and as unto the Lord.

Joseph, with humility before God and divine confidence before all the men he served, took the proactive approach by gently commanding, not asking, the cupbearer and the chief baker to recount to him the dreams that had troubled them. He said, "Do not interpretations belong to God? Tell me your dreams." The passage clearly states that Joseph attended them and not the other way around. And yet, the cupbearer obeyed Joseph and began to tell his dreams to Joseph like he has fallen under a Jedi spell! Who do you think is in command here? He had no business telling the details of his mysterious and disturbing dream, which was something very personal, to an abominable Hebrew slave who has been attending him...unless he was deeply moved by the way Joseph served him. But we must ask who, or what, is the cupbearer? Is he like a butler to a king Pharaoh? No, he is the one who stood beside the Pharaoh day and night, tasting wine and food for potential poison and listening in on the conversation that may decide the fate of the entire nation. To be appointed as the cupbearer, you must win the trust of the king by proving yourself courageous and worthy of character. It was the position of power that was highly esteemed by the kings and their courts. So the answer to that question is a no. A cupbearer is not a glorified butler for Pharaoh. For a man of such influence to open up readily to Joseph, an abominable Hebrew slave, again speaks volumes about the integrity and character of Joseph. He didn't do it out of the fear of men but out of the fear of God, who is only one trustworthy in his mind.

Excellent and impeccable service, as unto the Lord, that Joseph was providing to all of his masters including this cupbearer, was like that gentle but relentless warm breeze of summer that caused the cupbearer to take off the veil of pride and suspicion over his soul and allowed him to see Joseph, not as an abominable Hebrew slave, but as a man of God he can trust. That's why he is telling his dream to Joseph. This is not a work of trickery and there is no spell involved here but only God and his timing through the work ethic of Joseph. And Joseph was faithful to God in this season of life that And Joseph was faithful to God in this season of life that God has given him, excelling in every menial and important tasks, learning and absorbing everything around and in him, and realizing, above all, that all of this somehow was the necessary part of the training and journey toward his destiny in the Lord that was already revealed to him when he was 17. If it is our desire to win the souls of our bosses, coworkers, friends and family members who are not Christ followers, then we must first win their confidence and trust by being obedient to the Lord and going above and beyond the call of duty for all the tasks that the Lord has given you in this season of life you are going through. Many of us despair and lose motivations for being diligent and faithful to the work that God himself has placed in our season of trials and tribulations because we are too focused on the hardships of the discipline and training and NOT focused on WHY we are being trained and disciplined. We have to keep our eyes on our inevitable, glorious, and eternal destiny of kings and priests in Christ with thanksgiving. And the peace of God that surpasses all worldly wisdom will guard our hearts and minds in Christ, as we can gladly put up and even excel in all the works that are indispensable foundation for our glorious, eternal destiny.

He knew that his dream, given by God who never failed him, will have to come true eventually. Joseph continuously focused on the promise of God through all these unbelievably tough times, and excelled in everything he did in that prison in order that he can become the best administrator and the master politician in the eyes of God and all men. In other words, God was grooming him through all of his trials in order to turn him into the best ruler and king the world has ever seen, and the symbolic forerunner to Jesus Christ, who is the one true King. Imagine him busy and constantly running around, tired but focused, in order to keep track of all the inventories of materials and products of prisoners labor that are going in and out of prison, and the stress of keeping track of the whereabouts of the prisoner themselves. Imagine him interacting with the king's prisoners day by day being guided by the Spirit of wisdom, learning and discerning the thoughts and the intentions of the hearts of the most hardened and feared criminals/ politician in Egypt: the most powerful nation in the world at that time. He served all of his masters in and out of prison with diligence and wisdom. In the process he won the confidence of all he served and was given the key of trust to look into their minds and even dreams.

Being under the captain of the guard (for the most powerful military in the world, who was wise except in the case with his wife), Joseph was given the opportunity to share in the military wisdom of his master. And by interacting with the likes of the cupbearer, one of the most highly esteemed of king's officials, who stood by the Pharaoh and his officials day and night, he was exposed to the inner-working of the political world AND the mind of the king himself. When God sent Joseph into that prison, He was also sent him into the heart of every man, including all who were rich and powerful. Joseph discovered the essence of every human heart, which was the same whether you are "innocent" or guilty, in or out of prison. But he discovered something far greater than all of these. He discovered the blessings and the protection of God that gave him the strength to carry on through this hour of suffering. He believed with all of his heart that God, who gave him the gift of revelations, wisdom and the sphere of protection when all the people he trusted failed, will break through all these barriers and spiritual prison walls set up by the pride of the human heart and set him free. And He also understood that the people outside of prison, including the likes of his brothers, are not so different from people inside the prison in essence...including himself.

Has Joseph suffered enough for the wrongs that he did NOT commit at this point? If a man like this is not ready to claim his divine destiny at this time, then who is? Well, it is not God's timing for him to be released just yet. Obviously I'm saying this because we have the benefit of looking back and know that Joseph was not released until two years after his encounter with the cupbearer...or am I? I, too, have struggled with this question of why Joseph is not being released at this time and came to an inevitable conclusion.

Jonah's misinterpretation of divine destiny (materialization of God's loving intention) for all.

In short, Joseph is not ready to be released yet because God loves all people that he is going to redeem in His time and the desire of all people in God must converge on Joseph. Our divine destiny of kings and priests in Christ is designed for the redemption journey of hearts of ALL people who are and will be in Christ. The greatness of destiny is measured by the greatness of love demonstrated by it. In the case of truly great God given destiny, the great love of Jesus Christ for ALL people must be demonstrated by it. Now, let these statements just hang in your mind as we briefly look into the Book of Jonah.

The prophet Jonah was sent to the ancient Assyrian city Nineveh by God to preach the impending doom because of their sin and wickedness. In the eyes of Jonah, these ancient Assyrians were an abominable, prideful and ungodly people, not deserving of God's grace and mercy. He tried to run away from the Lord by getting on one of the ships headed in opposite direction for Tarshish. Soon, he was found out and was thrown off the ship to be swallowed by a whale. While inside this whale, Jonah prayed a great prayer of earnest supplication and praise. After being in the *fish* for 3 days and nights, he was vomited onto the dry land. As soon as he began preaching in the city of Nineveh about the impending calamity from God, every single person in the city and even the king himself, put on sack cloth and fasted. The whole city repented before the Lord, and the Lord relented from his judgment. However, Jonah did NOT like this one bit.

He became angry with the Lord because, in his mind, the great compassion of the Lord for the people of Nineveh was just too much for him to take. In Jonah's mind, a righteous man and prophet like himself should have never traveled and suffered like he has for committing such a minor violation of running from God's command to prophecy and predict a certain doom for such a wicked and abominable people. It just wasn't fair to Jonah! It is as if he was saying to God in his mind, "God, you are not being fair. Where is my justice!?" Even after seeing that God has made up his mind not to destroy Nineveh, Jonah still insisted on God to destroy this city in his own mind. We can see in Ch 4:5 that *"he went out and sat down at a place east of the city. There he made himself a shelter, sat in its shade and waited to see what would happen to the city."*

It sure appears that Jonah has picked out a prime real estate spot, like a spectator to a major sporting event of modern days. He really believed that God would judge the city even after seeing the whole city repent. He has the perfect shade to cover him and the best view of the city while he is eagerly anticipating the spectacular and glorious destruction of that city that deserves such fate from God. But God takes away the shade by the vine. While Jonah is contemplating suicide in anger, God says this to Jonah to help him understand why His time for exacting justice has not come to the people of Nineveh.

In 4:10-11, the Lord says, *"You have been concerned about this vine, though you did not tend it or make it grow. It sprang up overnight and died overnight. But, Nineveh has more than a hundred and twenty thousand people who cannot tell their right hand from their left, and many cattle as well. Should I not be concerned about that great city?"*

Now, what is the takeaway message from these passages in the book of Jonah and how do they relate to Joseph still stuck in prison? **God's timing is dictated by the love of Christ working through the repentant hearts of ALL people. In other words, God always waits for the very last possible moment, patiently suffering our relentless pride that is only exceeded by our own stupidity, to save and redeem as many as possible...TROUGH US, who are being redeemed ourselves by Christ.** We are saving people of the world through the message of love of Christ while our hearts are being actively redeemed by the same love of Christ working through us at the same time. I, too, realized that my mentality toward the world is like that of Jonah more often than I would've liked. Do you think I repented? Of course. I write this book in the spirit of repentance before the Lord and I have the peace and the joy of the Lord in my heart as I'm writing. I would like all of us to have this peace and rest in the Lord!

God had a great compassion for the city of Nineveh. I imagine that God had even a greater compassion for that mighty ancient empire Egypt, whose people lack the sense of spiritual direction and lived in darkness like the people of Nineveh...not knowing the right from the left. And I believe in the same God who has even greater compassion for our great nation and the world with all 7 billion people! If Joseph was to be released here and now, we do not know what would have happened to Joseph. But we know that he would have never risen to the height of power the way he did by the Divine timing two years later. He would have never had the opportunity to save the great empire and all the people. For all we know, the modern Egypt would have seen her last days when that famine struck the land during the time of Joseph. And the people of Egypt would have never come to know the saving power of God through Joseph.

God has something greater in mind than our own individual divine destinies that we may crave on our terms for our own agenda. What about his brothers? His brothers, who wanted to kill Joseph, are still in God's plan to be the patriarchs of the future nation of Israel at this time. What about their own redemption journeys that need to reach their full measure? How would they be able to recount and confront their own past and repent openly to claim their own destinies with Joseph if Joseph had not become the ruler of Egypt precisely at the right time?

God is not only concerned about the great divine destiny of Joseph, but He is also compassionate toward the brothers and concerned about the conditions of their souls. God is orchestrating all the events in His timing to redeem not only one but all twelve and beyond. He wants to save the nation of Egypt and the future of Israel with Joseph as His chosen instrument of Salvation. Joseph here is the foreshadowing of the coming of Messiah. In the book of revelation, we read that God has reserved exactly the same number of people from each 12 tribe of Israel in the last days. These are the descendants of the 12 brothers...yes, all twelve! He has his eyes on everyone, including you and me, all the way to the end of time. He is the very definition of love for everyone for all eternity! **Because we are still struggling with the concept of God's love through the flesh like Jonah, who thought His love seems to be too much when it comes to others but too little when it comes to us, we are often confused and frustrated by His timing of revelations and blessings. Again, we focus our desire on this temporary world and ourselves, but God's timing is based on His love for all people that Christ came to save for all eternity...through us in Him! That's the eternal perspective that we need but lack desperately! And whether we like it or not, each one of us is a necessary part of that global redemption plan by God.** And we will eventually understand in entirety, and with much pain and regret, that this global working of divine redemption through us is also to be a part of our own painful, and yet glorious, redemption process in the love of Christ.

God loved us first. Yes, when God — and anything of Him — was the furthest thing from our minds, He loved us first and orchestrated everything in our journey with Christ so that we can finally love God with all of our heart and soul, mind and strength AND love our neighbors as ourselves. Jesus said these two commandments of loving God and loving our fellow men as Christ loved us make up the very foundation of all of God's laws and precepts (Matt 22:37-40). It is the ultimate act of love that is the evidence of the hearts that are being redeemed by Christ. And when we truly begin to love one another, we begin to receive the same love of Christ from one another. That's heaven in the making while we are still here. That's why God commands us to love our neighbor because when we all love our neighbors with the true love of Christ, any burden, issues or unreciprocated and undesirable consequences of shallow loving disappears. But until we get there, we who are experiencing the eternal love of Christ can and must persist through the obstacles of Self in order for the world to glimpse that possibility of such heaven through us. We can do all things in Christ who strengthens us...yes, even loving the world. We have been designed by God for Him to do so through us. Again, His power is made perfect through our weakness. If our knees can just find the spiritual ground for them to plant, there is no telling what God may do for us and through us!

Journey of isolation away from the greatest evil in our lives: SELF in the world

But there is another spiritual dimension of the truth of God's love working here as Joseph is being confined and trained in this prison. That dimension is called the divine protection from the outside world, and all of the false and temporary opportunities that lead into spiritual darkness, despite all of its outward physical splendor and promises. The verse at the beginning of this chapter by King David *"Though I walked through the valley of the shadow of death, I will fear no evil; For You are with me. Your rod and your staff, they comfort me,"* are powerfully moving verses. We do take a great comfort in that verse on so many occasions...especially at the funerals.

However, I put the verse up there to reinforce the idea of God's protection and love for us the **living**. You have to ask yourself, why does a shepherd carry a rod or a staff? He carries a rod to apply the pain of loving correction and understanding to a sheep so that the sheep won't wander off and get stuck in a rock crevice or worse yet, run into a pack of wolves or lions and get torn to pieces. Yes, there are many lessons to be learned as Joseph is going through this valley of the shadow of death (the shadow side of humanity), but God is also protecting him from something that is beyond these prison walls. God may actually be protecting young Joseph from the outside world with all of its destructive influences — mainly power and temptations — that causes delusions and desensitization away from God. He needs God now more than ever but in the outside world, that need may be diminished significantly. Joseph is precisely where he needs to be at this time. For his great divine destiny to be realized for ALL people, He cannot ascend to power without having gone through the hardships of the humanity that was orchestrated by God.

If Joseph came to power and wealth without the suffering that produces character, he would not have been able to wield that power in the proper divine context. In fact, his glorious divine destiny that was acquired without the discipline from the Lord would eventually consume and devour him, like a helpless sheep by a lion. And His fate would have been worse than his beginning. This prison may just be that loving rod of God, protecting him from such catastrophic fate. Let's ask ourselves, who ascended into such great power and wealth with all divine wisdom, who was consumed and destroyed by his own destiny because of the lack of such discipline? Sadly...the answer to that question is King Solomon. If you read his life story, you will understand that what I'm saying is true. Solomon had it all! And all that he had destroyed him in the end. It was not the case of Solomon not relying on His God-given wisdom as much as he was walking away from God Himself...into the arms of all these attractive, idol worshipping, foreign women.

There was a person named Sampson who was the strongest man in the history of the world. He was not only a physical specimen to be feared, but one of the judges of Israel with God-given wisdom to judge and execute justice. What happened to him as all that power and wisdom went to his head? He became a thing to be toyed by a girl named Delilah and spent the last years of his life in the confinement in misery and bitterness. Yes, He did kill many Philistines as he died but do you think he himself was proud of how he had just wasted all that wisdom, knowledge and strength on the things of the world and the girls?

Joseph, to a certain extent, had a combination of gifts and talents that could rival that of Sampson and Solomon. You can say that his character makeup is the perfect recipe and set up for a monumental rise and even greater downfall had it not for God's direct interventions in his life, including putting him here in the dungeon. He was well built, handsome and his wisdom was unequaled in his time. It would be so easy for anyone in his position to let all these God-given talents go to his head like Solomon and Sampson did and become puffed up to his own demise. God was not going to let this happen to Joseph. And Joseph obeyed the Lord in whatever situation he found himself in. Certainly Joseph already has proven himself more worthy of the task than any of us men by refusing the Potipher's wife's advances day and night. However, his life could not be wasted by battling such temptations constantly when he needed to be trained in all manners of the king. And God wanted to protect Joseph from the most powerful of all temptation: The temptation of power, the pride of life, gained through SELF in the world. In the outside world, there would have been no telling how his fate would have been shaped with all the lures and temptations that beckoned his talents and wisdom to be utilized for much less glorious purposes than what God intended for him. Certainly God of love, with his eternal perspective, is protecting Joseph at all times and from all things. You may even say God is protecting Joseph from what he would be, without the working of God's love and discipline in his life. And God is protecting us today the same way that He is protecting this great man of God in this story.

When we are walking through hardships and tough times — that valley of the shadow of death — we have to ask ourselves, did God put us there? **If the answer is yes,** as in the life of Joseph, then we are exactly where we need to be and we should be diligent and faithful in all of our tasks in the marketplace and in our families as unto the Lord. If you truly believe that God has all things in control, your destiny will be realized in such a sudden, unexpected and glorious fashion that it will make your head spin. If such destiny does not come your way in this lifetime, then you can be sure that your destiny in Heaven will be far greater than Joseph's destiny as a king here on earth. This is what the Lord meant by saying in Matthew 11:11, *"Truly I tell you, among those born of women there has not risen anyone greater than John the Baptist; yet whoever is least in the kingdom of heaven is greater than he."* I love this verse! But **if the answer to the question is no**, then God is letting you taste a little bit of that bitter taste of the consequences of your own sins so that you will be protected from even greater and much more devastating consequences of the ever-escalating sins of pride while giving you the chance to repent and even redeem yourself in such a glorious manner like Sampson at the end!

Has Joseph reached the end of his trials and divine discipline for the full redemption of his own heart...at least to the point of claiming his divine destiny as the ruler of Egypt? Is there any fine tuning left for God to work on his soul? Was it possible for God to orchestrate everything beforehand so that the world was ready to receive Joseph at the age of 28 instead of 30? Has he waited long enough? Did Joseph discern through wisdom that this was his last real chance at freedom? What kind of emotional turmoil did he go through as days became weeks, weeks became months, and months became years after the cupbearer left the prison?

Chapter 10

ASCENSION OF GOD AND HIS PEOPLE IN JOSEPH'S HEART
(GENESIS 41)

I lift up my eyes to the mountains— where does my help come from? My help comes from the Lord, the Maker of heaven and earth.—Psalms 121:1-2

*Not only so, but we also glory in our sufferings, because we know that suffering produces perseverance; **perseverance**, character; and character, **hope**. And hope does not put us to shame, because God's **love** has been poured out into our **hearts** through the Holy Spirit, who has been given to us.—Romans 5:3-5*

*His divine power has given us everything we need for a godly life through our knowledge of him who called us by his own glory and goodness. Through these he has given us his very great and precious promises, so that through them you may participate in the divine nature, having escaped the corruption in the world caused by evil desires. For this very reason, make every effort to add to your faith goodness; and to goodness, knowledge; and to knowledge, self-control; and to self-control, **perseverance**; and **to perseverance, godliness**; and to godliness, mutual affection; and to mutual affection, **love**.—2ⁿᵈ Peter 1:3-7*

Pain and suffering in Christ ever nudging and guiding us to true hope and love in God alone

Please read slowly the following three statements by Joseph –

"My master has withheld nothing from me except you, because you are his wife. How then could I do such a wicked thing and sin against God?"

"Do not interpretations belong to God? Tell me your dreams."

"I cannot do it," Joseph replied to Pharaoh, "but God will give Pharaoh the answer he desires."

D o you notice any pattern emerging from these statements as you carefully meditate on them in this sequential order? You will notice that they are written in the chronological order, too. These are the reflections of Joseph's spiritual state at the most critical moments of his redemption journey toward his own divine destiny.

The first statement was said to Potipher's wife when Joseph was young and full of vigor. It was expressed in the form of a rhetorical question, because what Joseph is also saying to Potipher's wife is that she should know better than to tempt him after seeing how God has blessed everyone in the house through Joseph—including the wife. But that would sound more derogatory to the lady of the house so Joseph probably could not have said it that way. He was being as diplomatic as he can be while standing his ground in the righteousness of God. The order in which Joseph said all of these things to her, however, appears as though he is putting himself between everyone in the house and God himself. In Joseph's mind, there is no direct connection between the affairs of Potipher's wife and God. It is like, to Joseph, God only sees the lives of people around Joseph through his eyes and not God's. And while acknowledging the undeniable blessings of God in the life of Joseph and the entire house, it also sounds like Joseph sees himself as the only divine channel through which God's blessings can flow. He puts himself in the middle here.

Now, don't get me wrong. Joseph is still light years ahead of me even at this point of the journey. We all aspire to be such a righteous soul who is not ashamed of God's truth in any setting and who consistently, without single moment of hesitation, runs away from the most powerful of temptations. But God had in mind the most incredible divine destiny that Joseph could have never imagined nor wield if any part of his own pride rooted in his own limited view and abilities got in the way of God's revelations for all people of Egypt and beyond. The same pride of self that rages in every one was also found in Joseph. God had to chip away and remove this pride to the point where there is no "I" or "me" found in God's destiny for everyone. Conviction without pride is only found on the love of Christ that drives out pride and "self". St. Paul said, *"II f I give all I possess to the poor and give my body over to the hardships (flames in some translations) that I may boast, but do not have love, I have nothing."* But it is also interesting to note later that there is no "I" or "we" or "people" when Paul expounds on the idea of true love. He simply says, "Love is patient. Love is kind...", so on and so forth. He is talking about love of Christ that can only work through us when there is no "I" or "we" getting in His way of true love.

Now if you look at the second statements, "Do not the interpretations belong to God? Tell me your dreams." Again, Joseph sees himself as the messenger or instrument of God who can solve the problems of life and mysteries regarding anyone's future. He is not intentionally being prideful here. There is a difference between intentional and unintentional pride. Unintentional pride is a part of the twisted glory of this world that has integrated into the very core of our hearts and only through the supernatural illuminating power of the Spirit can we clearly see this pride working in us. With his incredible gifts of wisdom that can unlock even the mysteries of dreams, Joseph likely have witnessed his interpretations of the dreams for many people becoming reality time and time again. This is the statement of divine confidence, wisdom and conviction. But the focus is still on what he can do for this person. He is still putting himself between God and the cup-bearer. The bottom line is that Joseph believes in his heart that somehow he is still in control of his God given destiny. That is exactly the reason why he seizes the moment when the interpretation was favorable to the cupbearer. As soon as the interpretation is over, he pleads with the cupbearer to get him out of prison and...kind of forgets about the baker. Oops...It is the baker who has to engage him in order to tell Joseph his dream. He thought that he had finally gotten his improbable chance at last to bust out of this prison. This is Joseph trying to seize the moment the only way he knows how. Actually, it was probably the most logical thing to do for anybody in that situation. We all empathize with Joseph here. But God had a far greater and more magnificent position that was being prepared for him than even the best possible outcome in which Joseph would find himself to be if he were to be released from prison at this point. He was not quite there yet in the eyes of God. He needed just a little fine tuning...but that fine tuning would take two years. Joseph would not have known that he would have had to wait 2 years or forever. Days would turn into weeks, weeks to months and months to years after the cupbearer left the prison. That fine tuning may have caused Joseph to despair once again. That fine tuning once again reinforced the idea that men, including the cupbearer, cannot be trusted. That fine tuning may have caused him to doubt even his own divine gift that defined him and separated him from the rest. That fine tuning drove the self out of Joseph and caused him to surrender everything he believes about himself and the world. That fine tuning by the finger of God would finally convince Joseph that only God is in control and he is not. And that fine tuning would turn a strong conviction of this righteous tormented soul into even stronger and higher compassion for ALL PEOPLE.

Divine wisdom in Pharaoh?

Now let's get back to the present time of the story. Pharaoh had two dreams that greatly disturbed him. The cupbearer told him about Joseph and his ability to interpret dreams. When Joseph was brought to Pharaoh, the Pharaoh didn't actually ask a question or make a request but made a statement designed to elicit a certain response. The Pharaoh said, "I have heard it said of you that when you hear a dream, you can interpret it." Notice he didn't say, "I know that when you hear a dream you can interpret it" or "Is it true that you can interpret dreams?"

This is not the Pharaoh of Moses that we normally associate with the king of Egypt whenever we study the Bible. This Pharaoh is *different*. This is the same Pharaoh who put the cupbearer in prison and then released him to serve him again. It would be highly unusual for a king of any ancient world to imprison someone and then restore him back to his original position, especially if that person in question was so close to him before he was thrown into prison. This is also the same Pharaoh who recognized the divine wisdom in Joseph, not just his ability to interpret dreams, which is something else entirely, and made him the ruler of all Egypt. All of these reflect the Pharaoh's character. He is not being controlled by God like a robot or zombie when he makes Joseph the ruler of his own nation. He is SEEING and UNDERSTANDING the superior wisdom and power of God working through Joseph through his own humble wisdom and experience. If all of these conclusions do not convince you of this Pharaoh's character then examine the first encounter between Jacob, Joseph's father, and the Pharaoh and the exchanges between the two. The Pharaoh even allows Jacob to bless him! That's a little detail that we can easily miss or dismiss but everyone knew in the ancient world that the greater blesses the lesser. He displays his wisdom in humility, even there, as he was being blessed by an abominable Hebrew. By the way, do you know that God allows us to bless Him? How ridiculous! How marvelous and wonderful is His grace! A little side note here...when Pharaoh transfers his power over his kingdom to Joseph, this act becomes the foreshadowing of God the Father giving all the authority of heaven and earth to His Son Jesus Christ.

It is this same wise Pharaoh that throws out this character test statement in front of Joseph. More than the answer itself, Pharaoh wanted to know the character behind the man who may have the answer. It may not have been the statement that Pharaoh had rehearsed for this particular encounter as much as a reflection of the routine, probing and systematic approach to everything that Pharaoh had already incorporated in his own life. What is Joseph going to say here now? We know what he said.

"I cannot do it," Joseph replied to Pharaoh, *"but God will give Pharaoh the answer he desires."*

This statement by Joseph just blows me away. We need to pause here and let this sink in a bit.

The statement is a worship statement. It is a love letter statement. It is the statement of perfect rest in the perfect power of God. It is the statement of self-denial and self-control perfected in God of total control. This is the declaration of Joseph's absolute and unshakable confidence in God's providence for all people. This is the statement of the ascension of God in Joseph's own heart. There is no Joseph between God and Pharaoh, so it is the statement reflecting God's direct love and intervention for Pharaoh as well as all people. We often hear ourselves say "Praise God, we give Him all the glory." Or "I know I can't do it but He can." Whenever I hear these statements, my heart discerns that the people who are saying these things say them very casually or without much contemplation. I'm not saying that we are not sincere people as much as we don't really know what we are saying most of the time. Certainly I have been guilty of it, too. However, we need to look at the situation he finds himself in first before we can understand what he is really saying. This situation is not predictable at all. Even if the Pharaoh is satisfied with the answer and frees this abominable Hebrew slave, what would he do or where would he go in this hostile foreign land? If he was to remain as one of the advisors to Pharaoh, would he be happy? Wouldn't that be like being a slave to the captain of the guard all over again? Would he try to make his journey back to his homeland, not knowing whether his brothers would try to kill him again? Or even worse, Pharaoh can kill him or throw him back in prison if he doesn't like the answer. Pharaoh killed the baker after contemplating about his future role in serving the king's courts. He doesn't know anything about this Pharaoh personally.

But the strange and powerful thing about Joseph here and now is that while his mind in divine wisdom can consider all possible outcomes, his focus is always on God who is in control of all situations and all possible outcomes. He is finally SEEING God for who he really is and also SEEING everyone, including himself for who we really are. Every single person has failed him, even himself. His own wisdom, given by God, failed him when he relied more on the gift rather than the Giver of all gifts. He has found in himself the very same thing that caused all men to fail. In that dark pit of despair and evil, he took a journey into the heart of every man and became intimately aware of sin even before sin became a word. Only God has proven Himself worthy in his eyes. Only God stood by his side through all circumstances. Only God was in control. And only God can AND will give what Joseph or Pharaoh or anyone desires in his or her heart! Where is "I" in this statement? "I" is associated with "cannot." Who is between God and Pharaoh in this statement? No one. In fact, what Joseph is really is saying to Pharaoh is, "God will directly reveal to you your own heart's desires that you may not even know."

Joseph has completely emptied and removed himself from the divine path through which God Himself will personally and directly reveal Himself to all people according to His good pleasure and time, including Pharaoh. And Joseph knew that God will lift him up to his divine destiny eventually regardless of the decision of the Pharaoh here. Remember the lessons that we have been taught up to this point. God holds the key to your ultimate destiny. No one else is. Not even you or your God-given gifts/talents. Joseph knew that his own gifts and wisdom had failed him. Everyone he knew and trusted failed him. You see…If we had anticipated our divine destiny to be materialized in certain ways then please, we need to have a peace of mind that it will never happen the way we imagined. Joseph knew that Pharaoh will also fail him and deny him the path of his destiny unless God himself intervenes to make his destiny secure somehow. Pharaoh, or anyone in power in this world, has absolutely nothing to do with our destiny. Only God! And God has direct control over those who are in power. So the only one that we have to worry about is…God? I'm not really asking you and you know that. But even if the Pharaoh were to deny Joseph of his freedom here, Joseph knew that his destiny in God will always be secure because God has always remained by his side. So, all these trials and tribulations caused by men produced in him the character to trust God and only God alone. His hope was in God alone. As the character produced hope in the above revelation by Paul in Romans 5 given above, Joseph had come to that place of hope in God and God alone. But that same character produced in Joseph gave him a compelling desire to bring this hope to ALL because the same God who was producing this character through trials and tribulation was God of love to ALL including Pharaoh here. So the final destination of all of our trials at the hands of men is the love of God for all people mentioned in 2 Peter 1 as above.

We know that a life without hope of true love is not worth living, and God does not want that for any of us. And God is the author and the source of all true love. As Joseph was getting to know more and more about God, he also came to know God who wants to give that eternal hope to all people. We must understand that his hope in God is not limited to God rescuing Joseph from this dark prison of isolation, but rescue all humanity from this thing, this sin nature, that has placed a person like Joseph in his dungeon, which symbolically represents the sins of humanity. You see, your sins may propagate or create the bondage of sins in others and vice versa. You may not experience the consequences of your sins right away, but someone always does. But that someone always has a chance to break the link in that chain of sin. No one knows that concept better than Joseph and he knows that, while God of justice keep account of all of our sins, He wants us to see that His love is the only thing that can stop such propagation of sins! That's why Joseph NEVER contemplates retaliation and there is no mention of personal vengeance or vindications anywhere. He himself is such a sinner, he knew, and the vengeance belongs to God or otherwise everyone, including Joseph himself, would be subject to God's exacting justice should he desire it now. In fact, Joseph knows everyone will be annihilated instantly if God were to judge people according His perfect standards — yes, Joseph in his wisdom knew this even without the "law" or the "ten commandments."

Joseph came to know, through his suffering by humanity and the loving nature of God for all humanity, that this is the hope that all of our hearts are longing for: that desire to be saved and freed from the dark, mutually and globally induced, ever-perpetuating bondage of sins of all humanity. That's why he is finally able to say, at the end of his character building journey, *God will give Pharaoh what he desires.* God is the only hope for us because He is the only one who can save us from ourselves. Why does he save us? So that we can truly love one another in Him. By the way, Joseph doesn't say the word "love" anywhere but he is without a doubt the most loving person that the world has ever seen outside of Christ Himself. That will be proven later in the story. That love in Joseph, too, was built by suffering and isolation at the hands of humanity and the love of God for all humanity. The suffering or isolation has a way of removing all distractions and deceptions, and revealing what or who really is helping you and protecting you; thereby reinforcing your trust and love for that Person more and more. As in the life of Joseph, as well as in ours, that Person is none other than God and God alone.

First shall be last. Last in this world, for the sake of His Kingdom, shall be first for all people.

You see when you take a hard look at yourself in that spiritual mirror called God's law, you know you will fail. You will fail your families, friends, coworkers and even yourself when the insurmountable storms rise in your life. It is only a matter of time if you continue to insist on bringing everything under your control. And to your dismay, the most noble and loving people around you will also fail you given enough time and circumstances. This sin nature in your flesh that rages against your very soul also rages against God. God is the only one who will stand beside you. It only takes one stupid act, mistake or decision to make all that you hold dear and true to your heart come crashing down and fall apart. And you will never be able to put it back together again the way it was. You never can. But when you bring all these broken pieces of your heart to God — broken and contrite heart the Lord will not despise — he is going to put it back together again....not to its original state before it fell from its high place self worship but up to that high spiritual plateau where your heart will be so magnificent; it will be truly new and unrecognizable. The foundation of the universe, Christ himself, will build it back up with the power of His own blood!

Each and every step of the way, the forgiving power of the blood will bring all the pieces together and heal. And as we watch the Lord bring all the pieces together to "recreate" his masterpiece, we will begin to wonder why we had loved the things of the world so much. The world and all that is in it will continue to destroy us through our flesh. Each and every step of the way God removes the power of the flesh by the blood of Christ, the only thing worthy of our affections in light of all the empty promises and counterfeit affections in this world. This is the spiritual battle we will continue to engage in until the coming of our Lord as the King, who will truly expose all that is haughty and deceitful and bent on destroying all our souls, including even that of Joseph's own. Joseph finally understood the

121

spiritual battle within himself so well that he was able to abdicate himself from his self-throne so easily and readily everyday. This is what Christ meant by "take up your Cross daily and follow Me." Understanding of His love through the blood will expose in us and around us the desolate domain that tempts, deceives and ensnares us in order to take all that God has in store for us and even our very souls! Only God can save and only God can love. And this statement, "God will give the Pharaoh the answer he desires", is more than a declaration of divine confidence in absolute humility, it is the statement of the direct intervention and love of God for EVERYONE. Because only God can, God has and God WILL. It is the statement of Divine revolution in all of our hearts! There is no one standing between God and you but only…your SELF.

In the book of Haggai 2:7, the Lord says: *"I will shake all nations, and what is desired by all nations will come, and I will fill this house with glory."*

Even before this revelation from God to prophet Haggai some 1100 years later, Joseph has already persevered through that arduous journey of understanding: that the core desire of everyone and everywhere in all kingdoms in all histories is nothing less than the glory of God. It is the glory of God that our hearts truly desire because our salvation, from ourselves, only belongs to our God. It is the glory of God that our core yearns for but does not recognize. It is the glory of God that finally culminated in Jesus Christ and will be raised up to even greater in magnitude, honor and glory when He comes again as the Judge, the Lion Judah, and the defender of our souls! Nothing else will satisfy and nothing else will save our hearts because they were made by God! They belong to God but our hearts, full of pride, denied God's rightful ownership! No wonder why we are so broken and do not have a clue as to how we got here...

Our hearts were forged in the very heart of the Trinity. All others, men or things, will deceive and fail our hearts. Just take a look that the life of Joseph up to this point. Isn't that true? His brothers failed him. His master has failed him. The cupbearer failed him. And all the people who are not mentioned in his story, in essence, have failed him. He was buried in that deep dungeon of sins of humanity and became non-existent to the world. But the real world is where God is. He is the creator of ALL. And God is where our true hope lies. Just a take a look at your own life and meditate carefully all that have transpired. Am I out of my mind? And that glory of God, this passage is talking about, is found in totality of our Lord Jesus Christ. What Joseph was grasping here, as through a veil, is the glory of our Lord Jesus Christ, who is the ultimate love and true justice, even before

He had been fully revealed in the flesh about 1700 years later. The ultimate justice and true love that our hearts have been yearning for is found in no other but the One true King and the High Priest; our Lord Jesus Christ. And His life has truly become Christ-like that proclaims by both actions and deeds, "Not my will but Thy will."

In the spirit of total surrender and absolute dependence on God, Joseph finally understood the love of God; that God Himself desires to seek out and reach out and reveal Himself to every single one of us in spite of what our hearts have become. There is no other way for us to know Him and be saved from ourselves unless God Himself directly intervenes and reveals Himself, and Joseph came to know THIS more intimately than any of us. Now, he is ready for God to truly manifest his mighty works through him as an empty vessel with nothing of himself getting in God's way. Now, he is ready to be that foreshadowing of Jesus Christ, who is the essence of love. Now, he is ready to properly wield his divine wisdom and power to save all people of Egypt and beyond…even, and especially, his brothers. Now he is ready to be a king. He has truly humbled himself in the eyes of the Lord, and God is about to lift him up in the sight of all men. **He sees himself as someone absolutely expendable and irrelevant in the lives of all people and now, God is about to make him indispensable to all people.** He is about to make him a king. His thoughts and the intention of his hearts are dominated by "I cannot" and "God will." He has gone through the heart of every man to the ends of the universe, only to come back and find our Lord praying at the garden of Gethsemani, "Not my will but Thy will."

He is so far from seeking his own glory that his own divine gift has become worthless and NOT applicable when it comes to his own desire or destiny in his (Joseph's) time. What do I mean by that? Listen to what he says to Pharaoh after interpreting the dreams in Genesis 41:32:

The reason the dream was given to Pharaoh in two forms is that the matter has been firmly decided by God, and God will do it soon.

This is a true and yet a very strange statement from Joseph. Wasn't it 13 years ago that God had revealed to a certain person a certain dream of great divine destiny in two forms back in the household of Jacob? Yes, it was Joseph to whom a great dream of divine destiny came in two forms. But Joseph, after having that dream, had been on this exile for 13 years in the foreign land until now. His own dream didn't come true soon at all. So how can he actually say with conviction here that God will bring about Pharaoh's dream soon? What's Joseph's state of mind concerning this paradox?

Joseph had the gift of dream interpretation. He was blessed with the divine wisdom to explain any and all dreams. He has seen and witnessed dreams coming to fruition in the lives of others without fail. As the sun rises from the east every single morning, his interpretations were always consistent with the reality or the representation for every single dream with such unfailing precision EXCEPT that of...himself. Year after year, the wisdom of God and the divine power of interpretation working through Joseph seem to have the immediate effect on everyone around him EXCEPT...himself. He was sent down to Egypt by force for being a faithful son and a good brother. He was thrown into king's prison for doing the right thing where most men would have crumbled and failed. And He was totally forgotten by the cupbearer and allowed to suffer two more years in prison when all fibers of wisdom in him screamed that truly this cupbearer was his last chance, the ticket out of the prison, that God Himself had sent his way! But we must realize...Joseph finally understood the difference between the gift and the Gift Giver. It is not the gift itself or the possessor of that gift that makes this dream a reality or that wisdom a path to success and prosperity. It is only God, the giver of life and the world and all the wisdom therein, that can give you dreams and the power to interpret the dreams that He himself gave to Joseph or anyone. God was the one who was always saving Joseph, remember? **His own gifts themselves did not play any part in sustaining Joseph up to this point but the character that God Himself forged in Joseph through the gifts did.**

Moreover, God himself defines the rules inherent in all things and He is not afraid to change it in our eyes in order for us to finally see that God is the only one in control and only one we can truly trust and depend on... not anyone and NOT even our own divine gifts. Joseph knew the difference between the gift and the gift Giver. God is always in control. And this lesson learned gave him the understanding that his divine gifts, if it is truly from God, cannot be used for Joseph's own gain but for the love of God for all people. And God will extend the time of fulfillment for all of our desires because that is the only way we can learn the lesson of the true meaning of our Divine destiny: Our destiny in Him is for God's glory for ALL people. And the divine timing produces patience, perseverance, character and eventually love...for all people. We all crave that thing or that desire of our hearts to happen soon. Our individual selfish desires will only gratify ourselves for a short time and does nothing for God's people that Christ came to save. And that very selfish desire, disguised as love, honor, wealth or even spiritual acts, will destroy lives and boomerang back to haunt all of us. We are made to be more than what we want out of ourselves in this world. We are made for that mutual glory in Christ for all eternity.

Moses was the most humble man on the face of the earth (Numbers 12:3). There is a difference between being a coward and being humble. He was not a coward. When he witnessed a man oppressing his fellow Hebrew, he killed him. It was only when he was confronted by his own Hebrew "brothers" that he had to flee his home and the palace in Egypt (sounds kind of familiar to us now, doesn't it?) He was being trained as an instrument of God for what seemed like an eternity (40 years) until he was personally summoned by God at the tender age of...80! Yes, his journey was much longer than that of Joseph. He was so humbled to the point that his humility, for which God had sent him on this exile if you will, had even frustrated God himself. I have a hard time grasping that sometimes. God did too good of a job, if I can say that, in making Moses humble to the point where he confessed that he was pitifully weak in speech and no one would believe him! But we know from the martyr Stephen's testimony (Acts 7:22) that Moses was not only powerful in speech and action but also in all manners of wisdom. Now, if you think God knew it to be necessary for a person like Moses to take on this journey of self rejection and humility for 40 years all for the sake of HIS people and God's glory, how long do you think it will take us to complete our own redemption journey? But we have our Lord, who himself took on the burden of going on this journey for us. All we have to do now is...take up our cross daily (in order to crucify the self in ourselves with Christ) and follow Him. Let us partake this journey of the Cross. Only through this journey will we find true love and hope that God wants to reveal and instill in all of us...for beginning of that heaven to materialize while we are here.

Joseph will realize that when he is catapulted into the position of being the supreme ruler of Egypt, 13 years of perseverance and character development is just a speck in God's eternal spectrum of time. To our Lord one day is like a thousand years and thousand years one day (2 Peter 2:8). God's timing is always based on His love for all people. God is love and love is patient. If we do not know God who is patient for all people, then everything He does will appear to be delayed and out of time in our minds...all to our own personal disappointments that will only fuel our own restlessness and wandering tendencies of our hearts. God has all of eternity with our eternal destiny in Him in His mind at all times while we are so often concerned with days and years in this temporary life with all of our temporary desires for ourselves. Joseph somehow came to understand God, who will fulfill his destiny only when God Himself can finally use it to save as many as possible in HIS time; thereby allowing Joseph to experience God's love in the most powerful way that he couldn't even imagine retrospectively let alone orchestrate. And all of this was possible because of God's timing that is first based on His love for ALL PEOPLE. And Joseph will know in retrospect that 13 years was a very short time for anyone to have his heart transformed to make it worthy of the royal priesthood to be working powerfully through him.

Our Lord has gone through the redemption journey of all histories and all eternity. Unlike our spiritual forefathers like Moses and Joseph, He didn't have to go through this journey of redemption for His own heart's sake. He was the perfect Lamb of God. He went on that journey of redemption for our own hearts. We have to understand His journey from the beginning to the end, not just the crucifixion and the resurrection, in order to claim our journey and our destiny in Him. As I have said in the first two chapters, we have to understand that Jesus Christ in totality is God of justice as well as mercy and love, and justice itself is based on his love. We are supposed to find our path of journey in Him in totality. He knew what resided in the heart of all of us and He did not entrust Himself in any of us and YET was willing to be crucified for all of us. His parables and miracles were designed not only to move our hearts in order to put our trust in Him but to expose what was in our hearts so that we can see why He had to die in our place and why He alone is worthy of our trust. He truly was the best of us, the bright Morning Star, the purest of the pure, and the love beyond this universe. He did nothing but healed the sick, blind and crippled, fed the hungry, blessed the undeserved, cast out demons, forgave the unforgivable and loved everyone, yes even the Pharisees, and for ALL that...people put him through HELL.

Joseph came to know by all of the tragic and painful lessons of his own redemption journey that there is absolutely nothing worthy of his pursuit, worthy of his time or energy, worthy of his devotion or worthy of his heart in anything in this world or in the hearts of the men, including himself. There was only God who has been the only constant protector and provider, and his own visions and gifts had nothing to do with God's protection. As he is standing before the Pharaoh, he is not consciously trying to lower himself to appear humble. He is not conscious of himself PEROID...except the presence of God and His intentions for ALL the people that God loves.

Do you think that maybe Joseph knew that he was about to be made the ruler de facto of the whole Egypt? Likely not, given that he is NOT self-conscious at all at this moment. Does he care either way? No, not really. The wise king Solomon, who gained everything that his heart desired, lost his ways in the end because there was no presence of God in his heart at the end. However, Joseph's heart finally belonged to God and he knows and believes in his heart that whatever glory, fame, pleasure, success or wealth in this world, even if it is by his own Divine destiny (like Solomon), is doomed to fail himself and every one around him without the presence of God, the true protector of his heart. And in this revelation, the heart of Joseph could truly begin to rest in God who works to orchestrate everything in and outside of him for the true desires of all people, including Joseph himself. And the true desire of all our hearts is nothing short of and nothing less than the glory of God, our Creator, who is love. The glory of God is the desire of all nations even though the nations themselves, still yet to be fully redeemed, may not be aware.

At this moment in time, Joseph is truly ready to dispense true justice to all people because he is solely dependent on God and sees that God's glory itself is the true desire of all people and all nations. There is no longer "I" but only God and His people! In God, we will find our ultimate and true destiny in Christ, our Lord, who came as the Lamb of God to take away the sins of the entire world and made us royal priesthood of His coming kingdom into our hearts and for all eternity. The time has finally come for Joseph's ascension to claim his own divine destiny for the destinies of ALL God's people...including you and me! Through 13 years of long and arduous journey into the hearts of all men, God was systematically instilling in Joseph the most important character attribute found in any of His mighty instrument at any point in history. The true desires of all people cannot converge on anything other than this singular character trait. None of us will ever see the highest of our God intended destinies in Christ unless our journey actually produces — yes, it is acquired by training — this necessary and foundational trait. What is it?

Patience. My Christian brothers and sisters in America, God is patient. Love is patient. No one was, and no one will ever be, more patient than our Lord Jesus Christ. True godly leadership or kingship begins with patience forged in suffering and pain. If Christ was not as patient with us, none of us would be in existence today. And Joseph is the foreshadowing of Christ, who is the essence of love that begins with...PATIENCE.

127

Chapter 11

PREDESTINATION VS PERSECUTION?

TIME MACHINE

I just saw this movie and it kinda made me think....

All right, what's it about?

It's basically about this guy who travels through time to save lives, but he dies in the end anyway...like altering one's destiny for the good of many. Really moving.

All right, tell me more. Lots of action, with a sad romance to boot?

Well, there's been movies like that...with impossible and ridiculous storylines, but this movie was actually done well...I don't want to spoil it for you. You should go see it.

Do you actually think it would be possible to invent a time machine in the future?

I don't know. I really don't know what that would all mean. I'm pretty sure it is much more complicated than how the movies make them out to be. Right?

Yeah... I know for a fact that it will never happen.

Dude, how do you know for sure?

Because we don't have people from the distant future constantly invading the present and our past in their time machines. It will be like an eternal cycle of invasions from the future altering the past, altering the future, altering the past, altering the future...It's going to be like a loop that would've spiraled out of control long time ago

into an uncontrollable, global mess. We who are caught in the middle would be just a continuously changing, almost a formless scramble of worthless information. But we are doing fine today…turns out. I'm not getting blurry or ghostlike…And we have the ability to choose what we do. Someone gave us that power to choose…

GREAT WHITE JOE

There was a great white shark named Joe. He was a healthy and powerful beast. He wreaked havoc everywhere he went, causing decimation of all life forms that he came across. One time, he came upon a herd of seals that were completely oblivious to his presence. Joe was not very hungry at the time, but the sight of the seals ignited the excitement of the hunt in him. He thought, "well, I think I should eat one of these so I won't be hungry until tomorrow." So, he aimed for the middle of the moving herd and positioned himself directly below for an ambush attack. He ascended with such power and ferocity that his body was propelled well over 8 feet above the surface…completely airborne. He exploded out of the water with the disoriented seal already being devoured and the spritz of water bursting out of his mouth in all directions. Joe's body contorted furiously and majestically in the air with the tail of the seal draping over his large mouth. Joe thought he was the king of his world. He began to think that not only was he the king of his own universe but he was *making* his own universe wherever he went. He reveled in the power of his freedom and became more and more convinced that nothing in the ocean was his equal.

One day, he drifted into a territory that he wasn't familiar with. In his continuous attempts to expand his territory, he was always venturing out to new and unfamiliar places. The ocean is vast and deep, and he has only so much time in his magnificent life to conquer it all. And no matter how unfamiliar the new area was, Joe always recognized the unchanging and unchallenged pattern of his own universe…that whoever sees him is, and should always be, afraid of him and terrified. That has proven to be the absolute truth every single time. He reveled in it. "So this new territory should be no different," he thought. "I will dominate just like I did before and drive out all other fake kings…I will bring my universe into this place. I will be the king here and I will do whatever I want and I will create my own happiness with no one to oppose me."

129

The water was cold, which wasn't unusual, but something was a miss. There seemed to be a subtle disturbance in the current and he felt the presence of *something* watching his every move. He got a very strange feeling that this thing or presence *knew* Joe was gliding in his direction but didn't seem to care. And then...*SWOOSH.*

Joe didn't just hear it, but felt it rocking his body. His world was spinning out of control as he was suddenly engulfed in a strong and unexpected vortex. There was nowhere else to go but up. And then out of the corner of his eye, he saw a massive, monstrous *thing* approaching him at an impossible speed. The thing was bigger than him! And as it was just about to collide with Joe near the surface, it circled around and positioned itself before it landed its massive tail on his body. *THUD!* As he was still reeling from the impact that jarred through his mind and body, he felt a searing pain on his side as if a massive mouth has clamped down on it. Before his disoriented mind could recover from panic and fear — two things he has never known until now — he was being turned over by this *thing*... this monster!

A dreamlike state overtook him as his body was being paralyzed by this unnatural position in which he has never found himself before this day. It is as if this monster knew something about his body that even he didn't know. Somewhere in the vast ocean of fate and free will, Joe took a last glimpse of his small world — the world that he thought was his — that was slipping away quickly and quietly from his consciousness as he was being dragged into the depths, upside down...by a killer whale, the true king of the ocean.

And the infinite and magnificent ocean just went on being what it always has been.

But we have this treasure (of Jesus) in jars of clay (our bodies) to show that this all-surpassing power is from God and not from us. We are hard pressed on every side, but not crushed; perplexed, but not in despair; persecuted, but not abandoned; struck down, but not destroyed. We always carry around in our body the death of Jesus, so that the life of Jesus may also be revealed in our body. For we who are alive are always being given over to death for Jesus' sake, so that his life may also be revealed in our mortal body. So then, death is at work in us, but life is at work in you.–2 Corinthians 4:7-12

Therefore we do not lose heart. Though outwardly we are wasting away, yet inwardly we are being renewed day by day. For our light and momentary troubles are achieving for us an eternal glory that far outweighs them all. So we fix our eyes not on what is seen, but on what is unseen, since what is seen is temporary, but what is unseen is eternal.–2nd Corinthians 4:16-18

We often make a mistake of pitting the idea of predestination against free will. Our free will does not and cannot interfere with God's predestination. One of the greatest minds of the last century, C.S. Lewis, tried to clarify the perennial, ill conceived premise of positioning God against Satan as in the idea of good vs. evil. We agree with C.S. Lewis that Satan is equal to Michael the arch angel, for they were both created to be arch angels. Michael is the ultimate defender of God's people and Satan the ultimate accuser. God is far above Michael and Satan, or far above anything our finite mind has conceived. God vs. Satan? Please...there is no such thing. God is ONE. He stands alone. But He wants to bring all of us into Him through Christ and He will not do that in the absence of our free will! How interesting... But why?

We can think of predestination as the infinite ocean of God's omniscient presence bathing and infiltrating every fiber of our being and all of creation for all eternity and our free will is just a part of that infinite ocean. Paul says in Acts Ch17:28, "For in Him we live, and breathe and have our being." ALL creation is being sustained by God by all times...yes, even Satan. Everything is under his control. He is everywhere at all times. In fact, the very concept of time is irrelevant in the mind of our great God. Now, that's hard for us to grasp and yet I think you are beginning to understand what I'm trying to convey. Like in the story above, our collective free will does not change the character of the ocean of His predestination nor does it move the ocean in one direction or the other. It will remain the same forever.

Let's expand on the concept, however. Even if you believe in the chaos theory and the butterfly effect, it is still limited in this finite planet. As for the rest of the universe, a little hurricane near Florida is of no effect or consequence. And there is an inherent flaw in the theory itself that contradicts its own model. We have ships bigger than the Titanic traversing the oceans all the time and yet the ocean has maintained and never deviated from its essence all these years. In the same manner, our free will should have absolutely no effect on God's predestination. The concept of predestination, however, becomes very confusing to our minds when the foundational and global love of God for every single person enters into the whole picture of predestination. It is confusing because we are not filtering all the information with all surpassing love of Christ that designed His own predestination. Jesus said even the small things like the sparrows do not fall to the ground outside of God's predestination. Even the very hairs of our heads are all numbered so we should not be afraid. We are worth more than many sparrows (Matthew 10:30). This is actually a loving retort by Christ. Can you imagine God being aware of every single thing going on in every single cell in our bodies as well as all of His creation for all eternity all at the same time? He is. And Jesus saying that same God has his eyes on your heart and soul for all eternity and He is the only One who can make it secure and last for all eternity…in Him. Jesus is gently scolding his disciples, and us, for not believing in the omnipresent power of the loving Father, because our ever-wandering hearts — constantly focusing on the temporary and fleeting things of the world that limits our vision on his infinite power and predestination — are always doubting the power of God's love that controls all things. Trust me, all of our free will is being effortlessly being absorbed and integrated by the vast ocean of His predestination…and yet, He is the one who is giving our free will its weight, value, distinction and glory in our eyes, however misperceiving they may be. We know now that the Love of God is the very thing that built His predestination. We must understand that it has been very difficult for us to understand God's predestination because of our pride in our minds and hearts are continuously resisting the active redemption of love of God by the Word. The pride always opposes true love and when our intellectual pursuits are influenced by our pride, we will not understand the love of God that built the foundation for everything in this universe, including His predestination.

Let's continue on the concept of free will so that we may understand His love better. Suppose that we have been created like robots that have been entrusted with the task of worshipping him for all eternity without any other duties or purpose of existence. He can still be glorified through such worship but will it have the kind of weight and worth and glory that God desires? There are angels and heavenly creatures that have been made to worship in the presence of God in such fashion and yet God would rather be worshipped by one redeemed soul than any of those beings who have been wired to do nothing but worship. Why? It is because the weight and the glory of our freewill-driven choices to worship God depend on nothing less than the surpassing power and love of the blood of the Lamb, His only begotten Son! Our worship becomes inexpressibly glorious in our hearts and minds when its foundation and object is the very Foundation and the Capstone of this universe and beyond: Jesus Christ the King.

God has given us the free will. When we choose, by our free will, the blood of Jesus Christ as our only possible and overwhelming salvation, the same free will validates our worship of our God. Nothing else validates our beings in the core like the true worship founded upon the blood of our God, the Son of Man! Our free will itself does not validate God or anything else that comes from God; for free will itself was designed by God. But when we choose the blood of our Lord Jesus Christ over all the other things of the world, we impart to our own worship the kind of supernatural strength, weight, power, honor and glory that no other beings, not even angels, will ever have or experience. We truly have been made to be kings and queens of His universe. So the purpose of our God-given free will is that God can truly be worshipped in and among us. True worship is worship by choice and not by a threat of force. True worship is true relationship between God and men and not false religion, philosophy or ideas imposed by ourselves.

But it is perfectly OK for us to ask why Joseph was made to suffer so much. It is not so much that God is trying to derive worship out of Joseph for such unanticipated pain and persecution but He is trying to demonstrate to Joseph that there is nothing or no one in this world that is worthy of worship in Joseph's heart. Joseph learned from his own painful experience that all the things and the people in the world will eventually fail him and turn on him and so will we. God orchestrated all the events in his life so that Joseph will freely choose God over all other potential substitutes for his heart, even himself. Again, we are reminded that the "broken and contrite heart" the Lord will not despise. And the King David said only through the broken hearts that the Lord is worshiped. Ultimately, our free will was designed and given by our God to validate our existence and truly set us apart as His ultimate prized beings in His predestined universe *when we choose Him over all else.*

It is intriguing, however, and consistent with our own fallen nature, that we should only begin to question the validity of God's predestination when bad and "evil" things happen to us. We never question the sovereignty of God's will through predestination when we are happy and satisfied. But it is the idea of persecution that causes us to question the very loving nature of God, even by the believers. All this misunderstanding comes about because we are so consumed by the actions and the consequences of this temporary life and not focused on the eternal love of God. Let's take an extreme example. Ready?

Let's suppose that a teenager was repeatedly raped over and over again by her own family members...like her father, uncle or maybe even her brother. My brothers and sisters in Christ, you and I both know that this type of monstrosity is going on everywhere. That kind of act is not only the violation of her body, but her very soul. Its effect is so destructive and lasting that the same person who was violated will likely either contemplate revenge, suicide or turn into an abuser of some kind to drown out the abuse and violation that was done to them. Many of them turn into sexual abusers themselves. Now...let us not make that mental jump in our minds that Jesus Christ can heal all things physical and spiritual just yet. I know most of you believe that with all your hearts and so do I. But please, stay with me here spiritually and really identify with the hearts of all these people who have been violated against their will and understand that at least they *know* that they have been brutally violated.

When the omniscient and omnipresent God looks down upon the humanity, He perceives all things all the time in all places. He knows 99.9999 percent to the infinity of the things that we do not know. Our awareness is finite. In His eyes, all of our destructive consequences are being played out and perceived and put into their proper places in proper time, so as to effect not only His glory, but to reveal to us that our salvation can only come from Jesus Christ and Him alone. He not only knows everything, but orchestrates everything. And He knows in more detail than we can ever imagine the degree to which we are destructive to each other and yet He is the One who has chosen to reveal only the things that will really touch and affect our hearts in a way that only He knows how and why. Let me give you another example.

Suppose that I'm not a very good doctor, but no one knows that. And suppose that I myself do not know that because I'm a victim of my own self-delusion and self-grandeur. I am a doctor after all. I read and interpret many diagnostic studies and help the oncologists (cancer doctors) to properly stage their patients and formulate the most appropriate cocktail of treatments. If I fail to identify certain small focus of cancer that is making a comeback because I was either neglectful or incompetent, then the patient may have potentially lost months or even years of his or her life. My neglect or incompetence, however unintentional they may be, has cost the portion of that patient's life and the lives of those around the patient building into him or her. But because no one knows exactly how my part, as well as other myriads of factors, played in the whole process of care, the potential life depriving, or even possibly extending, consequences of my actions as well as all the others are almost never brought into *accurate* questioning by anyone...except God. God knows exactly how everything we do, and the consequence thereof is being *weighed* on his perfect eternal scale.

The sad thing, like the example of the doctor above, is that we may be spiritually violating one another and not even *know* it. It is not the physically abused who find their true salvation in Christ from the nightmare that we are to pity and empathize. We need to pity ourselves who are spiritually violating one another and dying in our own world of self-delusion and don't even know it. In God's eyes, the shame and the devastation of the bodies and souls caused by the monstrous acts of humanity — mainly rape — may not be so different than continuous and insidious violation of our souls by the ways of the lust, power and the pride of life, which has become so pervasive in this world and the culture that we are living in. God can fully reveal what lurks in the every corner of our hearts at anytime but that will absolutely horrify us...and may even cause series of heart attacks on global scale. He will not do that...yet. He is love. He will simply resign to say, I regret that I made human beings...like He did before the Noah's flood. He also said, I regret that I made Saul the king of Israel. Why is omniscient God of predestination "regretting" here? Did he make a mistake? If He made the mistake, then what is His mistake? Us? No, we are not His mistake, but we are his ultimate creation. We are His royal priesthood. He is saying the word "regret" (in some translations it says, "it *repented* the Lord that He created humans because our hearts were filled with evil all the time) because that is the *only word* that he can say here for the human beings that He loves so much. It is the only word He can use for us who have walked so far away from Him. He is being very kind and gentle to us here...that's why. If we were to put ourselves in God's shoes, we will never say these words. The word "regret" is not a reflection of God's unchanging character, but our ever-changing wandering hearts lost in sin and darkness. And He sent His only Son to turn that *Divine temporary repentance* into everlasting victory in our Lord Jesus Christ. There will be no regret by God or any of us in Jesus Christ the King in heaven. I bank my own soul on it.

For those of you who have been sexually abused against your will, God bless your precious souls. If you are one of the victims who are finding yourself in the true love of Jesus Christ, then your soul has truly been refined as by fire and the supernatural power and strength of the Lord is already working through you. The Lord can use you to save many who would not be saved otherwise. Your redemption in Christ will affect and touch both the victims and the perpetrators. Please do not give into the fear of men or buy into the notion of your self-worth weighed by the standards of this world. Only God is the judge! The concept of true validation and glory will be perfected in our new glorious bodies in Christ and we will never feel more loved and affirmed as all of our temporary suffering and seemingly insurmountable shame will be gloriously obliterated in the blood of the Lamb! And He will raise you up with Him in the last days and even NOW. And He will wipe away every tear from your eyes...of your eternal heart. I know that whatever suffering or pain in this life is just a speck in God's eternity of happiness and joy. He will make all of us new. Whatever violation you had suffered in our bodies will not affect the glory of heaven that you will enjoy with Him forever in our new bodies. In fact, I suspect that your joy and celebration in Christ will be more powerful and magnificent than those of us who have not known such pain and sadness.

And for those of us who have not been a victim to such life altering violations of our souls, we will be very surprised to find some startling revelations when we get to Heaven. We will find so many things that we dismissed as just a little more than inconsequential to be such a devastating and life altering forces in the lives of others as well as ours. And we will give true and heartfelt glory to our God as we perceive everything in His love and how He had sustained us through them all (1st Cor. 13:12). Trust me. All of our souls have been, and are still being, deceived and violated by the forces and evil working through the world of men in and out of our consciousness or awareness. In many respects, we who are ignorant of this are to be pitied more than the ones who know that they have been violated. It is as if you put a frog into a cold water and seeing the frog being boil to death as you slowly bring up the temperature of the water. The frog never jumps out! Self-delusion by the way of self-entitlement will have such insidious and destructive effect, and our nation is drowning in the world of self-entitlement. But if you place the frog in hot boiling water, then the frog jumps out. God has to bring a hot boiling water to our lives at His appointed and predestined times in order for us to see the devastating and ever escalating consequences of our own sins and self-righteousness. And that same hot boiling water will give us the wisdom to help such people who are drifting into delusion of destruction in that same hot water. And there is one singular evil that we ourselves, unknowingly, have infiltrated into every aspect of our daily living. We will discuss this **general of all evil** soon.

So, we are beginning to understand that our limited perception of reality and God, not the unchanging and all surpassing love of God, is causing us to ask the wrong questions at the very beginning and to set up false premises for the impossible argument of God's predestination vs. free will. But what about the idea of persecution? We can accept the idea of pain and suffering in the world that causes us to ask relevant questions regarding the true cause of pain and suffering, but what about the questions concerning our own suffering as we are walking in faith with God and our Lord Jesus Christ? Jesus said in this world, we will have troubles as His followers. It is not a question of if but when. Jesus said *"Blessed are you **when** people insult you, persecute you and falsely say all kinds of evil against you because of me. Rejoice and be glad, because great is your reward in heaven, for in the same way they persecuted the prophets who were before you"* (Matthew 5).

It seems as though the suffering in this life as a Christian is the only sure thing or the guarantee in this unpredictable life by the rules of God's predestination. I know you don't like it. I don't like it either...not one bit! But God never says we have to like it. God didn't give us the choice in the matter of existence of persecution against the Church but how we choose to respond to it. We all have experienced some form of persecution in the form of demeaning comments, social isolations, humiliations, physical abuse or combination of any and all of these as Christians. And Jesus Christ our Lord has suffered all of these forms of persecution to the most extreme degree. When you juxtapose the above *blessed are the persecuted* statement by our Lord with the two passages from 2nd Corinthians 4 by Paul that I provided at the beginning of the chapter, they all begin to come together. Paul said that he was willing to go through all that hell (persecutions for being a Christ follower) in order to demonstrate the death of Christ working in him so that life of Christ can be manifested through him as well as the body of believers addressed in his letter. What does he mean by that? It's very simple. When we see believers being persecuted and killed for no other reason than being a true and loving Christian — in the Muslim world for instance — their suffering and death becomes the very life giving force that powers our walk with the Lord, especially here in America devoid of such extreme persecution. In our story, Joseph was persecuted by his own brothers, Potipher and his wife, and forgotten (another form of persecution when it comes to unjust suffering for being godly) by the cupbearer. All these persecutions have a way of coming back to weigh down and crush the hearts of the perpetrators unto true redemption.

When Jesus Christ became the perfect loving canvas for which our sins poured out in the form of most vile and violent persecutions, He already foresaw our hearts being pierced and convicted unto true redemption by seeing retrospectively the monsters of our own sins murdering the Son of God, who did nothing but LOVE! When we, in turn, are being persecuted for following Christ, our Father God is foreseeing the future where the hearts of

137

the ones persecuting — either by participation or by apathy — being pierced by what they did to us. The hearts of the people who are persecuting and who were passively letting the persecution take place will be pierced and tormented to the point of opening up their hearts to the way, the truth and the life our Lord Jesus Christ, who will come into their cold, dead hearts and make them alive again! And those of us in America who are no where near being persecuted to the degree by which some of our brothers and sisters around the globe are being persecuted, the persecutions suffered by others become the example of the true life giving force in Christ — the power of true redemption of eternal life that saves even the ones that tries to destroy it — by which we are to be walking with the Lord. The suffering for our faith in the Lord Jesus Christ is God's predestination at its finest hour. And through all this pain and suffering in Christ, our own mind and hearts are being renewed and actively being redeemed. No other galvanizing tool is more effective or divine...both for the victims and the perpetrators.

Please don't get me wrong. I'm not saying at all that we should welcome persecution, and impose unnecessary suffering on our bodies. That's heresy. The false humility and self-imposed physical pain comes from our own religious pride, which is the most destructive form of pride. And pride can never oppose the working of the flesh, including sexual desires outside of marriage. Even Paul warned of such groups who were imposing self-mutilations, mainly circumcisers, and self inflicted physical pain that does nothing to curb the sensual and destructive desires of the flesh as in Colossians 2:23 where Paul says, *"Such regulations indeed have an appearance of wisdom, with their **self-imposed worship**, their **false humility** and their **harsh treatment of the body**, but they lack any value in restraining **sensual** indulgence."* God wants to bless us in more ways than we can imagine even on this earth. But in this world we can only get the glimpse of it because only the fully redeemed hearts can perceive and enjoy that perpetual true happiness in God and in one another. We will just have to wait for that world in Heaven where our hearts will be fully redeemed in Christ. But it is also God's desire for us to take the journey of heart's redemption because the world needs to see that kind of Heaven's love in Christ flowing over from and among us even now! That is the purpose of His blessings while we are here. All the Heavenly blessing is for us to not only enjoy but to be actively spread and shared while we are here. As much as poverty itself comes from evil, the persecution itself comes from the evil one by the way of other human beings who are bound by the forces of evil. But what the Lord is saying is that when we are being obedient to our call as sons and daughters of God, we bare His image and the world will persecute us just like we would've persecuted Christ on the Cross in ignorance and pride. That same destructive and evil picture of persecution will come back to haunt the hearts all who persecuted us, and drive them into their own spiritual torment and subsequent repentance and redemption.

Listen to what happened when Peter stood before a large crowd shortly after the death and resurrection of Jesus Christ. Look how the suffering of Christ, at the hands of the people He came to save, affected and moved the hearts of the very same people in Acts 2:36-39.

> *"Therefore let all Israel be assured of this: God has made this Jesus, whom you crucified, both Lord and Messiah." When the people heard this, they were* **cut to the heart** *and said to Peter and the other apostles, "Brothers, what shall we do?" Peter replied, "Repent and be baptized, every one of you, in the name of Jesus Christ for the forgiveness of your sins. And you will receive the gift of the Holy Spirit. The promise is for you and your children and for all who are far off — for all whom the Lord our God will call."*

Therefore, now we understand that we should be honored to partake in the heart transforming suffering of Jesus Christ. We cannot be ashamed of the Gospel or the name of our Lord Jesus Christ. Again, our Lord said, blessed are us when people insult us, falsely accuse us and persecute us because of Him. When we follow Christ, we become easy targets. We stand out like no other. We can't help it as kings and priests of His kingdom. We will experience persecutions in one form or another. But we do not have to be afraid at all. The consequences of all the persecutions in our lives will serve as the true faces of the demons that exist in every human heart for all the world to see — like Jesus Christ displayed for us on Himself on the Cross — and begin to weigh down on the hearts of many and cause spiritual torment unto the glorious redemption of our Lord Jesus Christ. Our brother Paul was such a person. His zealous persecutions against all the Christians went out only to come back to torment his own soul. And Saul, the number one persecutor of Christ, became Paul, the number one ambassador of Christ for all Gentiles and the undisputed weapon of mass destructions against all evil. He wrote half the New Testament: the sword of eternal truth and the unchanging word of God!

That, my friends, is how all the persecutions in Christ have been predestined by God of love for all of us, both the believers and the nonbelievers. And we should do everything in our power to support all these missionaries around the globe, especially the ones who are being persecuted...even to the point of rape and death. We need to pray constantly for all the Christians who are being persecuted for the name of Christ. They hold the banner of the glorious redemption of Jesus Christ working through their lives for the rest of the body of Christ: the Church! Like Paul said, the death and suffering (of Jesus Christ) is at work in any of us at any given time, the power of true life (of Jesus Christ) is at work in all of those who are learning from our suffering including the ones doing the killing and persecuting! And let's not forget what Paul said about having the eternal perspective on our temporary suffering; that we will trade all of these temporary sufferings in our temporary bodies (jars of clay) for all surpassing glory and the unspeakable joy in our new eternal bodies in our Lord Jesus, the King of Heaven! We will be vindicated and glorified in Christ in the end! That ultimate vindication and highest of all of our desires and destinies in Christ of glory, my friends, is only found God's glorious predestination forged in our suffering and persecution in this world.

Chapter 12

THE WORK OF THE KING, JESUS CHRIST: AUTHORITY TO DISPENSE TRUE JUSTICE, MERCY AND COMPASSION FOR ALL.
(GENESIS 41 AND 42)

Divine physical duty. Divine spiritual rest.

Joseph went from having nothing to having everything overnight. I believe he was absolutely floored as his spirit soared in the sudden and overwhelming glory and blessing that was placed upon Him by God Almighty. Life was beyond beautiful. It was more beautiful than where he left it as a free man. Words would have failed to describe what Joseph was experiencing as he ascended to the throne. The true and magnificent love of God has finally revealed its face and Joseph was truly ready to embrace all of its glory and triumph in proper divine context and perspective. The sudden ascension to power, the wealth and the splendor, and all the honor of the king bestowed upon Joseph could finally make him the most powerful channel through which the mysterious and foundational love of God can freely flow for all people. He will not suffer the fate of Sampson or Solomon. His immovable hope and trust in God Almighty wrought by the long season of suffering and pain have effectively driven out the *self* in Joseph and forged the strength of character, wisdom and compassion unequaled in his time.

141

With all the honor, wealth and power bestowed upon him as the ruler of Egypt, he could have enjoyed the life of luxury in the palace for a while. But that is not what Joseph did. He knew why he was put in this position of power and honor by God. He was a king for such a time. He indeed was given the life of luxury for him to not only dispense with the wisdom of God but for his own pleasure. He had suffered unjustly too long. But we see here, again, that Joseph's heart has truly been galvanized by God's own discipline in his life to see all people as God sees all people. And if you had studied the book of Jonah with me, that's how God sees people...with divine compassion that supersedes his rightful judgment. **Joseph, while fully understanding that he is just a human like any other man through his journey, also knew that it is God's all surpassing love and wisdom that made Joseph the supreme ruler of Egypt through that same journey. He came to really understand the concept of the word "undeserved". The unimaginable honor and power of Joseph's destiny came from the same incomprehensible love of God that put him through the painful, but necessary, redemption journey of his heart, equipping him with all the gifts of the King.**

Consider these statements. All will fail. You will fail me. I will fail you. I will fail myself. Every single one of us will fall and fail. All of us are fallen beings in the core. All will require the love of God. And the love of God will not fail us. Love never fails. The love of God working through us, when it reaches its perfection, will cause us to utterly depend on God and the people will see in us the love of God that does not fail... for the redemption of their own hearts. These are the redeeming, noble and pure thoughts of God of all people that are dominating the continuously renewing heart and mind of Joseph.

Now, with the gifts of the King that Joseph had acquired through his journey or "training", Joseph began to travel throughout the Egypt in the king's chariot (41:46). With all of his gifts of wisdom acquired in the years of prison-life under the warden, especially the gifts leadership, adminis-tration and wisdom of the King, he began to plan, organize and create the infrastructure and buildings necessary to gather and collect the huge amount of harvested grain in each city. Knowing the essence of human nature better than anyone in his time, Joseph felt it was necessary for him to oversee and prevent the human elements from interfering with this all important tasks at hand. That's why he himself had to travel throughout the land, making sure that everything was being executed as planned. Obviously, this riding of the chariot was not a parade of power and might for Joseph. Joseph understood that the real work for Joseph had begun. It was true labor of love and wisdom of God that was forged in that pit, in that household, and in that prison. It is for this very purpose of glorious labor of love that Joseph had been chosen to go through the journey of hardship and discipline. And he knows he has to get to his work as soon as he is able.

But now, he is not stressed at all. He does not feel burdened at all. For someone who has been in prison for 10 years, it is amazing to see how he is adapting so well and operating at the supernatural level almost immediately in the outside world. But all of this should not surprise us, because he has been personally trained by the One who is omnipresent, omniscient and omnipotent. And he can truly labor in rest without any kind of performance anxiety or stress. He knows that this is God's calling and God himself will make it a success as he depends on Him. **Even though Joseph was working hard on the outside in obedience to his Divine and glorious calling, his restless heart was finally at rest and peace because it was resting on God, who works out everything for the good for all of His people in His time** (Hebrews 4:11; Romans 8:28). His work and burden of destiny was truly light in weight as his heart now soared through the stratospheres of all that insurmountable obstacles, temptations and trials that God himself helped him to overcome (Matt. 11:30; Ephesians 2:4-10). And we have the ultimate helper in Holy Spirit, who helps us in our time of need to get us closer and closer to our destiny in Christ.

For those of us who have studied the spiritual gifts mentioned in the New Testament, you know that the gifts of administration and leadership (or governance) that have been refined in Joseph through suffering are also spiritual gifts. The gifts of leadership and administrations are two of the many gifts of the King.

Zerubbabel: manifestation of Christ the King... through us.

In the book of Ezra and Nehemiah as well as in the Haggai and Zechariah of the Minor Prophets of the Bible; the last 12 books of the old testament beginning with the book of Hosea; there is a character whose name is not so easy to pronounce. Zerubbabel, son of Shealtiel, the governor of Judah and new Israel, along with Joshua the son of Zozadak, the high priest, was one of the leaders of the nation of Israel who were coming back to their homeland after 70 years of exile and captivity in the Babylonian kingdoms. The nation of Judah and Israel were exiled from their homeland 70 years before because the Lord had to break the cycle of continuously escalating sins and rebellion in their hearts. God comes to

Zechariah with powerful and overwhelming revelations about the fate of Zerubbabel, not only as the leader of new Israel, but the foreshadowing of the Christ the King. It is amazing how God has revealed Himself in such magnificent and mysterious ways to Zerubbabel, a human being like us. In fact, the old testament is full of characters where God used people like us to symbolically represent the coming Messiah, Christ the King. Joseph is one of them. It defies all of our logic for God to endow us with such honor, power and presence of revelations that powered through their hearts and soul with unimaginable power. It defies our logic because that's the manifestation of God's unmatched power of love that He desires in all of us.

When God said all these incredible things about Zerubbabel through the prophet Zechariah, I can only imagine him thinking (like all those to whom the revelations of God have come): *"Why is God saying all these wonderful things about me? I'm not this person! Woe is me! What is man that you are mindful of him? And the son of man that you visit him? For you have made him a little lower than the angels, and you have crowned him with glory and honor"* (psalms 8:4-5). In His love, God will forge our heart to be nothing less than Christ-like, His only begotten Son. That is how deep and wide the love of God is for us. Just listen to this one of many incredible, awesome revelations from God to Zerubbabel in Zechariah chapter 4:6-8.

So he said to me (prophet Zechariah), "This is the word of the Lord to Zerubbabel: 'Not by might nor by power, but by my Spirit,' says the Lord Almighty.

"What are you, mighty mountain? Before Zerubbabel you will become level ground. Then he will bring out the capstone to shouts of 'God bless it! God bless it!'"

Then the word of the Lord came to me: "The hands of Zerubbabel have laid the foundation of this temple; his hands will also complete it. Then you will know that the Lord Almighty has sent me to you.

Now, in the books of Zechariah and Haggai, Zerubbabel is a symbolic representation of Christ the King, whereas the Joshua the son of Zozadak, a symbolic representation of Christ the High Priest. I briefly mentioned Joshua in the verse at the beginning of the **chapter called FINISHED**. You will be able to understand the Minor Prophets much better if you approach them with these correlations for these two characters in mind.

The very first task given to both Zerubbabel and Joshua was to build the house of God. This process of building the house of God is symbolic representation of the Church, the body of Christ, being built up by the spiritual gifts of the King and the High priest our Lord through us. The gifts of the King and the High Priest are our spiritual gifts. All of us have at least one of these spiritual gifts if you are in Christ. And only through love of Christ for all people that we can use all these spiritual gifts in the proper and effective manner to build the body of Christ: the new temple. The capstone, or the keystone, in the above passage is the power of Christ that presides over and holds all things together in the physical realm, this universe, and the new spiritual temple, which is us the Church The foundation of that temple, again, represents the rock of our salvation Jesus Christ, on which the body of Christ the church, along with the physical universe, is continuously being built. He alone is the foundation AND the capstone! But we, the Church, are right in between! And the totality of our Lord Jesus Christ is just beginning to be grasped when we see the power and love of the King and the High Priest, working through and around us by the power of the Holy Spirit. Each spiritual gift has a strong leaning towards either kingship or priesthood. Categorizing which gifts belong to which office or which person is not that important, but following Christ of love, who is the giver of all gifts, is. He himself will give you and teach you how to identify, cultivate and maximize them, but you must trust in His love first. The gifts are to be used to build His Church. And God himself will lift up these individuals for His purpose of building His Church. The gift itself will remain irrelevant until the person understands that the gift was given by the Giver of love for ALL people.

Joseph used his gifts of the King in order to dispense God's justice and wisely collect and fairly distribute the wealth that God had blessed this land through a critical season of abundance. We should desire all gifts, but excel in the gift of love that gives true meaning and purpose to all gifts. And the gift of prophecy, which brings all gifts together, is perfected in the gift of love. Love is not really a "spiritual gift" per se, and yet it is the greatest gift of all. We see mature Christian brothers and sisters in Christ who appear to possess nearly all of spiritual gifts of kings and priests because they saw all the gifts in Christ: the essence of love that all gifts flow through, and they asked God for them continually in order to be more and more like Christ (1 Corinthians 14:1). As we continue to walk in Christ by the power of the Spirit, the line between the kingship and the priesthood becomes more and more blurred, and you will see in yourself the true making of royal priesthood in Christ. And who, beside Moses, is the perfect example

145

of this royal priesthood in the Old Testament? As we will see, by the time that Joseph was ready to become the ruler of Egypt, he was also ready to become the high priest for his long lost brothers and the future nation of Israel. And the brothers symbolically represent all of us who were lost but who are now being found in the love and forgiveness of Christ. The brothers represent the Church of today and all history. The Church is the body of believers in Christ throughout history who are coming back to God from their old ways of sin. And Joseph is a foreshadowing of Christ the King for all people and the High priest for the new spiritual Israel, the Church.

Pastor Tong Hwa Pak, my counselor, my best friend and my dad.
April 2013. Washington D.C.

146

Chapter 13

THE WORK OF THE HIGH PRIEST, JESUS CHRIST: REPENTANCE AND FORGIVENESS BY INTERCESSORY LOVE FOR ALL (GENESIS 42–45)

He who does not love does not know God, for God is love. – 1 John 4:8

Then He said to the disciples, "It is impossible that no offenses should come, but woe to him through whom they do come! It would be better for him if a millstone were hung around his neck, and he were thrown into the sea, than that he should offend one of these little ones. Take heed to yourselves. If your brother sins against you, rebuke him; and if he repents, forgive him. And if he sins against you seven times in a day, and seven times in a day returns to you, saying, 'I repent,' you shall forgive him." –Luke 17: 1-4

Joseph knew the nature of the love of God better than anyone in his time. We will see the intercessory power of love in Joseph for his brothers in this chapter that is finally coming to fruition. The work of the high priest is more than just understanding what the high priest did in the Old Testament: representing all God's people to offer up lambs or bulls that their sins were transferred onto, in order that God can "symbolically" take away their sins by their sacrifices. The work of the high priest comes **first**

147

from understanding that our High Priest Jesus Christ became the perfect and ultimate sacrifice to take away all of our past, present and future sins once and for all and **second,** that same love is now moving our hearts to love and forgive our brothers and sisters and our neighbors and ALL people. It is the understanding that our hearts are not only made to receive the love of God from God but made to receive the same love of God *from* one another, who are finding themselves in the love of God.

Can you imagine what Joseph must have thought and felt when he saw his brothers for the first time in 21+ years? These are the brothers that tried to kill Joseph and sent him on this journey of exile and slavery that lasted 13 long years. How would we feel in such an unexpected turn of events? How do you think he had looked back on his dream at the moment? But we already know, through his journey of redemption and introspection, that Joseph understands the necessity and inevitability of God's love for all of our hearts that orchestrates and controls all events for His glory, which is the desire of all of our hearts. He understands the purpose for which God had allowed his brothers' hate to materialize in such a horrifying fashion, forcing him to face the universal reality of man's unchangeable state and the true decrepit condition of his own heart and soul.

He knows that the love of God, the only thing that sustained him and caused him to prosper beyond his wildest dreams, was the same love that demanded his love for his brothers. Joseph knew he cannot rest in his soul until he can bring the same love that he, himself, is now experiencing in God. The love of God is the supernatural love that can change the unchangeable. It is given to the repentant heart of the undeserving. The same love that exposes, purges, trains and finally shapes the heart of the king also desires to come into every person to do the same. Joseph doesn't have any fiber of appetite in him for vengeance. He has experienced the grace and love of God in ways that he could not have imagined. Joseph understands that only God can orchestrate and demonstrate this kind of supernatural love in order to change our hearts; that thing that is full of hate, jealousy and murder. He will not stand in God's way. In fact, he will do everything he can to help his brothers understand that God Himself had orchestrated all of his trials and tribulations to bring Joseph into this unimaginable place of glory and love. Life itself has become love of God for Joseph.

God's love is the only thing that can remove the things in our hearts that caused the beginning of the painful journey of Joseph in the first place. But it is only through that very same painful journey that we begin to see and feel the supernatural love of God breaking through. **It is a strange and awesome journey of divine cycle of love and pain, which became** necessary in our lives ever since the sin and pride entered into the world. And that very same love of God culminated in the death and the resurrection of Jesus Christ. He died for the undeserving and unredeemed people like us. He not only saved us, but seated us with Him in heavenly realms the Bible says! With all of the coming authority and power and might of our Lord Jesus, we have already begun this eternal life in Him! We do not see it yet....but as surely as the love of God was fully realized in Joseph's ascension to power, we will surely find ourselves in that magnificent destination that Christ Himself is preparing for us. Again, why would God himself send his only Son to die if not for that glorious purpose of redemption and our final glory in Him? He is love yesterday, today and forever. If we feel any grateful at all to our Lord for this unimaginable grace and honor, and if we can ask the Lord just how we can make a feeble attempt at repaying at least a part of that infinite love debt, do you know what the Lord will say? He will say, "**Feed my sheep.**"

When Apostle Peter experienced complete forgiveness and acceptance by the Lord after he denied him 3 times, he was not only humbled, but grateful beyond his ability to repay the Lord. The Lord, perceiving now that Peter loved Him with all of his heart, soul, mind and strength, tells him how he can repay this debt of this incomprehensible love. Jesus says, feed my sheep, feed my sheep, and feed my sheep. What Christ saying here is, "I know you love me Peter, more than you can possibly express, but if you really love me then channel that love to the people who really need it. As much as I came to love you and save you, I came to love and save as many as possible. I need you to love them like I have loved you."

Jesus says to love your neighbor as yourself. I don't know about you but I need that kind of love to dominate and sustain my life. It will free us from all pride of self-love, bondage and worthless striving that we get caught up so easily. If we confess that we love the Lord, who loved us who are undeserving, then we must love our neighbors and even our enemies, with the same love that Christ loved all of us. We must decrease so that He, working through the hearts of our families and friends, can increase.

Forgiveness is the singular most important reason for which Christ came to earth. Forgiveness is the ultimate revelation of God's love for us. If we have no choice in the matter of love, then we have no choice in the matter of forgiveness. **It is only through the forgiving of our enemies that we can truly break the cycle or perpetuation of our sins**. The true litmus test of the repentant and redeemed heart is its willingness to forgive others as well as one's own. Joseph is finally at that place in his journey where he understands that forgiveness, in himself and of other people, is

149

the singular most important reason why God has saved him from all that he trusted and believed in, including himself. And the first supernatural ability (powered by the true understanding of God's love) that He desires from all of us is the act of forgiveness. Our flesh cannot do it. But if we have gone through the redemption journey like Joseph, and if we have experienced the love of Christ that was intended to destroy the prideful and destructive desires of the flesh, the power of the flesh is being weeded out by His love. The flesh will not have power over you as the Spirit will give you the understanding and power to overcome the flesh, and forgive in ways that you never thought possible. He wouldn't even have to give us the power to forgive because He has already made in us the forgiving hearts in Christ. This power of forgiveness in Joseph through the love of God is what we are about to witness here.

Joseph's divine strategy in true forgiveness and redemption

Strangely, however, Joseph does not reveal himself here when he first sees his brothers. Even though it is his immediate desire to embrace his brothers and let them know everything has been forgiven completely, he simply cannot do it at this time. Why do you think that is the case? He desperately wants to reveal himself now so that he can forgive them and to bring the entire family to Egypt, including his father and his younger brother Benjamin that he misses so desperately. But instead, he appears to play this strange mind game, accusing them of being spies and secretly putting back the silvers — their payment for the grains — into their bags. And he demands that the youngest brother be brought to his presence to prove that they are not lying while keeping Simeon, one of the brothers, in his care as collateral. All this is very strange and dizzying indeed.... But he is not orchestrating some kind of mind game just to see Benjamin or confuse his brothers just for fun. Even when the brothers brought Benjamin with them on their second journey to Egypt, he still restrains himself and chooses not to reveal himself. Why all this patience by Joseph? What is he trying to accomplish here?

We begin to see the clue to the answer when the brothers finally reveal what has been weighing down on their hearts all these years. That dreadful weight of guilt that's been weighing down on their souls and wearing out their hearts is finally brought to surface when the brothers were confronted with the impending unjustifiable punishment by Joseph. In their mind, this punishment is perfectly justifiable because they believe in God who is just. In their eyes, somehow they are getting exactly what they deserve.

Their sins have caught up to them. Their sins will demand their payment of their bodies and souls. They could not escape God's justice even in this foreign land. All they can do now is ask for mercy. All they can do now is to beg for their own lives. Every single one of the brothers tore his clothes when the silver cup, planted again by Joseph, was found in Benjamin's sack. Every one of them threw themselves down before Joseph in terror and anguish. However, all of these demonstrations of heartfelt regret and remorse could not have been revealed had not Joseph orchestrated and devised this "testing" of the hearts. And He is testing the hearts of his brothers with the kind of longsuffering patience of love that could only have been forged by 13 long years of exile and slavery in the presence of God. Patience is the operating force behind this test of hearts. This is not a silly mind game. Love of Joseph for his brothers' hearts and souls began with patience. Love is, first and foremost, patient.

Joseph was trying to test the hearts of his brothers and the test was absolutely necessary. He understood that by applying this impending and "unjust" punishment, which is perfectly justifiable and deserving in the mind of the brothers now, he will know whether the brothers have truly repented of their old ways: the terrifying and unjust punishment to a young life who loved his brothers some 20 years ago. We can see from the heartbreaking, gut-wrenching confession and pleading from Judah, who has gone through his own redemption journey of the heart, that the pride that caused him to sin against Joseph cost him the joy of his heart. If you carefully examine the plea by Judah, we will see that he would gladly become a slave to Joseph than to see his father suffer and his family broken apart by this. Why? Because he knows that the sin that he had committed against Joseph as well as the very sin nature that caused it cannot be reversed or repaid in the eyes God. His confession is the confession of the repentant hearts that resonates and echoes through all of our hearts throughout history. It is the desperate confession of the heart yearning to go back to that place before the sin and its destruction entered into it, and willing to do anything — even being a slave — to get back to the place of its birth in God if at all possible. He knows full well, however, that such return to home is humanly impossible. Nothing is impossible with God of love, however. But Judah doesn't know that...yet.

In the parable of the prodigal son in Luke chapter 15, Jesus tells the story of a rich man who had two sons. The younger demanded his inheritance from the father before the time came and the father gave him his portion. After squandering everything he was given with wild living, he had no choice but to work for a citizen of the world who barely gave him anything to eat. When he finally came to his senses, he came back to his father with a repentant heart. Seeing himself unworthy of being his father's son anymore, he was fully prepared to be like one of the slaves of his father. Now, when Judah is pleading with Joseph, he too is more than willing to be a slave to Joseph. If he could only return to that place of peace and happiness for his family, that he was too prideful to understand before his sin destroyed the life of Joseph and thereby destroyed his own soul, he would gladly come into a possession of another man without a moment's hesitation! Judah's journey of redemption is finally reaching its divine destination. He is coming to the Lord on his knees with his repentant heart in his mouth. His heart is finally coming home. And as the father in the story ran to the prodigal son, the Father God in Joseph compelled Joseph to run to his brothers!

The love of God the Father through our son Jesus Christ, which culminated on his death and resurrection, is always waiting for us. He is always there. But only through the eyes of repentant prodigal son's heart that you will truly see the love of the Father for what it really is. If you do not have the repentant heart, you will not see God's love for what it is and you will only recognize it as something to be used and abused. That's why Joseph is being patient here. That's why Joseph is waiting for his brothers' hearts like God had waited for ours. He has to make sure that his brothers' hearts have been redeemed through repentance so that, when he reveals his heart's intention to forgive them, they can actually see it as all liberating forgiveness from their guilt and spiritual torment that they desperately needed. A heart full of pride does not want forgiveness or needs forgiveness because that would imply its own shortcomings and inadequacies. No one can be truly loved by God unless he sees the need to be loved and be forgiven. And all of us have such a great need to be forgiven. Our heavenly Father is running towards you through Christ even now. But if you, whether you are a Christ follower or not, do not repent and turn from your ways, you will not see Him. We will only recognize his incredible love as a fantastic toy or resource, something to be used, enjoyed and wasted for a while, and to be tossed aside when we get bored with it...just like in the attitude of the prodigal son at the beginning of that story. Before I go further, let me just say that we should forgive everyone at all times in our minds first whether or not they are ready to be forgiven. Forgiveness will free your heart from ever-festering bitterness and hate. Forgive them in your heart. I'm just saying it is probably not wise to reveal your heart's willingness to forgive openly to that person until they are ready and repentant — or otherwise, you may suffer even greater consequences from them and the forgiveness of God will be in danger of being taken out of context. Joseph has already forgiven his brother before they came to him but he waited to reveal the true intention of his heart as he was testing their hearts.

And Joseph saw that Judah and the rest of his brothers, by their actions and words, wanted to be forgiven desperately. The journey of redemption has crushed the sins of pride and jealousy out of them. They finally cared more about the life of their younger brother Benjamin and their father than their own. This transformation of their hearts stands in stark contrast to the state of their hearts as they were contemplating on killing Joseph some 22 years ago. They have all reached their destination where their hearts are ready to be forgiven and loved by one another. That place of love and forgiveness WAS the ultimate destiny of Joseph and all the brothers. Their hearts have finally and truly arrived in the incomprehensible love and the true redemption of the Lord!

In Christ Jesus, we have been made, not only to be loved by and to love God, but to love and be loved by one another through the love of Jesus Christ. Why would Jesus make a point of emphasizing that loving God AND loving our neighbor is the culmination of all of God's laws and the prophets? Heaven is the place where we can love each other in Christ without the presence of sin and pride. Joseph's heart, powered by the love of God, ran to his brothers like that father in the prodigal son story!

His heart ran. He wept over them. Only the heart of love makes you weep like he did. He sat down and talked with them. He ate with them and calmed their fears. He restored them to that heaven like place that is even better than the original home before this journey of redemption began. He displayed the love of Christ long before the coming of Christ. He is the foreshadowing of our Lord Jesus Christ. This union between Joseph and his brothers mirrors the reunion of Jesus Christ with His disciples after His resurrection. Jesus calmed their fears and restored their status as His disciples, especially Peter after his betrayal of Christ. He spent time with his disciples and ate with them to reconnect with them. He built into them again as they were beginning to see Him anew and true with eyes of the hearts that are being redeemed by the risen Savior. Joseph also made sure that they know that they are absolutely and completely and unconditionally loved and forgiven, so that they can finally forgive themselves. And here, we see a little glimpse of true heaven on earth, His Kingdom, that has come into the hearts of Joseph and his brothers.

The divine journey of redemption for Joseph and his brothers has finally reached its destination in the perfect love of God. God's timing has proven to be perfect once again. Even when the brothers doubted Joseph's love after Jacob's death, Joseph once again showed that his love for his brothers never wavered. They were finding themselves in the true love because now they can truly see God's eternal, global and foundational love for what it really is. God's thoughts are higher than our thoughts and His ways higher than our ways. His way is the supernatural and incomprehensible love that has been finally revealed to us in our Lord Jesus Christ... for all people, all the time. God has done it again! The journey has finally come to an end in true love and forgiveness by Joseph and all the brothers through the mysterious working of discipline and suffering that produced perseverance unto overflowing blessings of God's love. Joseph finally has reached that stratosphere of understanding where our hearts were created for the love of God to shine through AND to receive and share the same glorious love of God shining from one another and ALL people. And the glory of God is personified in our Lord Jesus Christ. This is exactly what Paul so powerfully articulates in 1 Timothy 2:1-5.

God desires this kind of glorious and perfect reconciliation in all of our lives in His good time. We don't know when it is going to happen but it *should* happen in our lifetime. Jesus Christ died for this glorious purpose of reconciliation in the body of Christ while we are here. This reconciliation does not just involve God and us. It involves rebuilding of that eternal bond in and among the body, the church, of Jesus Christ *between* each and every single one of us. Is this a new concept? No, not at all. But it sure sounds new, doesn't it? Is there someone in your life that you just can't bring yourself to forgive because what they did to you was not only unjustifiable but pure evil...as in the beginning of Joseph's journey? Is there someone in your life that you just can't bring yourself to ask for forgiveness because of your own pride or overwhelming guilt...like in the case of Judah and the brothers for a long time? Was there some misunderstanding that could not be overcome because of our self-righteousness? As we have gone through the journey of all the hearts through Joseph and Judah through this book, you have found yourself somewhere in the spectrum of redemption path between these two very contrasting individual journey of redemption orchestrated by God Himself. And the destination of their journeys as well as all of ours is One and the same: the unchanging, overwhelming and glorious redemption of our hearts and eternal reconciliation in our Lord, Jesus Christ, who died and rose for all.

But our journey is not over yet. In fact, it is really just beginning right now for us. You didn't think I would let you off the hook that easy, did you? But first, let us approach the throne of our God in deep gratitude and affection as we celebrate the true love and forgiveness of our Lord...in the next chapter.

Chapter 14

PRAYER OF INTERCESSION AND FORGIVENESS

Our Father in Heaven
Hollowed be Your name
Your Kingdom come
Your Will be done
On earth as it is in heaven
Give us today our daily bread... but wait
Here comes the part that I don't understand
A Divine mystery. Perhaps even a mistake?
Forgive us our debts
As we also have forgiven our debtors?

So I reasoned that unless
I forgive the ones from whom I took offenses
Then our Father in Heaven
Will not forgive my own offenses?
This is a hard teaching I said
Who can accept it?
The grace and the providence by the supreme authority
The inevitability of His coming Kingdom and the sovereignty of His Will
Only to be thwarted by this condition;
This contingency by which everyone will fail?

Then it all came back to me.
I was bound, I was lost, I was blind, I was undeserving.
Of all the reasons for His coming

First and last, He came so that I can be forgiven.
The only way that I can truly be free
The only way that I can truly be healed
From this bondage, this flesh, this sin.
That destroys, decays, that defiles
Was no less than God the omnipotent
To subjugate Himself, as the humble and perfect Son,
To His own exacting justice
To pay that terrible price on our behalf that He himself demanded
The mysterious juxtaposition of God's terrible justice and His incomparable love, the Cross!

As far as the east is from the west
Our sin has been removed from His presence
He was lifted up in ultimate humiliation
So that we can be lifted up in His ultimate glory
Through faith in Christ and in His works
We have become his sons and daughters
God's special possession, the royal priesthood
The rulers and intercessors of the Kingdom now and forever
This is His promise to us by the unchanging Word
But what, Lord, I asked again
Is the ultimate purpose for these blessings undeserved,
The glorious inheritance now and forever?

Then He said to me
First and last, I went through all that Hell so that you will love and forgive
Completely and always, unconditionally...but in My patient wisdom and timing
For my love on the Cross that you are beginning to understand
With all of its grace and mercy, all of its height and depth.
You will be compelled, yes, you will not have a choice
It will not even be a question, but rather a second nature.
If you have truly experienced my love and my forgiveness
This, "As we have forgiven our debtors, forgive us of our debts,"
Will be the core of your heart and prayer
For the redemption of My people
People just like you without Me
For the redemption of your own heart
Only one thing I require of you my son

156

To forgive seven times seventy
As surely as I, the Christ, abide in your heart
Forgive as I have forgiven you
Love as I have loved you
For that is the singular purpose for which I came
For you to grab a hold of that which
Caused the dawning of your eternal life in Me
Then, and only then, they will truly see Me through you

So that
Our Heavenly Father's name be exalted above all names
All other dominions and principalities that enslave our hearts be crushed
His Kingdom come
His will be done
In Me and I AM
In you

    I do not want to pray the same old prayer. I do not want to fight You for my own desires. I do not want to wrestle You but pray the new prayer and rest in Your everlasting power! I want to fight for Your Son Jesus Christ, who fought for me and for the world on the Cross and WON. I want to fight for the souls that you came to save, even if they would kill me for it because that is exactly what you did for me. You did it for ALL. If you had gone through all that Hell in order to save me, the undeserving and rebellious, then I must trust your reasons for wanting to save others like me, yes, even my enemies. I trust in your love and only your love truly saves… from ourselves. As much as Paul, who wrote half the New Testament, who still confessed his lack of knowledge of Your love, I confess now that I still don't know You well. I want to know Christ. I need to know Christ. I want to know His incomparable love that has taken hold of me for all eternity. In truth and love, I want to know who You are and all that You did for me to the fullest extent in all my knowledge, understanding, and most of all, actions motivated by your love that You yourself gave me with Your own blood. It is the love that surpasses all knowledge, power and wisdom. From Jesus Christ flows all true blessings and happiness…for my heart, which is designed by You for Yourself and for ALL Your people, including your humble servant.
    Amen

Chapter 15

THE CALL AND THE DUTY OF KINGS (AND QUEENS), THE CHURCH: THE DEFENDER OF THE WEAK

The Authority of the King over the kingdom of Babylon.

And the word of the Lord came again to Zechariah: "This is what the Lord Almighty said: 'Administer true justice; show mercy and compassion to one another. Do not oppress the widow or the fatherless, the foreigner or the poor. Do not plot evil against each other.'" Zechariah 7:8-10.

For the love of money is a root of all kinds of evil, for which some have strayed from the faith in their greediness, and pierced themselves through with many sorrows. 1 Timothy 6:10

*Give me five minutes with a person's checkbook (and credit card statements), and I will tell you where their **heart** is.—Billy Graham, an American crusader*

Then *Jesus* entered and passed through Jericho. Now behold, *there was* a man named Zacchaeus who was a chief tax collector, and he was rich. And he sought to see who Jesus was, but could not because of the crowd, for he was of short stature. So he ran ahead and climbed up into a sycamore tree to see Him, for He was going to pass that *way*. And when Jesus came to the place, He looked up and saw him, and said to him, "Zacchaeus, make haste and come down, for today I must stay at your house." So he made haste and came down, and received Him joyfully. But when they saw *it*, they all complained, saying, "He has gone to be a guest with a man who is a sinner." Then Zacchaeus stood and said to the Lord, "Look, Lord, I give half of my goods to the poor; and if I have taken anything from anyone by false accusation, I restore fourfold."

And Jesus said to him, "Today salvation has come to this house, because he also is a son of Abraham; for the Son of Man has come to seek and to save that which was lost." Luke 19:1-10

We have unknowingly looked down upon a person like this...even through some of the sermons that we have heard about this tax collector. But he is not so much different from you and me. In fact, he is doing better than any of us have ever done. Zacchaeus is truly doing the work of the King. His possessions were given up to God to help the poor. In the process, the glorious salvation of Jesus Christ has found Zacchaeus and his household for all eternity.

Contrary to what some may preach this passage as a message of repayment or restitution of **ill-gotten** gain, Jesus leveled the playing field throughout the Gospel by saying pretty much all of our hoarded treasures beyond the meeting of our basic needs are ill-gotten. Surprised? But do not fear...he has given us the way out and also not be yoked with the burden that we cannot bear. He also said he has given us the power to use the portion of our ill-gotten gain, which was gained through this fallen world — yes, it had no choice but to be tainted by the world — to glorify God! Even as a doctor, I must say that my possessions are ill-gotten because all the money I have earned must have passed the hands in this fallen world and got tainted before they came to me. Zacchaeus is doing the work of the King. He is helping the poor by giving up 50 percent of his possessions! Do we think we can do that? That truly is the work of the King. And we do not have to give 50 percent to do the work of the King as we shall see... He doesn't want to deprive us of the blessings that He himself has given. All that God requires is our heart that manifests itself in giving back of the true 10 percent of what God has given us. But it is not for Him. God doesn't really need it. He needs it because He can redistribute that returned portion of the wealth to support the weak and the neglected. He is testing our hearts through the command of giving up 10 percent for us to see whether we have truly experienced the magnificent, undeserving grace of Jesus Christ. He doesn't have to test our hearts to know them because he already knows our hearts even before a thought enters into them. But His testing of our hearts is to reveal what is in our hearts for our own benefit and redemption journey.

Our divine wisdom of Joseph in the King of all wisdom

As soon as Joseph became the most powerful ruler in Egypt, he went out immediately to do the work of the King. The gifts of the King forged and refined in the journey of suffering and expulsion of self love enabled him to administer true justice and show mercy with wisdom and compassion to all that he came across. We have to remember that God has been perfecting the heart of true justice in Joseph through the hope of true justice for all humanity that he could only find in God. We are no different than Joseph. When he rode throughout the land, people saw the power and wonder of God working through this once an abominable Hebrew slave. And he still is an abominable Hebrew but no longer a slave…but a king, who is better than 10 thousand Pharaohs in worth and weight. Do you think God was glorified by all in Egypt through Joseph? Yes, glorified and revered was God in the eyes of all Egyptians. While they still shunned Hebrews, they simply could not deny the saving power of God of Joseph. God of power was worshipped through the most unlikely and improbable person in the eyes of the Egyptians. That is true worship.

The books of the Minor Prophets, the last twelve books of the Old Testament, are full of prophecies that parallel the end time prophecies of the Revelation in the New Testament. They are also full of messianic prophecies about the coming of Jesus Christ, both the first and the second coming. The people that God is commanding with the above prophetic statement found in Zechariah 7 are the Israelites coming back from the 70 years of exile in the Babylonian kingdom. They were exiled because of their sins, mainly idolatry and sexual depravity, against God and each other. He is restoring them to their homeland and along with it, the authority to do the work of kings; that is the administration of justice, and the demonstration of mercy and compassion. As kings and queens of God's coming kingdom, which can very well come into your heart this very day, you are not only kings and queens by title or name only, but you have the power and authority of Christ the King to administer true justice and show mercy and compassion.

The first REVOLUTIONARY step of the KING according to Paul and James.

Paul was probably the most intellectual mind to ever walk the earth. He wrote half the New Testament. His defense of the Gospel on behalf of the Gentiles in the first Jerusalem meeting set the course of church history in a totally different direction than our church fathers, like James and John, had envisioned (Acts 15). We Gentiles (non-Jews) often take the precious gospel of Jesus Christ for granted as the universal free for all grace. But had it not been for likes of Paul, the same Gospel would have been off-limits to all Gentiles for ages...maybe even to this day. He was given the incredible revelations of Jesus Christ and all the spiritual gifts (yes, ALL spiritual gifts). In defense of sound mind and sound doctrine over that coveted mystical gift of tongue, he said he was glad that he could speak in tongues more than any of those who boasted such gifts. He not only had the gift of prophecies that brought understanding to all mysteries and knowledge, but the convictions to carry them out (1 Cor. 13:1-3). Oh yes...he was describing how *himself* would be without the perfect love of Christ in these verses. He had the gift of wisdom and knowledge, as they are evident throughout the Epistles (the books in the New Testament that he wrote). He was counted as one of the apostles. He had the gift of healing that was truly Christ-like in proportion (this is a representation of the "greater works" that Christ himself preached) (Acts 19:11-12)! He was persecuted, abandoned, struck down, and chained for advancing the gospel, the good news that Christ came to save all. He was powerful in speech (Acts 14:1, 14:12 and 17:16-31).

It is traditionally believed that Paul was not a good public speaker on account of his own confession. That's not true and contradicts everything we know about him through the New Testament. He was the one who was speaking nearly all the time when he and Barnabas went out in tandem to evangelize. Some of the people actually worshipped Paul as Hermes, the Greek god of speech and persuasion. He spoke before the philosophers. He persuaded the governors and the kings alike with such power of persuasion that instilled not only divine conviction, but fear! (Acts 24:25)

When he was "confessing" that he is not a good speaker, he was subtly being sarcastic in humility for the purpose of conviction. And everyone in the church of Corinth knew it. He said he was an untrained speaker (2nd Cor. 11:6), or persuader, in order to prick the conscience of the people at the church in the city of Corinth because they may not have been willing to give the offering that they had initially promised him; not for Paul's use but for the poor churches in need. Paul was supporting himself in his ministries as well as others in need! He used this "divine sarcasm" to make his point every now and then...even encouraging some of the circumcisers (those that insisted on being circumcised in order to be saved) to go all the way and emasculate themselves! (Galatians 5:12)

But with all these incredible gifts and the revelations, Paul was also given the thorn in his flesh to be constantly reminded of the weakness of the flesh. He knew that the thorn was given by God to keep the pride out of his heart and keep him humble. When the flesh was strong, then the flesh will use all of these gifts we have, yes...even the incredible divine gifts and revelations, for its own self glorification and elevation at the expense of other souls. Paul knew that to be true better than anyone (2nd Cor. 12:1-10). It is this same Paul who found himself complete and sufficient in the love of Christ. Paul wrote about the love of Christ more than any of the apostles. The all famous LOVE Chapter 1st Corinthian 13 was written by Paul, a single, never-married man with the power of self-control in the Lord.

In the middle of this love chapter, Paul says something strange and seemingly out of context with the rest of the "love" passage. He said, *"When I became a man, I put the ways of childhood behind me."* All the things that are being listed in the 1st Corinthians 13 are **not** the list of love does this or love does that. They are character attributes of our Lord Jesus Christ. When you substitute the word "Love" with "Jesus", you will understand this chapter. Go ahead please. Read like, "Jesus is patient. Jesus is kind..." When you truly find yourself in the love of Christ, you will see everything more clearly (like an adult, not like a child). You will begin to truly think and act like kings and queens and not like immature children. **If you are truly being sanctified by the Lord, the litmus test that you are getting closer to your true divine destiny in Him is the manifestation of the love and forgiveness of Jesus Christ, as in the life of Joseph, in your own life.** And there is a **first, most urgent and most fundamental step** that you must take in order to begin this process of sanctification by the truth in order to reach your God-given destiny of royal priesthood: God's love and justice. This first step is the singular, the most important reason why I began writing this book. No amount of theology, gifts or conviction will set you on that path of true divine ascension in the eyes of God unless you take this first step. What is this first revolutionary step of the King? The Lord gave us no other choice. Let's find out through Paul, shall we?

In Acts Chapter 20:13-38, Paul is saying goodbye to the Ephesian church elders. It was a heart heavy and sorrow filled goodbye and everyone wept because they all knew that Paul will soon be on the journey of no return. Paul's heart was torn to pieces. These are the brothers that would die alongside Paul but this divine journey of glorious suffering was reserved specifically for Paul. His love for them was truly great because his love was like the love of our Lord. Wasn't Paul the only one out of the entire Bible who said, "Imitate me, as I imitate Christ?" Paul said they will never see his face again and their hearts were broken. In the love of Christ; the love that was forged and refined in his heart by unspeakable suffering and pain, Paul delivers the most gentle but revolutionary message at the very end of this farewell. It is not only an encouragement, but the very last request of this highly esteemed man of God on his way to final series of suffering and the eventual martyrdom. Turn with me to Acts 20: 32-35. Now, WATCH and LISTEN.

> *Now I commit you to God and to the word of his grace, which can build you up and give you an inheritance among all those who are sanctified. I have not coveted anyone's silver or gold or clothing. You yourselves know that these hands of mine have supplied my own needs and the needs of my companions. In everything I did, I showed you that by this kind of hard work we must help the weak, remembering the words the Lord Jesus himself said: "It is more blessed to give than to receive."*

Please remember that Paul could have said anything in this short crucial time that he was given. With all of his wealth of knowledge, all of his unmatched spiritual gifts and all of his surpassing revelations in Christ, he could have said something *magnificent* and most *edifying* that they will take away and remember him for a long time. Well, he didn't ask them to remember him but to never forget the forgotten ones that Christ came to save. Instead of expounding upon some theological precepts or unraveling the most mysterious revelations of Christ, he addressed the most urgent need that we the Church, then and now, must act upon! He put the exclamation mark to his farewell by pleading with the elders to fulfill their duties as kings of God's kingdom. The first step of the kings and queens of God's kingdom is that we must, and I say again, **we MUST help the weak,** remembering the words the Lord Jesus himself said: "It is more blessed to give than to receive." The first revolutionary step that we must take as kings and queens of God's kingdom is that **we MUST support the weak.**

Here is the divine order of things. We must help the weak first materially and financially, and then, and only then, can we address their spiritual needs. Otherwise, all of our words become empty and without power. We have to be the kings first before we can be the priests in Christ. And their spiritual needs are the same as ours, which is the love of Christ through forgiveness first and last. If the order is reversed or neglected, the weak may not find their way to our Lord at all...certainly not by us! If their physical needs are not met by us, their hearts will not be moved by our testimony of Christ. Our Gospel will be rendered ineffective if we fail to help and reach out to the needy; first in the Church, then the world. We cannot say that we believe in God of impartiality and God of justice when we discriminate against or neglect the poor, especially in the Church as James expounds continuously and repeatedly in his letter! And we cannot and must not discriminate against certain race or gender or people of certain background or nation. If we see certain Christians being persecuted in certain nations, we must not discriminate them in our minds and divert our resources elsewhere.

Apostle James strongly warns against such hypocrisy and says "I will show you my faith by my works." First, we have to redefine this pervasive but often misunderstood concept of "It is not religion but relationship." When we project our own ideas of relationship to this statement, then all kinds of false theologies emerge from it. Only God can teach you how to have a true and loving relationship that will last for all eternity. In order to learn what eternal relationship really is and what it means to us, we have to learn from Christ, the author of all relationships. And how did he teach us about "relationship"? He taught us about relationship by dying for us, who were undeserving of such generous gift of eternal relationship and inheritance. We are NOT commanded to help the poor because they DESERVE our help. If we love someone because they deserved to be loved in our eyes, then none of us would be loved the way we are being loved by God. In fact, none of us will come to know how to really love PERIOD. Just as much as we needed that amazing, undeserved grace for forgiveness of our sins in order that we can be saved and have eternal life with Christ, there are many out there who desperately need this "undeserving" help to break the cycle of poverty, neglect, dehumanization and deprivation. If we do not do that, how can we say that we have truly experienced the amazing grace of God that we did not deserve? Here is the divine order of royal-priesthood. Like Joseph in the story, we must fulfill the duty of the king first in order to demonstrate the intercessory power of the priest: the true power of love and forgiveness in Jesus Christ to our brothers and sisters first, and then, to all people.

For our salvation to be God's amazing grace, we had to be so undeserving...and we were. That same amazing grace is truly seen and understood for what it is only if the receiver of that grace is undeserving. We must help the poor and the most neglected PRECISELY because they are UNDESERVING. Here is our opportunity to take the first step to be like Christ to one another. We help them because they have nothing to do with us but everything to do with God's predestined destiny in them...just like us. And it is not only the desire of our God, but His mandate, for us to be the hands and feet of Christ for them. We, the Christ followers, are the physical manifestation of Christ in His absence. The grace of God cannot be seen or manifested in any other way. Our divine destiny orchestrated by our Savior Christ was designed to impart that same saving power to others.

So, it is not about religion but relationship. Yes, that is absolutely true. But the foundation of that relationship is the undeserved grace that compels us to love the undeserving (just like us) by the love of Christ, and to embrace the true religion of James 1:27:

Religion that God our Father accepts as pure and faultless is this: to look after orphans and widows in their distress and to keep oneself from being polluted by the world.

If we are being purified by the word, we will see God for who He really is: that He is the provider and the defender of the most neglected of our society...in us and through us, his children who are his kings and queens in His kingdom. He is the defender of the weak. We once were weak and lost. We were undeserving. We still are undeserving kings and queens for this very purpose of helping those who are undeserving in our eyes. Please... God will not be mocked. He will see right through us.

Before we start this practice of giving, however, we need the wisdom of Joseph to execute God's justice, love and mercy in the manner that will maximize the distribution of God-given wealth, and truly glorify God. We can clearly see how God himself forged that very wisdom in Joseph. This is not as hard as we think. His yolk is easy and his burden is light. His redemption task builds up our own souls, but the world wants our souls in exchange for the wealth that will destroy our souls. The LOVE of money is a root of all evil. But the money itself, even the ill-gotten (Jesus said) and dirty money from the likes of Zacchaeus the tax collector or any of us, can be redeemed for God's glory. As I said earlier, Jesus said pretty much all of our money is ill-gotten if you had acquired much more than you ever needed in this fallen world (and God will be glorified through our ill-gotten money today if your heart is being redeemed by the Lord).

Wisdom of saving and generous giving before the over-whelming blessings from the Giver.

In Chapter 41 of Genesis, Joseph collected a fifth of the harvest during the first seven years of plenty. Now, this 20 percent of the harvest was to be kept in reserve for the entire country and NOT individually. That collection of grain belonged to the Pharaoh because Pharaoh himself commissioned Joseph to build the storehouses. What does this all mean? The tithing, or the 10 percent of your income that belongs to the Lord, is the basic required offering. It is the demonstration of your gratitude and understanding that you are simply giving back to the Lord the 10 percent of all that the Lord has given you. But in essence, all the money that you have and all that is in the world belong to the Lord. God says, the gold is mine and the silver is mine. Offering is the reminder that you should let go of that 10 percent, acknowledging that the Lord is in control of your wealth in the first place. It is the Lord who gave you the talents, gifts and the opportunities to create wealth that you have now. Now, I'm not going to *bracketize* anyone here. Every one's financial situation is different. On paper you may be making more than 95 percent of the people in this country. But if you have 4 or more kids, that changes the game as far as your ability to save. But if you cannot save 20 percent of your income no matter how much you make — 10 percent minimum for the Lord and 10 percent minimum for emergency fund (not just for you but for all of God's people, especially your family) — you may be living above your means. And that *living above the means* will break your bank quickly and overnight with one "unlucky break" or one "mistake in judgment" or any of the unforeseen events or tragedies happening to your loved ones or to you.

It is not the low income that prevents us from saving. If you abide in the Lord, the Lord said, do not worry about what you will eat, drink or wear. He will provide for you He says. *But seek ye first the kingdom of God, the Lord said, and all these thing shall be added unto you* (Matthew 6:33) because as kings and queens of his kingdom, we have much more important, higher and eternal things to worry about than our temporary physical needs. If you work hard for your boss as unto the Lord as Joseph did during his time of trial, He will bless you and your family will be provided for. And we must realize that it is the indulgent, living above-the-means lifestyle that will bring your financial situations to ruin, NOT the low income. God stands behind His words.

If you abide in the Lord, you will be able to save at least 20 percent of your income. Again, 10 percent for the Lord and 10 percent for God's people (including yourself). I perceive, however, that most of the Christians in this country do not give 10 percent to the Lord, let alone save 10 percent! This calls for our repentance before the Lord and the lifestyle change. If our desire was to live the life full and abundant in the Lord, don't you think the Lord, who is in control of everything, will bless you beyond measure? But if it is your desire to find fulfillment and abundance outside of Christ, then you will be left to the devices and whims of the power and the principalities in the world that are much smarter and stronger than you. Those powers in the world will lure you to take your money and soul, and you will be left to wonder why all these smart, creative people of the world who don't believe in God or Christ are so rich while we are so poor? We will find ourselves in this kind of spiritual confusion when we strive towards the things of darkness in this dark fallen world. We are often confused because we do not understand God who gives us all things in His time so that we can know He is God, and that only He can truly provide. Most of the unbelieving people of the world who are very rich do not see God because their wealth has become their god. And their hearts and souls are in turmoil. If our hearts and minds are constantly running after the wealth of the world, we are seeking the very thing that will replace God in our lives. And God will withhold that thing from you — that wealth, that someone special, that dream job or whatever else — because He loves you. He will not see your life come to ruin! Again, your heart has the heart of the King so you should concern yourself with the things of the heavenly Kingdom...not where your next meal is going to come from or who's got the new 4 bedroom house or that brand new sports car. They are blessings, yes, but they can never be our obsession or the idols to replace God in our hearts.

Two things I ask of you, Lord; do not refuse me before I die: Keep falsehood and lies far from me; give me neither poverty nor riches, but give me only my daily bread. Otherwise, I may have too much and disown you and say, "Who is the Lord?" Or I may become poor and steal, and so dishonor the name of my God. Proverbs 30:7-9

Now, this passage clearly states that God desires to give you enough that we will not dishonor him but not too much that we will replace Him with the wealth that He Himself has given us. But we may say, "There are plenty of examples of overflowing richness and abundance throughout the Bible. What about Abraham? What about King David? Who can forget about Solomon? What about the miracle of feeding the 5000 men, not including women and children, with five loaves and two fish? I used to believe for a long time that the over-abundant material blessings are an integral part or even the undeniable sign from the Lord that I was walking with the Lord. Nothing could be further from the truth.

You have to understand that in all these examples, the wealth and abundance and the blessings all came from the desires to pursue righteousness in the Lord and to pursue the love of the Lord our God for ALL of God's people, not just the person in question. The reason for abundance in our blessing reflects God's desire for us to dispense and distribute that wealth to as many as possible. That is the lesson of five loaves and two fish. That is the lesson of all of God's stories regarding abundant blessings throughout the Bible!

If your desire was to give more than 10 percent to the Lord, your action is already speaking for yourself that your possessions truly belong to God and His people. Your action of giving is the reflection of your desire for God and His kingdom for all of God's people. The percentage of your offering is inversely related to how much of your wealth has taken a hold of your heart and not God. Do we think God actually needs anything from us? Why would a loving God, who sent his Son to die for you, command you to give 10 percent and save the other 10 percent if it wasn't really for you? He is not petty and He will not be mocked. And He does not want us to turn into a laughingstock in the eyes of the world! God will honor you and will not put you to shame if you honor Him with your first fruit: the true 10 percent.

If we have the mindset of God in control of all wealth and possessions; God has already blessed you and secured your divine destiny in Christ now and in that glorious rich heaven, then we give because we trust in the love of the Lord and His loving command for all people for all eternity, NOT because we are seeking to be wealthy and self-glorified in this temporary fallen world. And that's exactly why God blesses certain godly individuals financially because their motivation for giving generously was not obtaining financial wealth to begin with. They are not seeking to be secure in the gifts itself but they already know that they are more than secure, more than conquerors in the Giver of all gifts! Anything extra is just an icing on the cake that is already so magnificent that it doesn't really need any more icing. To such godly individuals, God will give generously beyond their expectations, because these individuals have significantly less probability of spending the blessings outside of the will of God in the first place. They know that outside of the will of the loving God, no amount of wealth, power or pleasure in this fleeting, dark, deceiving and temporary world will make them happy. All these things, tainted by sins, will only make them empty, miserable and without meaning in this meaningless life. If we have understood all this, then this passage of great blessings below will finally make sense. We can all aspire to be free from the ultimate entrapment: the love of money that is a root of all evil, and freely give them up to God. And God can finally bless us like crazy because He knows we will not enjoy the blessings outside of Him and His people.

"Will a mere mortal rob God? Yet you rob Me.

"But you ask, 'How are we robbing you?'

*"In tithes and offerings. You are under a curse—your whole nation—because you are robbing me. Bring **the whole tithe** into the storehouse, **that there may be food in my house.** Test me in this," says the Lord Almighty, "and see if I will not throw open the floodgates of heaven and pour out so much blessing that there will not be room enough to store it. I will prevent pests from devouring your crops, and the vines in your fields will not drop their fruit before it is ripe," says the Lord Almighty. "Then all the nations will call you blessed, for yours will be a delightful land," says the Lord Almighty. Malachi 3:8–12*

God warns the people, through Malachi the prophet, to abstain from marriage outside of God's people and offering up defective, left over animals for sacrifices. To us, this last book of the Old Testament serves as a mirror for the 21st century America. Sexual sins outside of marriage between a man and a woman, and neglecting the poor and the oppressed (including the lack of money offering to the Lord by us the Christ followers) dominates the culture of our nation today. Before we can address any issues of society or problems/sins in the world, we must address the most basic fundamental needs of the people. Was God angry because He was short on cash for Himself due to the lack of offering or because certain people were neglected and oppressed in His people because of the lack of offering? We all know the answer to that question. If all of us were to tithe, yes just 10 percent to the cause of Christ to help the weak and poor, there will be no poor in the Church Period. That is the promise of God in the passage from Malachi 3. But because there are so many people in need in the global Church, I must conclude that we as the Church are no where near giving our true 10 percent back to our God for redistribution!

True 10 percent given by all of us in the Church, the body of Christ, will effectively remove the poor in the Church and evangelize the people of the world even before we speak a word about Jesus. God is telling us to test Him. This is a fearsome saying, I must say. If we read the Malachi passage carefully, this passage is not really about individual blessings as much as the global Church wide and nation wide financial blessings for all to partake in, so that ALL the people around us will see that God truly is the ultimate provider for His people! And ALL will give the glory to God. This great nation was founded upon the Constitution forged in the hearts of our founding forefathers who were also men of deep faith in Christ our God. When we love God and His people through our money, the people of this nation will see the love of Christ in the Church. They will begin to abandon the notion of hypocritical Christians. They will begin to see the true love of Christ in us and through us. Our tithing out of love will trigger the floodgates of heaven to open and allow us to enjoy all of God's overabundant blessing in love for one another. When the world sees that, they are being evangelized. They will *want* to know our Lord Jesus Christ, Who is responsible for all of our blessings. They will call us blessed and they would want to be a part of what we have: the love of Christ for ALL people culminating in abundant blessings of God both physically and spiritually.

Now, many of you are already giving 10 percent and even more, and I thank God for you from the bottom of my heart. Why am I thanking you? Even though you don't know me, you have given up the portion of your God's blessings back to God. And God will use it to bless His people. If I ever find myself in a dire financial situation, part of your love offering will find its way to me somehow by God's mysterious power and it will not only bless me but revive me. Again, God does not want you to give up 50 percent. God knows exactly what you need and what you is need is never more than 90 percent of what God has given you. And many of us living in this country, including myself, have been truly blessed. Our 90 percent is much more than what we need. Has any of the kings or emperors of the ancient world has seen the kind of array of food and travel options that we as the first world people, especially in the US, are enjoying — and complaining at the same time — right now? We live better than the kings of old. We shouldn't look at all of our millionaire friends and be dissatisfied with what we don't have in comparison. We really need to see what we have been blessed with already. It just may be that lack of gratitude for His continuous overflowing grace from our Lord that is causing us to hold on to what God commanded us to give away. Brothers and sisters in Christ, I implore you.

We need to start thinking more creatively and wisely about giving so that we can give even more. Not for God — He doesn't need it — but for His people. And we must keep in mind that we cannot bring to the altar of God our leftovers or surplus after calculating all the write-offs and deductions. We have to make this offering a priority, the first fruits of our labor. Just set it aside with love and forget that it ever belonged to you. And He will bless you by opening up the floodgates of Heaven.

Act of giving through our children for their own divine destiny.

If our tithing is 10 percent to your local church and that's our conviction, please continue to do so as long as your local church is the Christ loving and God fearing church founded on the sound doctrine of the Bible. But even then, you **must** still do your research as to where all of your money is going and how it is being used. You must keep your church accountable and make sure that most of the money is going into the advancement of the gospel and meeting of the physical needs of the people so that they can tangibly feel the love of Christ in their hearts. And those of you who are not tithing but who is now really motivated to tithe now, I urge you to do your research with all due diligence. Trust me that this will be the most significant thing that you will ever do this year. It is the highest duty of the King. God gave you the money to give away so that you will know the joy of giving. If you do not know where that money is going, then your joy will not be complete. The organization's first priority must be the advancement of the Gospel of Jesus Christ for the salvation of our souls. There are many mission organizations, both local and international, and small Christian ministries advancing the love of Christ and His salvation in the poorest neighborhoods across our nation. Go ahead and pick three after careful research and contemplations in prayer. The ones that are dear to my heart are Christian urban youth ministries active in poverty stricken areas. But there are whole array of ministries and programs ranging from rescuing sex traffic victims to single moms struggling to make ends meet. And I strongly encourage you to get your children involved in the whole process of researching all these organizations for which you can potentially be a financial partner for a long term. If you have never been involved in this kind of endeavor with your children...it will move their hearts. They will say, "What's going on with Mommy and Daddy? We've never seen them so passionate about something. This is...kinda cool." Do this before they grow older. Do it today, in fact. We don't know what's going to happen tomorrow.

If the Christian charity organization of your choice appears to advance the gospel and puts the salvation in Christ as the cornerstone of all of their programs, then you have found a good place to start. Do not go by the size of their programs or their reputation in the secular world. Start by donating small, like 10 dollars a month. 10 dollars? Yes. The reason why you start small is mainly two fold. **Number one**, it is so easy that you won't even feel it. And that particular organization may have needed your money 2 months ago as opposed to 2 years from now when you will finally "feel" like you are ready to give 100 or even 1000 dollars a month. Guess what? That kind of ideal mentality, or road paved with good intention, almost never works. We tend to be very forgetful people...especially when it comes to money. **Number two**, you don't really know your organizations well at the beginning. Do your research and get to know the board of directors, the affiliated foundations, the program directors, paid staff and especially the volunteers. I highly recommend you going to one of these programs in the neighborhood and even volunteer if you can. And I recommend talking to the mentors/volunteers as well as people being loved and reached out to. Try to make your contributions relational as much as you can! There are many good organizations and missions out there, but every once in a while, you will come across a scam. We don't ever want to be victims to such evil organizations. All of the research efforts through literature materials and personal interactions/participation may serve as the redemption journey of our own hearts.

Please don't forget that they are people and not a charity case. God loves them as much as God loves you and me. However, please use your judgment and be safe first. Volunteering is my recommendation, not a command from the Lord. As you continue to do your research, one organization may stand out from the rest or you may like all three because they all practice what they preach on paper and on the web. After 3 months of research — that's giving 10 dollars for 3 months — pick one, two or all of them and increase the giving amount to whatever the Lord has been telling you in these three months. At the end of your 3 months of trial, you can complete your monthly tithing by including the organization(s) of your choice to your offering. Trust me, you are in for some incredible and heart-revealing, redemptive conversation between you and the Lord in that 3 months. The Lord will reveal to you that the amount is definitely larger than 10 dollars a month, which is just a Chinese take out for one person. Again, no one will ever know but the Lord who is in control of all things and the Giver of all secret gifts will. And He will reward you for what you have done. Please do not forget about the international mission organizations, especially in the Middle East and other countries where Christians are being persecuted.

I believe that God will give you a number for each of these organizations. And your giving is a part of what powers these organizations: the hands and feet of Christ to the oppressed, abused, neglected and poor. Your mind will become more sensitized by the Holy Spirit for you to discern which organization really needs more of your money and which organizations are ineffective or possibly fraud. We need to be cunning like snakes even when it comes to loving with the money that the Lord has entrusted to us. Again, the salvation of souls through Christ must be their first and ultimate goal. And the organizations must meet the physical and spiritual needs of the targeted population. You should ask, "Do they have some kind of metric system to keep track of the progress of the population they are reaching out to? Do they have organized follow up and the record system? What kind of long term goals and visions do they have for the people and the organization itself?" If it is urban youth ministry or rescue mission, you may ask, "How effective is the organization in equipping the students to carry their Christian value and work ethic into school and beyond?" It's all about teaching one to fish and not just handing them fish continually… as they say. It's about nurturing and equipping them physically, mentally and spiritually so that they can not only become productive members of the society but strong men of women of Christ who will in turn train and equip the next generation likewise or even more effectively! If it is a shelter program of some kind, you can ask, "Are there compassionate counselors and volunteers who can make them see that God truly is the protector of our souls and there is no need to fear?" How are they being moved or displaced? These are some of the sample questions. Again, it's all about the organizations' ability to nurture and equip the populations they serve with the true gift of physical blessings, knowledge, wisdom, and most importantly, love that is only found in Jesus Christ! Certainly, most of us have been creative on the job and the market place, haven't we? Why not bring our creative business and intellectual minds into God's kingdom? Let us be shrewd like snakes when it comes to being righteous and generous in the Lord… for the sake of the most neglected in our society and also for our children.

We have neglected our creativity and efforts in this area too long, but I believe in you. As you do your research, the Lord will help you to ask the right questions. And as always, get your children involved as much as you can. The fate of our future generation may depend on this simple act of beginning to reach out to the poor and neglected because this is the most simple and basic mandate that Christ himself and all of his disciples, especially James and Paul, preached. This is the first duty of the King that makes us kings and queens. And you will begin to feel the love of our King Jesus Christ powering through you, not only for these people but for your children and your whole family. It is the trigger point to His kingdom and His heaven come! There is absolutely no other way. As our beloved brother Paul's last request to the Church, this is the first step in showing and proving our love to be genuine and eternal in Christ.

Children imitate their parents. Even though the world may deceive us and say the adults no longer have real power over children, you still have the divine authority to be their parents. Not all fathers or mothers act like parents but it's about time that we claim this divine destiny of being the parents and exercise the authority of the king and queen of true justice in our families...starting with our children. It doesn't matter if you were once a wayward teenager or even a drug/alcohol addict who lost the respect of your peers and even your own children long time ago. The authority of the parenting, again, is given to you. You did not deserve it. None of us know what we are doing when we become parents. I'm a single person and yet, I know this to be the absolute, unchanging truth when it comes to parenting.

What we need to do, however, is to repent before God and make sure that our children know our genuine desire to change. The fate of their souls may depend on this simple gesture of transparency and authenticity by you before God and them. God will certainly see you through. If your children do not want to participate in these activities, please do not force them but try to figure out why they don't want to. It is not their money that you are investing into these kingdom projects. It is your money that God gave you. So the issue is not the money for them. It is not the project itself either. You may be surprised to find that children actually like the idea of helping people. Well, I was being just a little sarcastic there for your benefit. Of course they do!

Nevertheless, you should just gently encourage them and try to let them know how the research is going on your end...give them an update every once in a while to see if that would maybe change their minds but please...don't demand. When children do not respond in kind to this type of noble gesture or invitation, there is a deep reason why they don't want to. And the main reason, I hate to say this, may be us...not who we want to be for them but who we have been knowingly and more often unknowingly. So, you must suffer through their defiance and persist even though their cooperation is not very forthcoming,and know that you are trying to change that very thing that caused them to arrive at this point of rebellion in the first place. In the meantime pray that the Lord will show you the wisdom to identify the potential frictional and problem areas in your life. Get into the prayer groups and Bible studies and find a mature loving Christian mentors or older brothers/sisters who can really guide you in truth and love of Jesus Christ. We all need to redeem our hearts in the Lord first, as I have been writing all along. We need to come before our God, the giver and provider of all of our treasures — especially our children — on our knees and ask for His divine wisdom that will save our children in spite of who we have been or who we will never be as parents. Whether it was caused by time not spent, emotions not shared, or spiritual life lessons not taught (all because we were too either busy pursuing our own dreams or pursuing our dreams through them and driving them mad without really figuring out what their true divine destiny in Christ might be), they have a cause or reason to behave this way. Please know that none of us are perfect. We all make mistakes. And even if you have been a mess of a parent, it's not too late to change but you CHANGE by obeying this simple, fundamental step commanded by the King who gave you your family. You must first show them by example that you are willing to support the weak and poor as the Lord commanded.

And please pray. Again, all of our journeys, even as a king or a queen, begin on our knees. You need to learn how to love in Christ again. No one's beyond redemption as long as that person is breathing! God can make your family whole again! And our children will eventually come to understand our true intentions and be proud of us and we just may have planted that divine seed of redemption in their hearts as well. And guess what? We may eventually win the respect of everyone around us! And we shall REJOICE.

If your teen is just straight up, downright rebellious and beyond "redemption", then again, we can all get on our knees and pray first. Why couldn't the disciples drive out those demons? They did not fast and pray enough Jesus said. If you can't get them to obey, they are past the age for spanking anyway. Just persist in doing good and God will take care of the rest for your family. Please don't yell, or get angry with them. Show them...in the love of Christ. Lead them...to the love of Christ. And know that God of love for all people is in control all the time. Get in the Word and pray consistently...to remind yourself that **God of love in total control** is our eternal reality and the destiny of your children. He has to be! Please let them go...into the hands of the Almighty loving Father! We must show our acts of kindness and generosity to the weak and the oppressed in the Church and have our children see us doing the acts of the King of love and be the kings to all.

For those of you whose children are not only willing, but enthusiastic about participating in such a noble endeavor, God bless you. You have raised them well. Meek and gentle children can be gently volunteered by parents...and that counts, and certainly the children who were raised with the loving — not angry — rod (a small stick, NOT your hand or any other instrument) of correction at early age will turn out well. That is the promise of God through Proverbs 13, 22 and 29. Do not raise them in anger but in truth and love of Jesus Christ. Don't wait until they are 6 or 7 to apply that loving rod of discipline. Now, get them involved in the act of giving as much as possible and feel the ultimate grace, love and power of our God as He is building the foundation of the Church in your family. The Church starts with the family. Let the love of Jesus Christ be revealed to you in all of its glory and power through these kingdom investment journeys. Christianity is NOT about trying hard not to sin, but being filled with the Spirit, and God's glory and power with sacrificial giving, spiritually, emotionally, and most importantly, financially. The sacrificial giving in the Lord for the souls of His people will eventually drive out all the evil and sin in our lives; for the love of money is a root of all evil. Let your children see you as you are truly becoming kings and queens in His eyes.

Out of all the things that you can do as a king or a queen of God's kingdom starting from this point forward, helping the poor financially in Christ is the most important thing you can do. Again, our esteemed brother Paul, unmatched in revelations of Jesus our Lord, said, "We MUST support the weak." There is no question as to what we must do. If we, the undeserving, have truly experienced God's amazing forgiveness through the Cross and believe in our unbelievable blessings of promise here and in heaven, then you have no choice but to give that same kind of overwhelming and generous grace to the undeserving, the oppressed, the neglected and the abused. The Lord came to save them too, and their destiny or destination is not so different from us in Christ. Some of us need to really meditate on THAT, I believe. The first way you help them is to be faithful in your tithes/contributions first. That 10 percent of your money belongs to God and His people. And it must be the first fruit. It is the true 10 percent as your conscience is guided by the Spirit. There is no point in deceiving God. The Lord weighs our hearts. And for those of you who have been giving 10 percent or more for all these years without fail, God's blessings will continue to flow for you. And we should always do our research to find out exactly where that money is going or how it is used in order to experience the redemptive power of God working through the money. Sit down with your children on a regular basis to do this. And reassess the organizations or ministries that you are giving to every 3 months. It will make your joy complete. We should get our children involved in this endeavor as much as possible and lead them by example. Don't just hand them 5 dollars on Sunday morning and be satisfied. That is not love. Let us make this a family tradition and they will love us and respect us forever. It will fundamentally change our family dynamics and trigger a movement that this nation has never seen before. We BELIEVE in the promise of God that will revolutionize our hearts.

Notice that I did not say that we should first get our children to receive Christ into their hearts. We must help them see Christ in us first! Then and only then we will know exactly WHO they are receiving into their hearts.

Let the kingdom of Babylon fall so that the Kingdom of God may come... in our hearts and the lives of our children.

Through our generous, sacrificial giving, God will bless all of His people so that the world will see that our God truly is the provider of overwhelming blessing. I believe in you because our Lord saved you for this very purpose: that we should be like Christ to all people! I pray that we will demonstrate the power of the King by proving to everyone that we love the Lord more than anything, including our money. We have heard the phrase, "Sex sells." Just like money, sex itself is not a sin. Sex was meant to be enjoyed in the context of the holy matrimony between a man and a woman. But when we take the divine blessings such as money or sex out of its divine context, that's when the blessings in our lives become sins of entrapment, bondage and strongholds. If the humanity did not love the money so much, there would not be such widespread, pervasive sins of sexual depravity in the America and the world. Pornography and sex-slave trafficking are being sustained and fueled by the love of money by individuals who gave their souls to the evil of money. The lust of the flesh has always been there. But these evil individuals have used our lust to profit greatly at the expense of our hearts and our children! And in this era of globalization through the media and the internet, the love of money, that root of all evil, has found an unprecedented power to wield, abuse, defile and destroy all things political, social and spiritual. Many people, who would not have succumbed to such evil of sexual depravity before all this globalization to bring about global economic "prosperity", have fallen and are falling in and outside of the Church...and all over the place. Just look at the divorce rate in the Church today. Look at all the broken relationships that have their roots in some sexual baggage or bondage that was the result of the love of money at the very beginning!

We can't let the love of our money control us. It will only bring misery and all kinds of bondage and sins...and it already has. It will surely destroy our future generations. Are we saving a little too eagerly for our children? They will not benefit from it. We need to use and give our money to the eternal cause of Jesus Christ, who is the only One who can truly save their souls. And in the process, our own hearts will be redeemed. We have the love and authority of Jesus Christ over everything including our money. The generous show of love offering, intelligently and diligently researched and the Spirit led, is the most urgent duty we have to fulfill as kings and queens. Listen, I'm well off...I don't need your money. God certainly doesn't. But our money was given to us by God to be more than we need specifically for such a time and place that we are living in. 10 percenters, are we listening? This is especially for the 10 percenters. I'm a 10 percenter myself so I have 3 fingers pointing right back at me. And the rest of us are not excused either because God has already given you enough so that you can give back at least 10 percent. Your children is looking at you and looking up to you. What are we going to do? Are we going to be passive and see the annihilation and self-destruction of our future generations because we have failed to act now? This issue of lack of proper and generous giving is more important issue than any of the other pressing issues of our days. Dealing with everything else, such as the problems of abortions, sexual immorality outside of marriage, homosexuality, teen pregnancy, violence or any kind of idolatry in our lives, will just have to take a back seat. Why? The love of money is a root of all these evil, that's why. We must strike the evil shepherd that nurtures and feeds all these evil in our hearts. How can we now say that we have experienced the undeserving and surpassing love of Christ if we don't?

In the book of Revelation Chapter 18:9-24, there is a great revelation of a dark and mysterious, spiritual city called Babylon that has continuously built herself up to be a great global financial empire (Please read the passages now). It is obvious as you read through these passages that the economy of the whole world has come to depend on her system for creating and sustaining material wealth. And we find, among many verses, especially in the last verse, that this spiritual city or *system* throughout all human history is responsible for all the blood of the prophets and the saints as well as ALL who have been slain. What does this all mean? It will be made very obvious to all of us as we read the passages the second time that this city that killed all the prophets and saints as well as all the people who are slain — as in war and not in natural death — is not necessarily a physical city or kingdom at any point in history but the love of money that fueled the rise of such great financial and economic empire!

This spiritual city is called the mystery and the mother of all harlots (Revelation 17 and 18). In the passage, the city is drunk with the blood of all the saints of Jesus Christ. The city is causing all the kings and all the people of the earth to be drunk with the wine of her fornication. The wine of her fornication is the love of money where all the kings and the people of the earth have fornicated and prostituted themselves. If any of you reading this book is in charge of a company or an office, and wealthier than 99 percent of America, you know from your experience that money has a mysterious way of revealing and infecting the hearts of the people. Am I right? Money has a mysterious way of ensnaring and subjugating people like nothing else on the planet. That is why this city is called the MYSTERY in the book of Revelation.

People will sell their bodies and souls to get rich and many of you wealthy powerful men and women have witnessed this first hand. Perhaps you yourself have become this citizen of Babylon and didn't even know it...until now. The insidious and mysterious power of money has the vice grip on the heart of this nation and beyond. All of us, and especially the wealthy — because you have the power given by God for such a time as this — to properly redistribute the wealth that God has given us. The Lord abhors dishonest scales. Are we being dishonest with our money in the marketplace because we love money more than our souls or the souls of other people? We need to STOP...lest we desire to face His judgment before our time. Are you being dishonest with your employees and holding back the money that is consistent with their efforts and productivity? You need to start paying them more and reverse this economic down turn. Don't let your hoarded possessions and money become a festering pool of self-decay of your souls and the souls of this nation. You will be absolutely miserable if you fail to understand this. For many of you, hearts of all those that desire to associate with you and the hearts that you want to be associated with are bound by the bondage of the glory of money and nothing more. They love you and you love them NOT because of who you really are but only because of the money you have. Your life has been defined by the money you have and nothing more. You already know this. There is no worse feeling of betrayal or emptiness than the reality of our hearts bound in the love of money.

In the same way, the love of money has also entrenched itself in the heart of nearly all people in this nation. Both in and outside the church, this mother of all evil has infected our hearts and blinded our spiritual senses to the point of stifling and interfering with the spreading of the true Gospel: that Christ has come down in order to give away everything of Himself so that everyone can be saved in Him through us! We have despised the weak, helpless, downtrodden and abused because we thought we were so much better than them. We are NOT. We are as undeserving of our glorious salvation in our Lord as they are. If this nation were to bring itself on its knees before the Almighty for true cleansing, healing and blessing, the church in America as a whole must repent and find herself on her knees once again.

The love of money is the desolate spiritual wasteland where all the eternal things of God, including all the authentic, deep and fulfilling relationships in His love that we could've had, have been replaced by empty and temporary promises driven by selfish, self-advancing ambition and desires of the flesh at the expense of our very souls. It is happening in many of our souls right at this moment! Our Lord said, what good is it if you gain the whole world but lose your soul? The love of money will break our families. The love of money will drive us apart. And IT HAS.

We will truly be alone and the love of Christ will not be there to console or comfort us because God and the love of money never coexist. We cannot serve God and money at the same time. We are just not designed that way by God. We are designed either to serve money or serve God. We cannot serve both. We need to choose this day whom we will serve. We need to serve God with our money...and we CAN! We need to control our money for God's kingdom and not let the love of money control us. Again, it is never too late for us. As Zacchaeus used his ill-gotten gain to glorify God, we can do so freely and generously with all divine wisdom for all people with our repentant heart. It is time for us to get righteously and rightfully angry at ourselves for letting our love of money get in the way of supernaturally loving and fulfilling relationships that we could have had so easily all these years in Christ!

This is the reason why the Lord is imploring us, saints, to come out of her, the mysterious spiritual harlot called the Babylon in the book of Revelation. He is commanding us to come out of that harbinger of all evil that brought death and destructions not only to all the prophets and saints but all the people who died in any battle or war throughout the history of the world. Isn't it true that all the wars can be traced back to the point of origin called money? In fact, all powers of the world derive their strength from money.

Even our Lord Jesus Christ was killed by the Pharisees and the law makers whose greed for money blinded their hearts to the point of only seeing their gullible flocks whose money was getting away from them over to Jesus, who demanded none of their money except their hearts! Sexual depravity and love of money are two headed monsters of the pride of life with all of its powers. But the love of money is the greater evil of the two. I challenge all of us to find any other singular destructive force in the U.S or throughout the whole world, right now. **By allowing the love of money to dominate our lives and to prevent us to come to our Lord with the whole tithes, we have become unwitting participants of death and destruction of all the saints and the prophets, including our Lord Jesus Christ. This is the kind of foundational truth that should strike the fear of the Lord in our own hearts unto the true redemption of our hearts in Christ.**

This fallen world is still beautiful in so many ways and God has blessed us with so much in this great nation. This world still belongs to our God who created it and that's why it is still beautiful in spite of what we have been doing to it. Are we going to trust once more in God of all creations and blessings and give up what little that He commanded from us to be used for God's people? Why would He need the money from us but for His people who really need it? The love of money is the admiral or general over all evil in all of history. It is the foundation for that great dark financial and spiritual empire of all ages called the Babylon. Crucify the evil general in your heart by the power of our Lord Jesus Christ the King! And all these evil soldiers whose names belong to all kinds of sexual immorality and idolatry will be scattered in chaos and will not be so hard to overcome in our hearts. Let us kill the evil general in our hearts and win not only the true respect but the very souls of the people around us for Christ and His Kingdom. We shall see the glory of our Lord and all of His blessings as the floodgates of Heaven open for all the people in the church!

For the sake of the souls of our children…are we going to act now and today? Will you give generously for the sake of our children and all the children out there? We don't know what will happen tomorrow. Jesus said, *"See that you do not despise one of these little ones. For I tell you that their angels in heaven always see the face of my Father in Heaven."* Let us not give the angels of our children any reason to see the angry face of our Father. We really don't know what's going to happen if that pattern occurs over and over again…God is patient and longsuffering. He is also God of justice for all people. Let us not test Him any longer. As a fellow brother in Christ, I implore and exhort all of you in the love of our Lord, Jesus Christ. Let us rise with supernatural strength of our Lord as kings and queens in the love of our mighty God Jesus Christ, the Defender of the weak!

Chapter 16

TORMENTED RIGHTEOUS SOUL?
(GENESIS 38, 44)

***A scene from the movie Godfather III: between Cardinal
Lambert and **Michael Corleon**, the Godfather.*

Look at this stone. It has been lying in the water a very long time. But the water has not penetrated it. (*cracks the stone on a concrete*) See, it's perfectly dry inside. The same thing has happened to men in Europe. For centuries, they have been surrounded by Christianity. But Christ has not penetrated. Christ does not live within them... What's happening?!

Is it possible, (*sitting down suddenly and out of breath*) that you can give me something sweet...some orange juice, a candy? (*a priest was asked to bring a tray of juice and candies quickly*) Diabetes...when I'm under stress, sometimes this happens. (*The tray arrives. He takes the juice and gulps it, and begins to shove the candy in his mouth*).

I understand...

To come to you on such a delicate matter...Accusations against your arch-bishop was...difficult for me.

The mind suffers. And the body cries out.

That's true.

Would you like to make your confession?

Your Eminence. I'm... It's been so long... It's been 30 years. I think I would use up too much of your time, I think. I'm beyond redemption.

Sometimes the desire to confess is overwhelming, and we must seize the moment.

What is the point of confessing…if I don't repent?
I hear you are a practical man. What have you got to lose? Huh?…. Go on.
Ah…hmm.
Go on my son. (*the Cardinal looks away from the Godfather*)
I…betrayed my wife.
Go on my son.
I betrayed myself. I killed men… And I ordered men to be killed…
Go on my son. Go on.
Ah…this is useless…
Go on my son.
I killed… I ordered the death of my brother. He injured me… (*He begins to sob uncontrollably*) I killed my mother's son… I killed my father's SON…
Your sins are terrible and it is just that you suffer. Your life can be redeemed…but I know you don't believe that. You will not change.

*For if God did not spare the angels who sinned, but cast them down to hell and delivered them into chains of darkness, to be reserved for judgment; and did not spare the ancient world, but saved Noah, one of eight people, a preacher of righteousness, bringing in the flood on the world of the ungodly; and turning the cities of Sodom and Gomorrah into ashes, condemned them to destruction, making them an example to those who afterward would live ungodly; and delivered righteous Lot, who was oppressed by the filthy conduct of the wicked (for that righteous man, dwelling among them, **tormented his righteous soul** from day to day by seeing and hearing their lawless deeds)— then the Lord knows how to deliver the godly out of temptations and to reserve the unjust under punishment for the day of judgment, and especially those who walk according to the flesh in the lust of uncleanness and despise authority.—* 2 Peter 2:4-10

The Godfather was absolutely right when he said that there is no point of confessing our sins if we do not repent before God. Mere confession does not go much beyond a show of emotions, however genuine or authentic that emotion maybe….But the confession driven by true repentance sets us on a path of true salvation toward the Lord of our salvation, who is waiting for us on the other side of the world that is free of all sins. The

Godfather simply could not bring himself to trust in God who can save him from all his sins and the past and the deadly world the mafia that he and his cohorts have created. He believed that he himself was beyond redemption. That's why he couldn't turn away from his sins and toward God. He could not bring himself to repent. His journey through life has forever been damaged in his mind by what he had deemed to be the apex of all unpardonable sins: fratricide. And his body cried out in suffering and pain. Even though this was a just a scene from a movie, all of us can identify with such a tormented soul. However, my friends, if we have been following God of Joseph through this book, we know that NO ONE is beyond God's redemption and the reaches of the blood of Christ as long as there is a breath left in him or her!

As I was writing this book, I began to realize in the Spirit the most peculiar and particular placement of a certain individual in the story of Joseph. But his story is absolutely critical and most edifying to the understanding of our salvation in our Lord Jesus Christ. God sometimes interrupts the flow of the stories or even in our lives to create that strange feeling of some divine intervention or revelation that we need to grasp but we just don't get right away. Can you guess who this man is in the story of Joseph?

The person is none other than Judah. As the story of Joseph is coming to an end, Judah's story also finally makes sense. It also makes sense why God placed the story of Judah and Tamar, his daughter in law, in such an awkward spot as Joseph was about to go on this journey of all human hearts. Judah's story was placed there by God precisely to evoke that feeling of curiosity, causing us to bring our attentions to it. In God, there is no such thing as accidents. God and randomness do not coexist. This is just another proof that God has his eyes on ALL people. Human beings look at outward appearances and gravitate towards our own ideal projections of ourselves. We limit our temporary visions and desires on one or certain group of individuals. God searches the hearts of all people because He is concerned about ALL people. That's why this story about Judah and Tamar is interrupting the story of the main character Joseph here rather unpleasantly in our minds. He wants us to know that He has his eyes on Judah as well as all twelve brothers and beyond while Joseph is going through his own redemption journey with Him. In fact…He has His loving eyes on you and me RIGHT NOW. He always has. We need to dig a little deeper into Judah's character and his redemption journey as well and how his destiny interconnects and intertwines with all of ours. It will be worth our time.

In Genesis Chapter 38, (and I am confident that you will read Genesis Chapter 38 right now, wont you?) Judah went away from his brothers to build his own family after they sent Joseph into the *permanent* exile. But Judah's first and second sons were wicked in the eyes of the Lord and God had to kill them both. Right away, Judah was allowed to experience the incredible pain of losing not only one but two sons. The story does not express his emotions here but what we know about his character from the rest of the story confirms that he loved his sons just like any good father would. This lesson of pain of losing two sons was the main reason why Judah did not want for Jacob to experience the same pain with the possible loss of Benjamin later in the story.

But the key question that we need to be asking right now is, "Was Joseph in the back of Judah's mind when all of these tragic things were happening to his own life? Do you think that he was getting God's just punishment for what he and his brothers did to Joseph?" The exchange between the Cardinal and the Godfather in the story above illustrates the spiritual torment for 30 years that ravaged the soul and the body of the Godfather because his brother, who was endangering his family, was executed and killed by his own order. How much more of a spiritual torment do you think Judah would have experienced when he looked back and realized that he helped delivered young Joseph to a certain death by exile of no return! Joseph was just a boy who was simply obeying his father! Joseph was an innocent blood in his eyes! Joseph was a smart and brave boy who did nothing but to help the family anyway he could! Do you think Judah may have had a nightmare or two that took him back to that place where Joseph was pleading for his life? Again, we know from the rest of the story that Judah himself was tormented in his spirit for what he did to Joseph. In fact, he is the one who was leading all the brothers to ask for forgiveness from God before Joseph just before Joseph revealed himself to them. It was one of the most gut wrenching, repentant plea before God in the history of mankind. He was willing and ready to be Joseph's slave. He was more than willing to sacrifice his own body, freedom and all that he had if that meant sparing his father from losing two sons like he did. Spiritually speaking, he was finally coming home as the prodigal son in the story of Jesus.

In the Chapter 38, Tamar, Judah's daughter-in-law, deceived Judah and got pregnant by him. Now Judah, in his righteous anger, wanted to burn her to death because he didn't yet know that she got pregnant by him. When he found out that it was him who got her pregnant, he saw the error of his ways and said, "She is more righteous than I..." A different way of saying this would be "I'm a worse sinner than she is." We know now that no one is righteous before God. It is Christ who makes us righteous in Him. He is our righteousness. He is our only salvation.

Judah was tormented between the desires of his righteous mind and the workings of his sinful flesh. In so many stories of the Old and the New Testament, we see man after man that succumb to the same pattern of delusions reinforced by pride and self love like Judah before his sin was fully exposed for everyone to see. It is this delusion that blinds you from seeing the monster in you that you are so ready to judge and destroy in the lives of others. Jesus says remove the plank in your eyes first but removing the plank is impossible when you don't even know it is there. That is the definition of delusion. This is not only the story of Judah but the story of our lives. And even if we have identified the plank and want to remove the plank ourselves, we do not have the ability in us to remove it. First, we have to understand the simple truth and love of Jesus Christ that says we are all sinners and we all need forgiveness from the Lord. We are not that righteous than we think. First we have to see the plank by the truth of God and about men.

Only the repentant and tormented souls will be allowed to clearly see the plank and what it can do to our souls. Again, what is the plank? The plank is self-righteousness that is mutually destructive and self-contradicting. The self-righteousness will cause that delusional state where the sins in your life is minimized, rationalized away or suppressed in your consciousness while the very same sin is maximized and horrified in the lives of others. But when Judah's delusional self righteousness was exposed by Tamar, he repented right away just like king David did when his own delusional self righteousness was exposed by Nathan the prophet regarding sins with Bethsheba. We can turn briefly to the story of Nathan the prophet and King David here. King David slept with one of his commander's wife, Bethsheba. When he found out that she was pregnant, he tried to have the husband Uriah the commander sleep with her in an attempt to cover his sin. When that failed, he devised a plan to kill Uriah and Uriah was killed in a battle. After sometime, Nathan the prophet came to David to tell him about a certain rich powerful man who forcefully took a poor man's ewe lamb — the only possession the poor man treasured — to entertain his guest. David, not realizing that Nathan the prophet was telling him about his own sin with Bethsheba and crime against Uriah, burned with anger and condemned the rich man in the story to be sentenced to death. Nathan told David that the rich and powerful man in the story was actually David himself!

If that kind of delusion of self-righteousness existed in the man after God's own heart, David, then the same kind of delusion of self righteousness exists in every human heart. Only the truth and the love of Christ can expose and cleanse it from our hearts. And we should be ready to repent every time the truth exposes our planks just like Judah and David. It is not the question of if but WHEN. We are all humans and sinners. The difference between the tormented righteous soul vs the wicked is simply the willingness to truly repent of our sins and turn from our self-deluding self-righteousness. That's our daily redemption and sanctification/purification by the Word. And only the love of Christ makes it possible for us to repent and find ourselves back in His love.

God was orchestrating all of these events in the life of Judah in order to expose that plank or splinter in our inner-being: the sin of pride that always tries to come out in the form of self-righteousness that seeks to destroy everyone and then comes back to destroy our own souls. Judah came to understand the nature of self-righteousness and its deception but found out that there was nothing in him that can remove this plank; this splinter in his heart and soul. In fact, he realized that everyone was like him in essence. In his mind, his salvation had to come from the Lord and the Lord only. The Lord Himself had to make him *righteous* somehow in spite of who he was. He desperately wanted to be righteous in the eyes of God but this splinter of self-righteousness would always drag him back to that place of darkness, deception and destruction of souls. His only option was to walk before the Lord with the repentant heart always and seeking the mercy and grace of the Lord that the salvation will somehow come from the Lord directly because God was the only one who can save his souls. God of love exposes and purges self-righteousness from our souls by the way of its own humiliating and destructive consequences.

Now, here is the grace of God breaking through. After his repentance, God restores him by giving him two sons through Tamar to replace the two wicked sons He had taken. Judah becomes the direct physical ancestor of David and our Lord Jesus Christ. While Joseph's destiny was glorified in all of its splendor while he was on the earth, Judah's greater and higher divine destiny was realized in the coming of our Lord in physical form and will be realized yet again even more majestically when the Lord comes again as the "Lion of Judah", the ultimate judge at the end times. He will come again as the "root and offspring of David". What an unspeakable and undeserving honor and power bestowed upon Judah by our Lord! It was all because Judah walked before the Lord with the repentant heart! The salvation of our Lord is granted first to the repentant hearts and the same repentant hearts, along with our repentant hearts, will be raised up in the last days with Christ! Broken and contrite hearts, our Lord will not despise and it is only through the repentant hearts that the Lord is truly seen and worshipped.

Judah here is the very definition of the tormented righteous soul of the Old Testament. He knows what's inherently wrong with himself and humanity. At the same time, however, he is helpless to do anything about it and cannot find the salvation in anything or any other souls around him. THIS is your spiritual state in torment. It is the state in which the person knows that he needs to be saved desperately and yet cannot find the salvation anywhere in this world. Tormented righteous souls constantly walk in the spirit of repentance. To such souls, the name of Jesus Christ will be given. And because we have the knowledge of our salvation, Jesus Christ the King, we are no longer in this perpetual spiritual torment.

Joseph was a tormented righteous soul. David was a tormented righteous soul and so was Moses. To such individuals, the name of Jesus Christ is given. Here is the wisdom that we have been looking for. People often ask, "How do you know whether or not all these people who didn't know Christ actually went to heaven?" **The mechanism of our salvation gives us the understanding of exactly HOW we are saved in Christ. But *what* makes us *believe* in that glorious mechanism of salvation in Christ in the first place is the repentant heart residing in every tormented righteous soul throughout history.** If you are not a tormented righteous soul, you will not accept and believe in the works of Christ even if you may know the mechanism perfectly. If you do not have the repentant heart, you will never feel the need for the necessity of that glorious working divine mechanism wrought in pain and suffering for our hearts and souls. If you are not a tormented righteous soul with a repentant heart, then you will reject the need for the necessity of such mechanism and reject the works of Jesus Christ even though you may be the expert of who He was and His works. What was the very first word that came out of the mouth of Jesus when he began his ministry? REPENT. It is only after repentance that we can actually believe and receive the good news of Jesus Christ. Here is the verse that some of us are familiar with.

Salvation is found in no one else, for there is no other name under heaven given to mankind by which we must be saved." (Acts 4:12)

The name of Jesus Christ is *given*. It is not earned. It is not understood by our own power or will. God himself gives us wisdom to understand who Jesus is. Again, salvation is given to us in Jesus Christ and it is only given to the tormented righteous souls with repentant heart for all ages. Anybody at any point anywhere in the history will be GIVEN, not earned, the name of Jesus Christ if that person was a tormented righteous soul with a repentant heart. Whether or not they actually knew exactly who Jesus was is not the issue here. In heaven, these individuals will instantly recognize and accept Jesus Christ as the only One powerful, holy and loving enough to truly save their tormented unanswered souls. It will be as if they have known Him all along. They will finally find the true love and justice in Christ that their hearts were desperately searching and longing for.

Moreover, there is something more incredible and supernatural about them. These tormented righteous souls, if you examine their lives collectively and carefully, were more Christ-like than any one around us now... weren't they? Even though they didn't really know exactly who Jesus was, their lives partially reflect the truth and love of Jesus Christ, as evidenced especially in the life of Joseph as well as many of our spiritual ancestors like Daniel, Job and Abraham. How can that be? Maybe because it is the privilege and the honor of these souls to demonstrate the power and love of God in such mysterious ways that the person themselves do not know exactly, but perceiving as through a veil, that shadow of the truth and love that they are manifesting through their lives with such power and glory is the culmination of all of our hearts' desire for all eternity: our Lord Jesus Christ!

Chapter 17

SUMMATION OF THE UNFOLDING OF CHRIST FOR KINGS AND QUEENS

The sayings of King Lemuel – an inspired utterance **his mother** taught him:

Listen, my son! Listen, son of my womb! Listen, my son, the answer to my prayers! Do not spend your strength on women, your vigor on those who ruin kings. It is not for kings, Lemuel – it is not for kings to drink wine, not for rulers to crave beer, lest they drink and forget what has been decreed, and deprive all the oppressed of their rights. Let beer be for those who are perishing, wine for those who are in anguish! Let them drink and forget their poverty and remember their misery no more. **Speak up for those who cannot speak for themselves, for the rights of all who are destitute. Speak up and judge fairly; defend the rights of the poor and needy.** *– Proverbs 31.*

Since His Life cannot be less in one being than another, or His Love manifested less fully in one thing than another, His Providence must needs be universal. – Helen Keller, a true deaf-blind American visionary.

Love the Lord your God with all your heart and with all your soul and with all your mind. This is the first and greatest commandment.

190

And the second is like it: Love your neighbor as yourself. All the Law and the Prophets hang on these two commandments.—Jesus Christ, the Vision.

Well, we are finally here! Thank you for putting up with me and my poor writing. I have never been a writer but hopefully I will write a few more, the Lord willing. I can rest completely in the Lord that no book, including this one, is perfect except the Bible. The Bible is the perfect and unchanging word of God. A good book will always lead you to that perfect Book of truth and I hope and pray that this book will do just that. The perfect Book of love and truth will always point to our Lord Jesus Christ, the perfect Lamb of God of love and the one true King of kings, forever...

How did sin enter into our world?—We know that the sin entered into our world because, out of their own free will, Adam and Eve ate the fruit of the tree of the knowledge of good and evil: the only thing out of ALL creation that God withheld from Adam and Eve.

Why did God allow the free will in them that eventually led the opening of the gates of sin and death?—We understand that God is truly glorified and loved as He has loved us when we freely choose God over the things that He doesn't desire in us. Free will gives the choice its weight and validation. Free will that chooses God is validated and glorified for all eternity in Him. Free will that chooses all things outside of God's will inevitably result in the world outside of God's love and protection.

Why, did Adam and Eve, ate the fruit in spite of all that God has given them?—We believe that they were easily persuaded and deceived by the serpent simply because they *doubted* the love of God: the love that gave them everything except a single tree. They doubted the love of God that gave them the whole world to rule and multiply in.

How does sin enter into our lives today? The sin enters into our lives when we *doubt* that God really loves us...that God really is for us...that God gives, orchestrates and commands everything out of His love for us. That is how **any sin** enters into our lives and begins to take hold of us. **I wrote this book in order to systematically destroy and drive out any lingering doubts in our minds and utterly convince ourselves of this simple and unchanging truth: Holy God is God of love all the time for all people, and the same God created and designed our hearts for the same purpose.**

And after we have failed as humanity in the Garden of everything we could possibly have in Eden, He gave us and sacrificed the only thing, the only One, that He treasured: His only begotten Son Jesus Christ, who was more precious to the Father than His own Being Himself…so that we can truly become his sons and daughters; his kings and queens by the proof of that undeserving and unsurpassed love of grace. God is love. When we finally understand God's love, we will understand all things mysterious in this God-given universe. If we really believe that God does everything out of His love for us, our lives will be the reflection of this great love. That is the true religion and true faith. But if we don't see why we need to love our neighbor, the poor, the abused, the rejected and the neglected, then we really didn't believe that God was the love for all people in the first place. **I wrote this book so that we, my brothers and sisters in Christ, can take the redemption journey of our hearts in order to take hold of that love of Christ for which He has already taken hold of us for all eternity… FOR ALL GOD'S PEOPLE.**

Our divine destinies lie in the heart of our God who sent his Son to bleed for ALL. Jesus Christ is the desire of all nations. Let this desire of all people in Christ converge on us as we readily abdicate ourselves from the throne of our hearts and make room in our hearts for all the people that Christ came to save, especially the poor, the downtrodden and persecuted in the church, locally and globally. Let us abdicate ourselves from the throne of self-love and self-entitlements in our hearts, following the example of our Lord Jesus and his glorious sacrificial love for ALL of us. Joseph as well as countless others has gone through the journey of all the hearts and the world only to return to this foundational eternal truth: **God is true love for all of us and nothing else is.** They finally realized that they can trust in nothing, even themselves, except God! And this simple truth forged in the journey wrought in pain and suffering made the process of self-abdication not only easy but…imminent and inevitable. Have we learned from their journeys of hearts and souls? Let us raise Jesus Christ the King to His rightful place in our hearts so that we can demonstrate His love sacrificially with power with the Holy Spirit empowering us. And I believe in our Lord Jesus Christ that people will believe in Christ as He is shaking the heaven and earth once more!

We look forward to the day when this flesh, which constantly blinds us to see the truth of His love by our selfishness and pride, will be replaced with new bodies and new eyes that will truly "see" the love of our Holy God in all of His glory for all of us all the time. Whatever situation or "prison" you find yourself in today, you are in it because God loves you and you are being made into something much greater than who you are for all of God's people. Let us do everything in the Lord and as unto the Lord with all of our heart, mind, soul and strength for all people that Christ came to save. Let us be the witness of the power of His love that drives out that ever-destructive *SELF* out of ourselves and usher in His kingdom of love and salvation for all people in our hearts!

I believe in you. I believe in the same God who has saved a sinner like me has also saved you. What am I? If St. Paul said that he was the chief among all sinners, then I'm nothing! I'm a fellow servant just like you. He has saved us because He saw something magnificent in us that He needed to reclaim. Let Him reclaim it. YIELD. SURRENDER. Let us demolish that harbinger of all evil and death — the love of money that is the root of the Babylon — that is raging in our hearts so that we can readily and generously help the weak, poor, oppressed and neglected around us. This is the proof of "love your neighbor as yourself", and "feed His lambs" in action in all scriptures including James 1:27. We **must** get our children to take this journey with us and see the glory of his Kingdom come into our hearts and everyone around us! It's never too late. 1st Corinthians chapter 13:7, it says "love always protects, trusts, hopes and perseveres." If I have the love of Christ in me, I have no choice but to believe in the purpose for which He has saved you and me. Unlike the prophet Jonah, I believe in you; sons and daughters of the most High God, to carry on with His good works that He has begun in us. Why would our Lord Jesus Christ, the King of the universe, go through all that Hell on earth if not for this ultimate and glorious Divine destiny: that we will truly be His sons and daughters and royal priesthood for ALL people? God does not waste His time. He saved us for this very reason. He will be glorified and magnified...in and through our hearts that are being actively redeemed by the eternal love of Christ!

We remember the statement by Joseph, "I cannot do it. But God will give Pharaoh the answer he desires." I didn't write this book to change the world. I cannot do it. Only God can and will give us the answer that our hearts desire. The answer that all of our hearts and all nations desire is Jesus Christ. **I wrote this book so that you may know our Lord and Savior Jesus Christ, who has already come to change the unchangeable, redeem the unredeemable and unravel the greatest mystery *of the universe*: our own hearts that were created by the greatest mystery *beyond this universe*: Jesus Christ, to be united in His love for God and for ALL of God's people.**

THE UNFOLDING AND CONVERGENCE OF OUR ETERNAL DESTINY IN THE LOVE TRINITY

When he had finished washing their feet, he put on his clothes and returned to his place. "Do you understand what I have done for you?" he asked them. "You call me 'Teacher' and 'Lord,' and rightly so, for that is what I am. Now that I, your Lord and Teacher, have washed your feet, you also should wash one another's feet. I have set you an example that you should do as I have done for you. Very truly I tell you, no servant is greater than his master, nor is a messenger greater than the one who sent him. Now that you know these things, you will be blessed if you do them." John 13:12-17

How does one wash someone else's feet? Don't you have to kneel down? Do we think Jesus knelt down in order to wash the feet of his disciples? Jesus our Lord has forced himself into this unnatural position of washing the lowest parts of our bodies. The love of Christ caused the knees of God to bend before human beings...even as Jesus knew that the same human beings will crucify Him very shortly. He has demonstrated his surpassing love in this way in order for us to readily cast aside our pride of self-love and begin to wash one another's sins and shames with true love, His Unchanging Eternal Love.

*For this reason I **kneel** before the Father, from whom **every family** in heaven and on earth derives its name. I pray that out of his* *glorious riches he may strengthen you with power through his Spirit in your inner being, so that Christ may **dwell** in your hearts through faith. And I pray that you, being rooted and established in love, may have power, together with all the Lord's holy people, to grasp how wide and long and high and deep is the **love of Christ**, and to know this love that surpasses knowledge—that you may be filled to the measure of **all the fullness of God**. Now to him who is able to do immeasurably more than all we ask or imagine, according to his power that is at work within us, to him be glory in the church and in Christ Jesus throughout all generations, for ever and ever! Amen. Ephesians 3:14-21*

The true knowledge of God, that He is God of love for all people all the time, begins on our knees in the fear and reverence of our Lord. It will continuously lead us to the surpassing love of Christ that surpasses all knowledge, even the knowledge that led us to Him. The more we know about His love, the more incomprehensible and mysterious He becomes. The more we grow in the knowledge of His love, the more majestic and beautiful He becomes. The closer we get to the wisdom of His love, the more intricate, magnificent and fearsome He becomes! That is exactly why His love stands alone as the only unchangeable truth beyond this universe that can overcome all things in this world, yes...even our hearts, and rebuild and reunite our families with everlasting power in Him...unto all things eternal!

And he showed me a pure river of water of life, clear as crystal, proceeding from the throne of God and of the Lamb. In the middle of its street, and on either side of the river, was the tree of life, which bore twelve fruits, each tree yielding its fruit every month. The leaves of the tree were for the healing of the nations. And there shall be no more curse, but the throne of God and of the Lamb shall be in it, and His servants shall serve Him. They shall see His face, and His name shall be on their foreheads. There shall be no night there: They need no lamp nor light of the sun, for the Lord God gives them light. And they shall reign forever and ever. Revelation 22:1-5

Yes, we will reign with Him forever! This world, and all of its empty promises, counterfeit affections and shallow, temporary glories, will pass away, but His kingdom and righteousness will remain forever. Until next time, my brothers and sisters in Christ, kings, queens and the priests of His universe...even though we have never met, I will miss you, and even more so, who you are going to be in the continuously unfolding eternal love of our God and Savior, Jesus Christ. May our Lord Jesus bless you in all things eternal.

The Day before the Dawning of Our Glorious Eternal Destiny in Christ

The Father, with his eternal eyes on EVERYTHING, is now focused on His Son's pleading and supplication. The physical manifestation of His spiritual and emotional torment was clearly visible as his sweat flowed like blood. The Son pleaded three times to the Father to take the cup from him: the cup that was the impending manifestations of all of our evil culminating in that violent Crucifixion. But the Son, full of Holy Spirit, also said, "Not my will, but Thy will be done." The Father's eternal heart perceived His Son's heart in anguish and torment. The Father's heart was in torment and anguish as well. He, too, was seeing what was causing this hour of anguish and pain in His beloved Son. He and the Son are One. He sent an angel to comfort Jesus. Jesus was about to undergo something that no human was ever capable of undergoing or understanding. The Father God Himself, however, remained silent.

Why was He silent in the hour of the most gut-wrenching sorrow? What did the Father see around his Son? What was He thinking? Did He see all of our hearts raging against the Son of Man? Did He see our sins, with all of its greed, malice, violence, lust, jealousy and pride; from the beginning of time all the way to the end, bent on destroying His only begotten Son, who came to save the very hearts by which all these pain and anguish flowed? Did He see our hearts, full of pride and jealousy, were also bent on destroying each other? Did He see our violent hearts with all of its evil and murderous intents swirling around His Son, who was the best of the best, the very definition of love, the purest, the bright Morning Star, our only hope and salvation? Did He see in Himself a true dilemma? Did He say to Himself, "Do I save my Son from this hour or do I save all *THESE* over my Son?" Did He say in His heart, "One more plea from my Son and I will surely come and destroy all *THESE* and WE will build another universe together where my Son, the only One holy, worthy and true, will not be crucified?"

But all the while, the Father's eternal eyes were fixed on something on the other side of the eternal chasm separating God and men. He saw the eternal destiny of the redeemed in Christ. He saw his sons and daughters, kings and queens, being redeemed through the blood of His only begotten

196

Son. He saw the power of the blood of the Lamb washing our souls and redeeming our hearts. He saw the coming of the King Jesus on that fearsome horse with the sword of truth and justice coming out of his mouth. He saw His Son coming with power and authority to throw down all evil into the fiery lake of eternal hell. He saw His Son who will answer all our hearts' questions and desires because we will finally and truly see Him through our fully redeemed hearts by the blood of the Lamb: the only true love. He saw that we will finally see the Lord, who makes all things new, anew through His loving eyes. He saw that we will know all things even as we were fully known by Him, who is love beyond this universe. He saw the power of the blood of the Lamb in its full glory with all of the redeemed saints of God following the train of His robe dipped in blood as the kings and queens of His coming Kingdom...to overcome and reign with Him! The Father God saw the FINAL REVELATION of the coming of His Son in His glorious kingdom.

As He was listening to His Son, full of the Holy Spirit, praying in unspeakable agony for the humanly impossible love and unity of the bride of the Lamb: the Church above all races and nations, the Father was also seeing the thousands upon thousands of saints, finally united in the love of the Son, rising up in worship to the eternal shouts of "God bless our Lord and God bless my soul! Blessed the Lord oh my soul! Worthy is the Lamb! All the salvation, honor, power and glory belong to our God! There is no one like our God! There is no one like our Lord Jesus Christ, the King of kings and the Lord of lords, forever and ever!"

Amen.